What Savta Told Me...

By: Daniela Livni

A Publication of JewishGen, INC
Edmond J. Safra Plaza, 36 Battery Place, New York, NY 10280
646.494.5972 | info@JewishGen.org | www.jewishgen.org

An affiliate of New York's Museum of Jewish Heritage – A Living Memorial to the Holocaust

What Savta Told Me…

First Printing: April 2023, Iyar 5783

Author: Daniela Livni
Cover Design: Irv Osterer

Printed in the United States of America by Lightning Source, Inc.

Library of Congress Control Number (LCCN): 2023936895

ISBN: 978-1-954176-76-8 (hard cover: 262 pages, alk. paper)

About JewishGen.org

JewishGen, an affiliate of the Museum of Jewish Heritage - A Living Memorial to the Holocaust, serves as the global home for Jewish genealogy.

Featuring unparalleled access to 30+ million records, it offers unique search tools, along with opportunities for researchers to connect with others who share similar interests. Award winning resources such as the Family Finder, Discussion Groups, and ViewMate, are relied upon by thousands each day.

In addition, JewishGen's extensive informational, educational and historical offerings, such as the Jewish Communities Database, Yizkor Book translations, InfoFiles, Family Tree of the Jewish People, and KehilaLinks, provide critical insights, first-hand accounts, and context about Jewish communal and familial life throughout the world.

Offered as a free resource, JewishGen.org has facilitated thousands of family connections and success stories, and is currently engaged in an intensive expansion effort that will bring many more records, tools, and resources to its collections.

Please visit https://www.jewishgen.org/ to learn more.

Executive Director: Avraham Groll

Director of JewishGen Yizkor Book Project: Lance Ackerfeld

About JewishGen Press

JewishGen Press (formerly the Yizkor Books-in-Print Project) is the publishing division of JewishGen.org, and provides a venue for the publication of non-fiction books pertaining to Jewish genealogy, history, culture, and heritage.

In addition to the Yizkor Book category, publications in the Other Non-Fiction category include Shoah memoirs and research, genealogical research, collections of genealogical and historical materials, biographies, diaries and letters, studies of Jewish experience and cultural life in the past, academic theses, and other books of interest to the Jewish community.

Please visit https://www.jewishgen.org/Yizkor/ybip.html to learn more.

Director of JewishGen Press: Joel Alpert
Managing Editor - Jessica Feinstein
Publications Manager - Susan Rosin

WHAT SAVTA TOLD ME….

For Maya, Ella, Ben and Anna

By

Daniela Livni

Woburn 2023

Third revised edition

In your warm houses,
You who find warm food
And friendly faces when you return home.
Consider if this is a man
Who works in mud,
Who knows no peace,
Who fights for a crust of bread,
Who dies by a yes or no.
Consider if this is a woman
Without hair, without name,
Without the strength to remember,
Empty are her eyes, cold her womb,
Like a frog in winter.
Never forget that this has happened.
Remember these words.
Engrave them in your hearts,
When at home or in the street,
When lying down, when getting up.
Repeat them to your children.
Or may your houses be destroyed,
May illness strike you down,
May your offspring turn their faces from you."

Primo Levi, Survival in Auschwitz

TABLE OF CONTENTS

Boston, 2019

PREFACE

I and my children are the last generation alive that heard of the atrocities of the Shoah first hand from Yossi my husband and directly from his parents. I know that in a very short while the Shoah will be a line in the history books and then perhaps that single line will be no more.

This is the reason I wrote this book. Although my parents lived through those horrific days they never spoke of them and growing up in Israel in the late fifties and early sixties we learned at school mostly about the Jewish partisans and their heroic operations, very little about the atrocities of the Shoah. Until I met Yossi I knew very little about this period that I now feel so strongly about and I want my grandchildren to know what being Jewish meant in other times and places.

This second edition of my book came into being because Avital Schlesinger Horn, the daughter of Eliezer (Vico) Schlesinger, my cousin, and her husband Joey Horn recently came into the possession of some valuable documents from the Swiss archives that shed light upon the story of my father and my father's family escape from the Nazis to Switzerland in 1943-1944 when the Germans occupied Italy.

There is controversy about the role Switzerland played in saving the Jews from the Nazis.

Every sovereign country has the right to determine who and how many aliens to admit at any given time and during World War II Switzerland severely limited the numbers of refugees admitted into their country.

The Government in Bern was quite legalistic and anti-Semitic in its approach. In 1938 for example they passed a law mandating a "J" to be stamped onto the passports of German Jews.

I find it also disturbing that during those horrific times Switzerland, a country that was supposedly neutral, would demand refugees that were running for their lives to deposit a very significant fee to be permitted entry. And after having being ....mercifully admitted, unless they could provide a permanent address of residency and could support themselves they were sent to labor camps.

These Swiss documents are painstakingly detailed, often redundant. All the documents record personal details about the age, place of birth, place of residence, legal status and occupation. They document the assets one possessed in Italy, in Switzerland or elsewhere. They detail the jewelry they wore, whether it was gold, with precious stones or diamonds and in one particular case they detail the fact that one piece was missing. They record the money they brought and deposited with the Swiss authorities. In my father's case in order to be admitted into the country, he gave them 50 gold "marenghi" and 10,000 Italian lire which today would be worth more than US$ 85,000! Marenghi were gold coins issued from 1862 until 1927 with the Savoy coat of arms on the reverse and King Vittorio Emanuele II on the obverse. Was this outrageous amount ever returned?

One document explicitly specifies that the "permesso di soggiorno", the permit to stay is granted for ..... 2 months! The expectation was definitely for a short temporary stay and their sojourn was regulated closely. Obviously the Swiss authorities were very well aware what awaited them on the Italian side of the border.

This most valuable collection of documents was issued by the border guards, the small towns' police stations, the Canton Police and the Federal Police. They are in Italian, French or German. I translated the personal testimonies which detail the hardships they went through trying to save their lives.

You will find these documents in the chapter Switzerland during the Shoah.

Mamma

So I am writing it all for Maya, Ella, Ben and Anna because you need to know where you come from. I know that you don't particularly care for these things right now but who knows perhaps one day you will, perhaps one day you will want to know more and since I will not be around this will perhaps give you some answers.

So Maya, Ella, Ben and Anna, this is for you.

But where do I start?

I don't know. One usually divides things into three but how can I do that? For example, so far I have lived in four places. Perhaps I can start from Israel, and then like in the movies go back and forth.

My first instinct is to start from there so there must be a reason. So much happened there! Good things, very good things, bad things.... If I compare those years to the years in Montreal or in Boston, well they don't compare. Those were wonderful years, lots of memories, some good, some not so good.

But I will start from the beginning.

THE LEVANTINE CONNECTION

KALONIMUS

Rav Gustavo Menachem Ben Yosef (Giuseppe) Calò

Alba Milla Caló

When I decided to write this book I knew absolutely nothing about the paternal side of our family. All I knew were the names of my paternal grandparents, something about their lives and nothing more. And then,

Covid-19 2020 happened. I watched a presentation by Luca Ascoli about The Jews of Ancona. Needless to say, both his name and the presentation captivated me. I contacted Luca and he provided me with significant information. I could now begin to trace my paternal ancestors.

The Caló family descends from a distinguished Italian Jewish family. The name in Hebrew translates to Shem Tov, which means “good" or "beautiful name".

Caló or Kalo is an abbreviation of the Greek name Kalonymos. Greek names became widespread among Jews of Second Temple Israel (Eretz Israel) during the Hellenistic period, when many of them adopted the Greek way of life.

The name Kalonymus also appears in Talmudic literature as the father of Onkelos, who converted to Judaism and translated the Torah into Aramaic, a translation (which is also an interpretation) known as Onkelos translation (Targum Onkelos). According to the traditional Jewish sources, Onkelos Ben Kalonimus (Onkelos the son of Kalonimus) was a member of the Roman royal family, a nephew of the Roman emperor Titus. His mother was Hadrian's sister, Aelia Domitia Paulina (75-130 A.D).

The first documented origins in Italy of the Calonimos, Kalonimus or Caló family dates back to 70 A.D. in Oria, Apulia. The family immigrated then to Lucca in the year 800 and we find a Calonimos ben Calonimus in Provence in 1286.

In the 10th century the Carolingians ruled over France, over the Eastern part of Germany along the Rhine and over North East Italy. They wanted to enhance commerce between their Empire and the Mediterranean and being aware of Jewish contribution to commerce, the Emperor Carl, (Charlemagne) invited Kalonymos the Jew, the courtier and friend of Emperor Otto II, in 917 to move to Mainz. From the 9th to the 13th century the Kalonimus family became one of the most eminent Jewish families in Germany, especially in the cities near the Rhine. The family is considered to be the founder of the Early Scholars (Hachmei Ashkenaz).

The Great Kalonimus from Lucca was thus an ancestor of Ashkenzi Jewry.

Other names deriving from the name Kalonymus include Calmus, the Italian Calo and Calimani, the French Calot, the central and Eastern European Calman or Kalman.

Lately I learned that some scholars maintain that the Calo are of Spanish origin.

They find the surname Calo or de Calo or de Callo in documents from the 14th to the 15th century in Castile, Toledo, Tarazona, Illueca and Calatayud in Aragon.

This evidence does not contradict earlier evidence from the 10th century for the presence of a Kalonimus in Lucca, Italy. Hence I dare say that our ancestors are ancient Italians and not Spanish.[1]

In this deeply rooted history one story carries a personal note, as I heard it from my father. The Rosh Ha-Shaná prayer includes a poem (a piut) called U'netaná tokef that gave birth to a legend. It is said that it was recited by Rabbi Amnon (Mainz, c. 11th century), who had failed to reject a proposal of immediate apostasy and instead asked for three days to consider it. When he refused to give up his faith, he was taken away and tortured brutally. It was Rosh Ha-Shaná and he asked his disciples to take him to the synagogue, where he interrupted the service and recited this prayer in order to sanctify the name of God. Upon completing the recitation, he died. Later, the legend continues, he appeared to Rabbi Kalonymus in a dream and asked that this prayer be recited each year.

Gustavo Caló was born in Florence on the 29 of August, 1879, one of the six children of Giuseppe Caló and Enrichetta Ghirone.

His grandparents, Abramo Caló and Rosa Orvieto lived in house #2 in the ghetto of Firenze that was established in 1571. His great grandparents, Moise Vita Caló and Gentile Uzieli still lived outside the Ghetto on Via della Nave.

---

[1] Ascoli Luca, Le origini della famiglia Calò; (luca.ascoli@ec.europa.eu)

THE SPANISH CONNECTION – GHIRON

The ancestors of my great grandmother, Enrichetta Ghirone, the mother of Gustavo Menachem Caló, came from Gerona, Spain, hence the name Ghirone.

Jews left Gerona, Spain already in the 1200, fleeing persecutions from the Catholic rulers. They first moved to Provence, France and by 1424 there is evidence of Jews by the name Gueyron, Ghirone and Ghiron in Piedmont, Italy. They also assumed names like Girundini, Girondin or Gerondin.

There is evidence of Jews by the name Ghiron or Ghirone in Casale Monferrato, Trino, Asti, in Piedmont back to the 17th century. Documents from Alessandria in 1860 tell of 23 families by the name Ghiron and one female by the name Enrichetta Ghiron.

Rav Gustavo Menachem Ben Yosef Calò was a distinguished scholar. He graduated in Liberal Arts and received the rabbinical ordination ("Semikhà") from the Italian Rabbinical College in Florence. In 1902-1903 he received the title of "Maskil" (a scholar or an "enlightened man") and then that of "Chakham ha-Shalem" (the title was used to distinguish well-known important rabbis). He is the Rabbi of Verona in 1907, of Corfu, Greece until 1918, of Bengasi, Libya in 1919 for 1 year only because the community could not afford to pay his salary, of Pitigliano from 1920 until 1924 (he is the last Rabbi there), of Parma from March 1924 until 1927, of Mantova from March 1927 until 1943 and of Biella and Vercelli from 1946 until 1956. He is the last Rabbi of the Jewish Community of Vercelli and Biella.

1924 Livorno, Hebrew Congress

A Libyan Jewish classroom in a Benghazi Synagogue before World War II.

LA SCUOLA RABBINICA « MARGULIES-DISEGNI »

(e nella foto i rabbini italiani quando erano ragazzi)

La Scuola Rabbinica « Margulies-Disegni » della quale fu fondatore, animatore e ideatore il rabbino Dario Disegni, rabbino capo di Torino fino al 1960, che dedicò gran parte della sua opera in campo ebraico alla ricerca di allievi, in varie parti d'Italia e del mondo (Grecia, Libia, Etiopia) da avviare alla carriera rabbinica.

Centro notevole di vita e cultura ebraica nella Torino del secondo dopoguerra, dalla scuola uscirono numerosi maestri e rabbini, gran parte dei quali ricoprono oggi le principali cattedre rabbiniche: Laras a Milano, Caro a Firenze, Kahn a Livorno, Viterbo a Padova. Rav Disegni se ne occupò fino alla sua morte, avvenuta nel 1967. Oggi è diretta da Rav Sierra, ma conta due soli allievi. Una sezione della scuola è stata aperta due anni fa a Genova da rav Zegdun.

Pubblichiamo su questo tema una foto del 1951 che è diventata quasi un documento raro: accanto al rabbino Disegni vi figurano in buon numero alcuni degli attuali rabbini delle Comunità ebraiche italiane, quando avevano i calzoni corti o quasi.

In piedi, da sinistra a destra: Raffaele Pacifici, Isidoro Kahn, Carlo Baconcini, Achille Viterbo, Giuseppe Laras, Roberto Bonfil, Umberto Sciunnach, Samuel Babbout, Luciano Caro, Eliezer Cohen. Seduti da sinistra a destra: l'insegnante Bergatin, Alba Calò, rav Dario Disegni, rav Gustavo Calò.

The Rabbinical School Margulies-Disegni in Torino in 1951; Seated, from left to right are the teacher Alba Milla Caló and Rav Gustavo Caló.

Torino, 1951

Gustavo Caló first row on the right, Alba Milla Caló first row second to the left.

He and Nonna Alba taught at the Margulies-Disegni Rabbinical School in Torino from 1952 until 1956 and at the Hebrew School "E. Artom".

The Caló siblings: from left to right: Aldo, Elsa, Camillo, sitting from left: Raffaele (Lele), Enrichetta (Ketty)

A book translated by Gustavo Caló, from Rashi script into into Italian.[2]

[2] L'Esilio e il Riscatto, Le vicende degli Ebrei Mantovani tra il 1627 e il 1631, Abramo Massarani, Bologna 1977

Gustavo Caló died In Vercelli the 1st of May, 1956

Gustavo Caló

Alba Caló

In the Italian synagogue in Jerusalem there are two Torah scrolls crowns (ketarim) with an inscription engraved on the inner bar that reads:

"The Jewish community of Vercelli in memory of Rabbi Gustavo Caló, 20 Iyar 5716 (1956)”

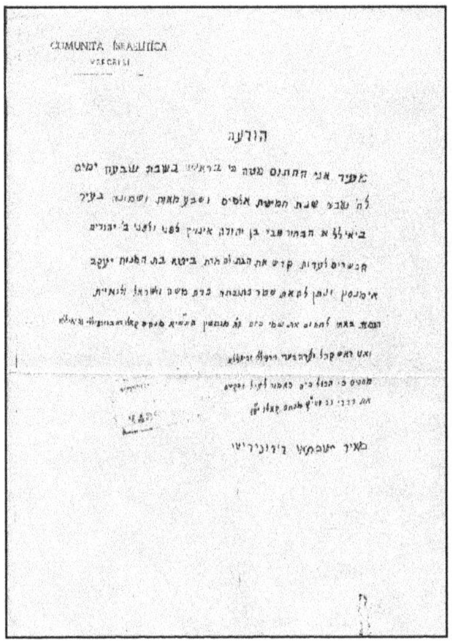

COMUNITÀ ISRAELITICA
VERCELLI

הודעה

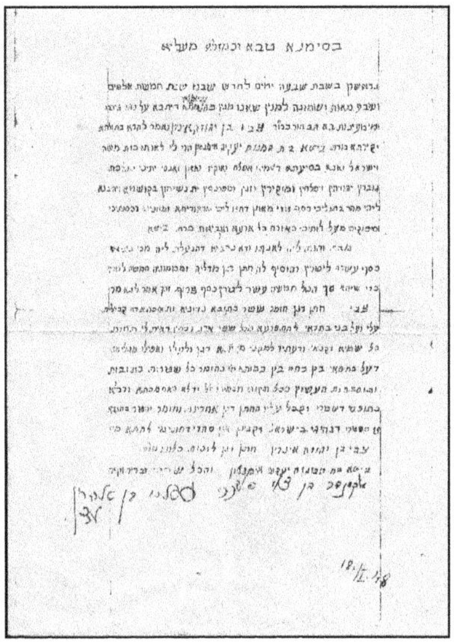

בסימנא טבא ובמזלא מעליא

A Jewish marriage contract (Ketubah), hand written in Hebrew
by Rav Gustavo Caló

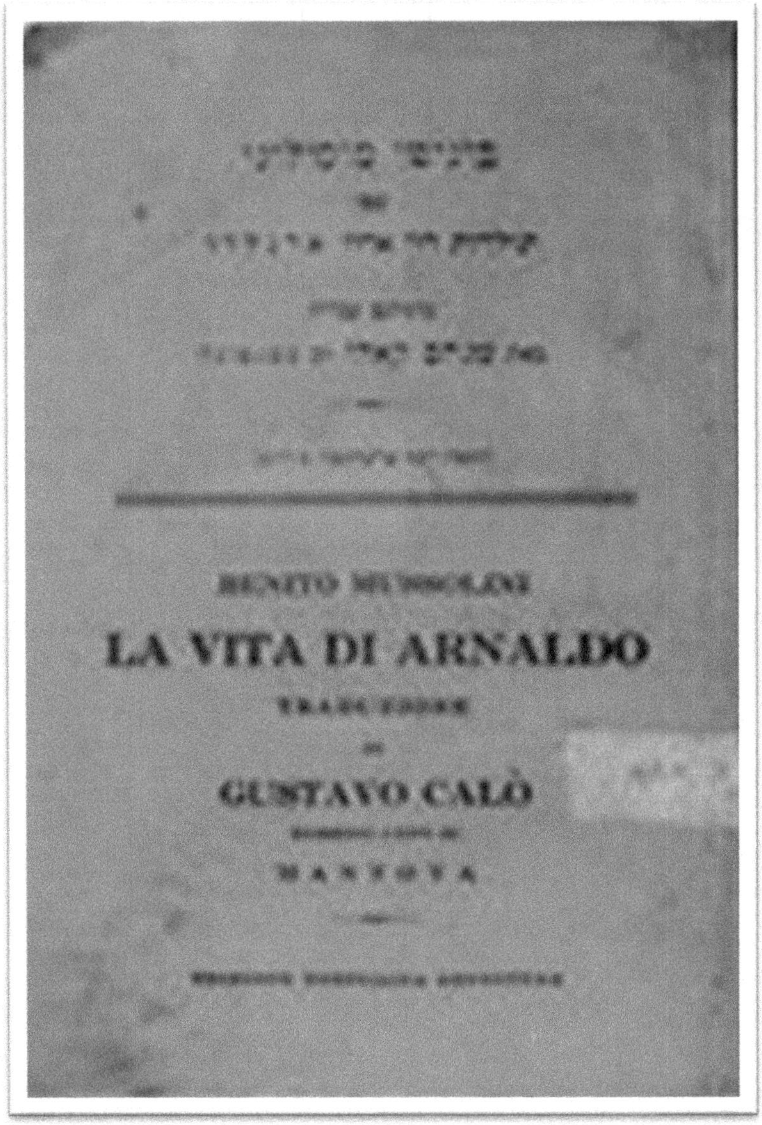
LA VITA DI ARNALDO

GUSTAVO CALÒ

MANTOVA

Toledot ḥaye aḥiv̦ Arnaldo
La Vita Di Arnaldo / Benito Mussolini

traduzione di Gustavo Caló
Rabbino Capo di Mantova.

The Calo' family tree

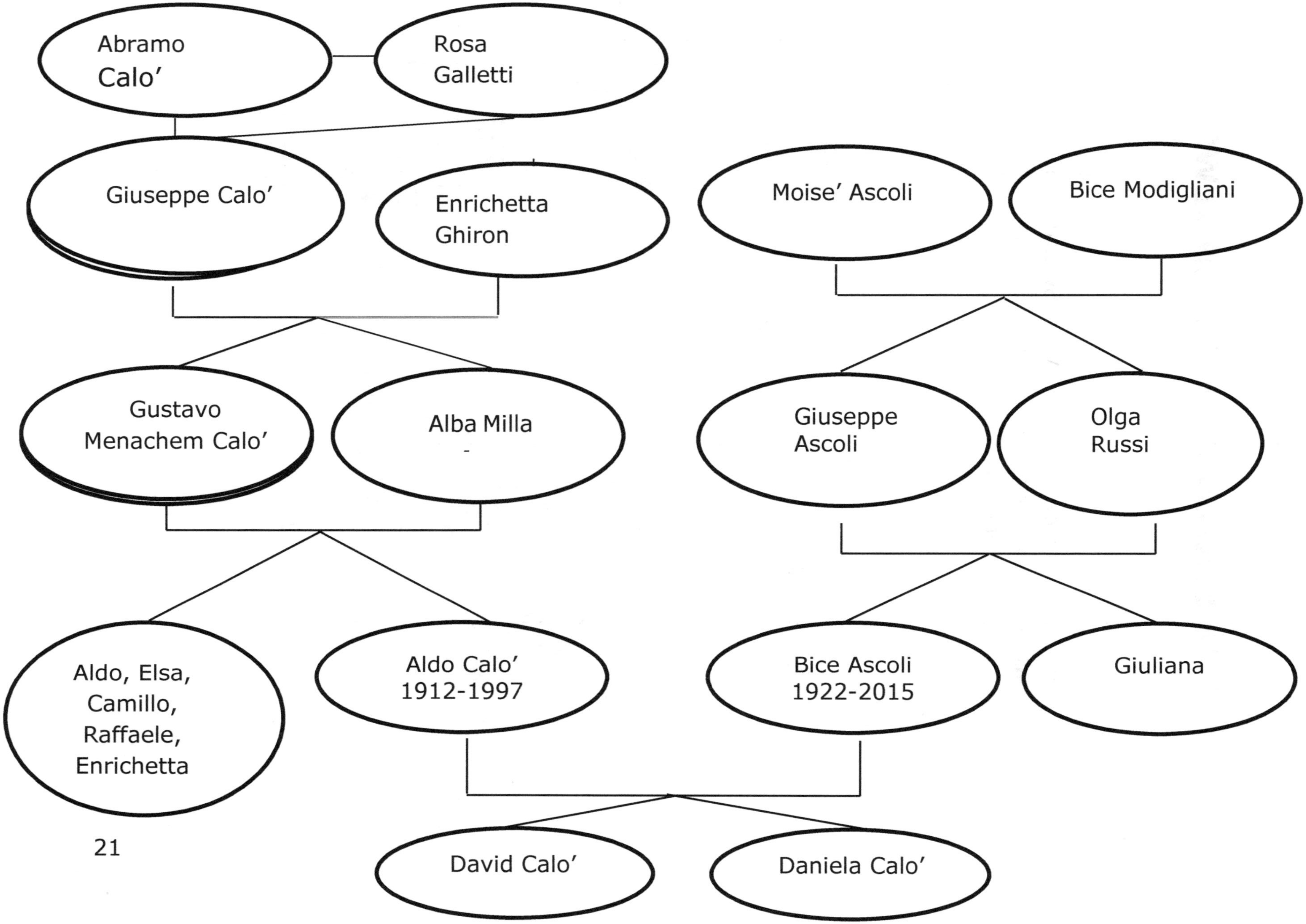
Abramo Calo'
Rosa Galletti
Giuseppe Calo'
Enrichetta Ghiron
Moise' Ascoli
Bice Modigliani
Gustavo Menachem Calo'
Alba Milla
Giuseppe Ascoli
Olga Russi
Aldo, Elsa, Camillo, Raffaele, Enrichetta
Aldo Calo' 1912-1997
Bice Ascoli 1922-2015
Giuliana
David Calo'
Daniela Calo'

THE SHOAH OF ITALIAN JEWS

What follows is an extended collection of Swiss documents that detail the hardships our families endured in trying to save their lives when the Germans occupied Italy.

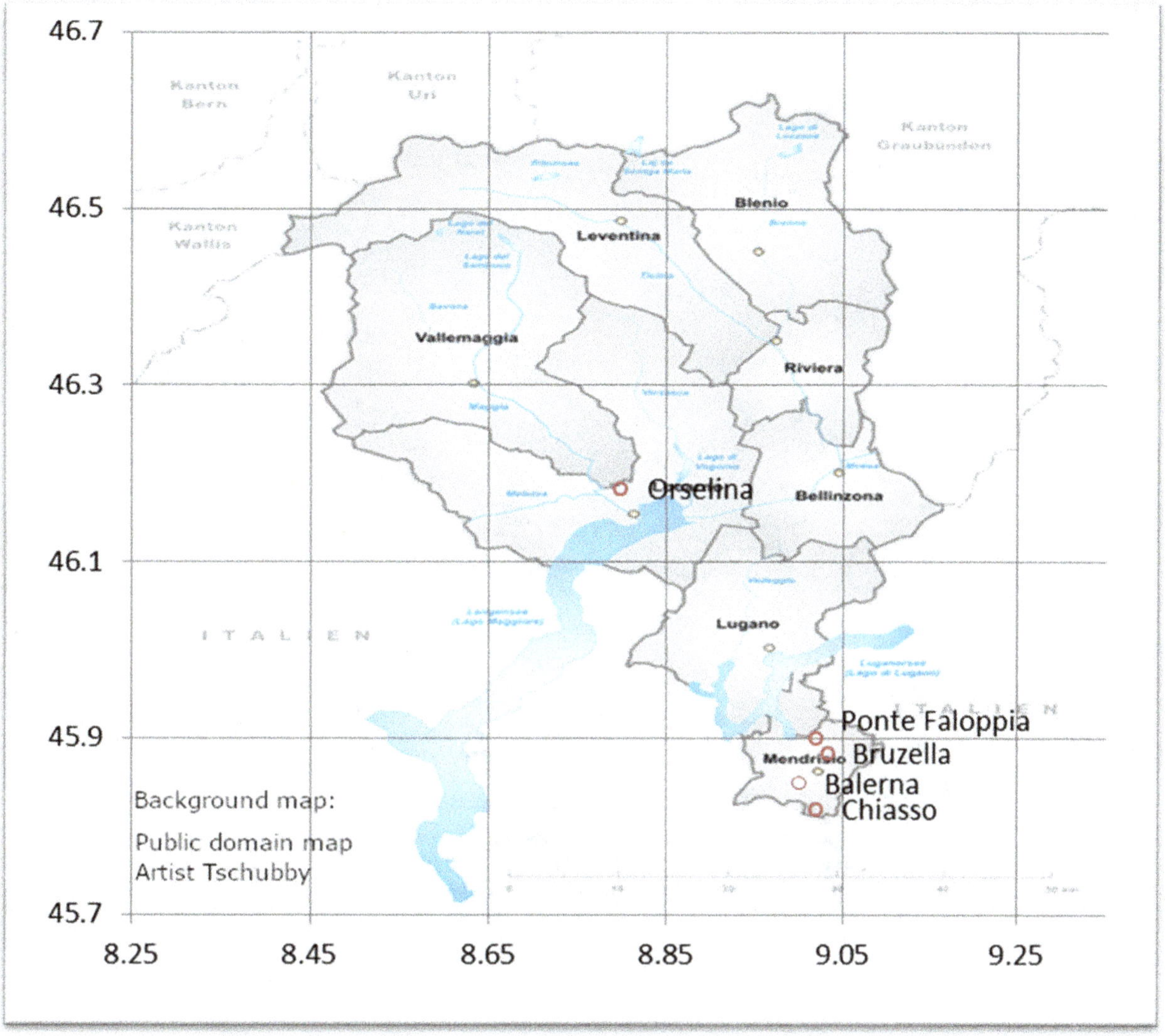
46.7
46.5
46.3
46.1
45.9
45.7
8.25
8.45
8.65
8.85
9.05
9.25
Kanton Bern
Kanton Uri
Kanton Graubünden
Kanton Wallis
Leventina
Blenio
Vallemaggia
Riviera
Orselina
Bellinzona
Lugano
ITALIEN
ITALIEN
Ponte Faloppia
Mendrisio
Bruzella
Balerna
Chiasso
Background map:
Public domain map
Artist Tschubby

Eidgenössisches Justiz- und Polizeidepartement
Polizeiabteilung

Département fédéral de justice et police
Division de police

Dipartimento federale di giustizia e polizia
Divisione della polizia

Einvernahmeprotokoll
Procès-verbal d'interrogatoire
Verbale d'interrogatoio

Bellinzona den / le / il 11.1.1944.

1. Name: / Nom: / Cognome: Calò
2. Vorname: / Prénom: / Nome: Aldo
3. Staatszugehörigkeit: / Nationalité: / Nazionalità: italia/na
4. Bei Staatenlosigkeit frühere Staatszugehörigkeit: / Ancienne nationalité (en cas d'apatridie): / Precedente nazionalità (per apolidi):
5. Vorname des Vaters: / Prénom du père: / Nome del padre: di Gustavo
6. Vor- und Geburtsname der Mutter: / Prénom et nom de famille de la mère: / Nome e cognome di nascita della madre: di Alba, nata Milla
7. Geburtsdatum: / Date de naissance: / Data di nascita: 28.12.1912.
8. Geburtsort: / Lieu de naissance: / Luogo di nascita: Corfu
9. Früherer Wohnort: / Ancien domicile: / Domicilio precedente: Biella
10. Beruf: / Profession: / Professione: dottore in legge
11. Zivilstand: / Etat-civil: / Stato civile: celibe
12. Konfession: / Confession: / Religione: israelita
13. Begleitende Familienangehörige: / Membres de la famille accompagnant l'intéressé: / Congiunti che accompagnano l'interessato: sorella Elsa Vitale nata Calò
14. Ausweispapiere: / Papiers d'identité: / Documenti di legittimazione: carta d'identità N21270 Mantova, 19.1.39. Tessera per a/bbonamento ferroviario N 336626 Biella valevole fino 31.5.44.
15. Militärische Einteilung: / Incorporation militaire: / Incorporazione militare: sottotente art. , ora in congedo assoluto
16. Grund und Umstände der Flucht sowie eingeschlagener Weg: / Motifs et circonstances de la fuite ainsi que route suivie: / Motivi e circostanze della fuga come pure percorso seguito: Dopo l'armistizio mi sono nascosto in campa/gna. A/i primi di Dicemre43 ~~ax~~ temendo persecuzioni razziali, mi decisi a lasciare l'Italia. Mi diressi prima a Como e il giorno 14.12. varcai il confine a Bruzella. L'indomani fui condotto a Chiasso.

F 115 / 82000

Interview report of Aldo Caló

Identification document (issued by the Police of Bellinzona): railway fare card, valid until May 5 1944,

Military records: artillery “sottotenente”, second lieutenant, , dismissed.

The following day I was taken to Chiasso.” Mr. Aldo Caló born on December 28, 1912 and resides in Biella, son of a rabbi in Mantova. His testimony: “After the armistice I hid in the countryside. At the beginning of December 43, fearing racial persecutions, I decided to leave Italy. I went first to Como and on December 14th I crossed the border at Bruzella. Italian Jew, admitted on December 15, 1943.

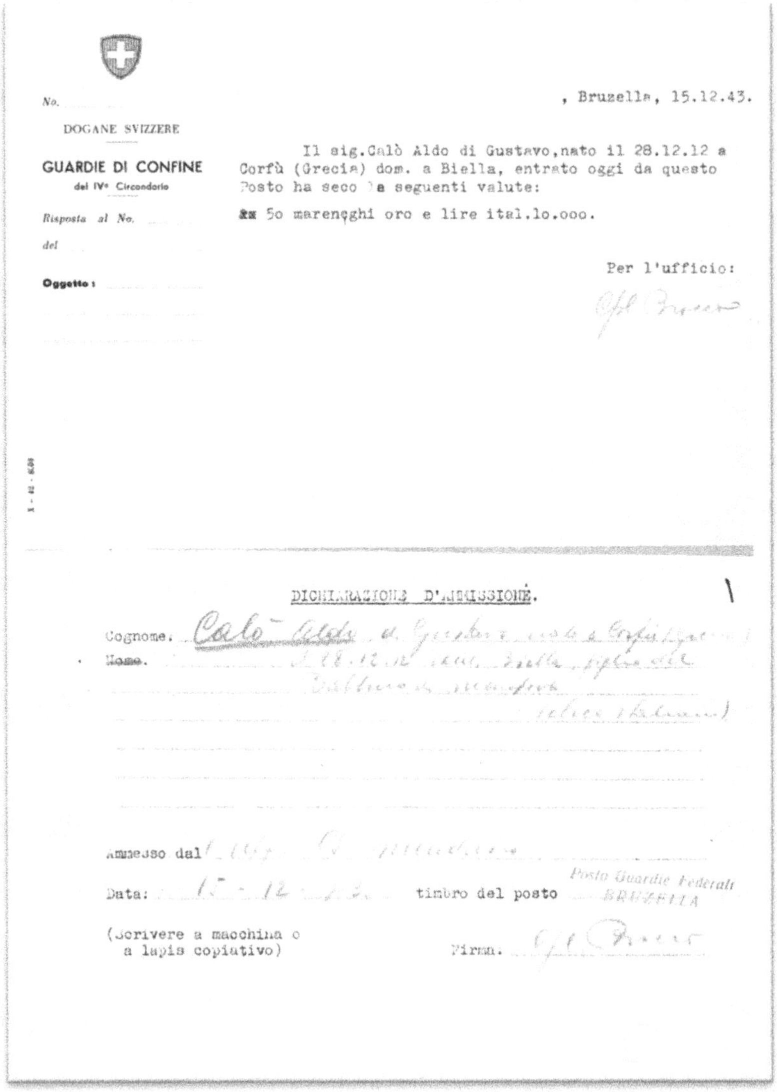

No.

DOGANE SVIZZERE

GUARDIE DI CONFINE
del IV° Circondorio

Risposta al No.

del

Oggetto:

, Bruzella, 15.12.43.

Il sig.Calò Aldo di Gustavo,nato il 28.12.12 a Corfù (Grecia) dom. a Biella, entrato oggi da questo Posto ha seco la seguenti valute:

50 marenghi oro e lire ital.10.000.

Per l'ufficio:

DICHIARAZIONE D'AMMISSIONE.

Cognome. Calò Aldo

Nome.

Ammesso dal

Data: 15 - 12 timbro del posto Posto Guardie Federali BRUZELLA

(Scrivere a macchina o a lapis copiativo)

Firma.

Declaration of civil status issued by Border Guards at Bruzella

Mr. Aldo Caló, born December 28, 1912 in Corfu, Greece resides in Biella

"I do not have any possession neither in Switzerland nor elsewhere. I brought with me 50 marenghi and 10,000 lire."

... he entered at Bruzella December 15, 1943. His parents have already been admitted and he had valuables to deposit.

He entered at 05:30 on December 15, 1943.

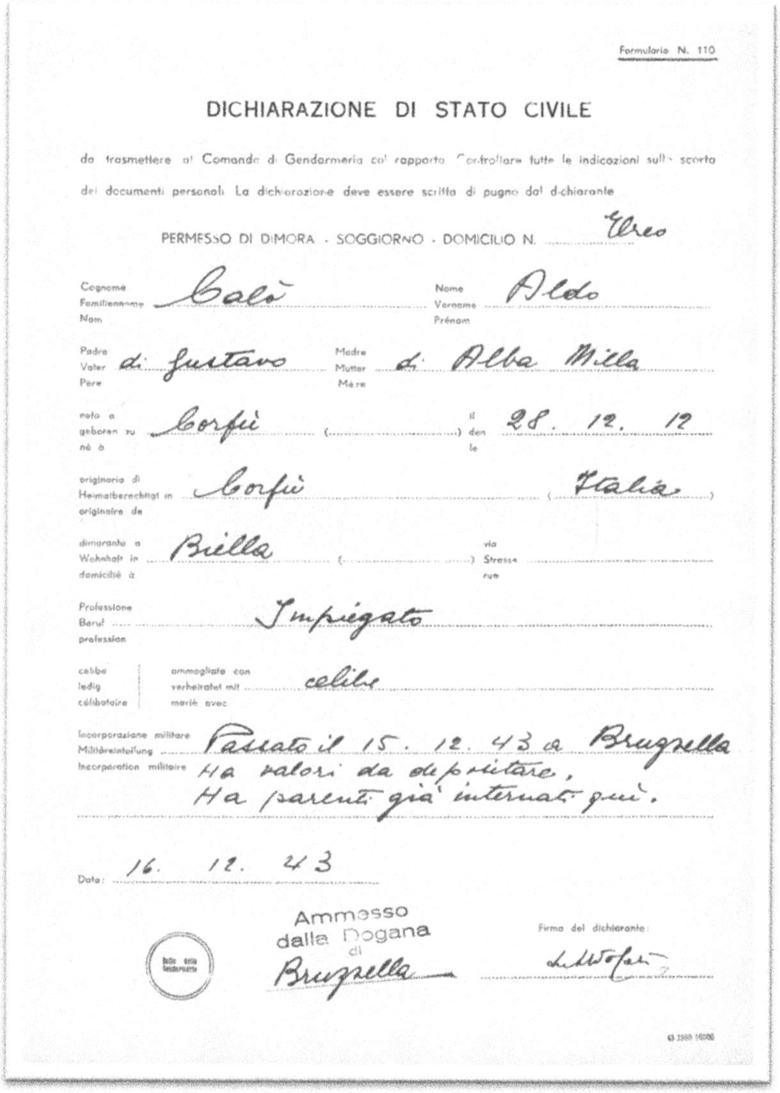

Formulario N. 110

DICHIARAZIONE DI STATO CIVILE

da trasmettere al Comando di Gendarmeria col rapporto. Controllare tutte le indicazioni sulla scorta dei documenti personali. La dichiarazione deve essere scritta di pugno dal dichiarante

PERMESSO DI DIMORA - SOGGIORNO - DOMICILIO N. Ebreo

Cognome / Familienname / Nom: Calò — Nome / Vorname / Prénom: Aldo

Padre / Vater / Père: di Gustavo — Madre / Mutter / Mère: di Alba Milla

nato a / geboren zu / né à: Corfù (…) il / den / le: 28. 12. 12

originario di / Heimatberechtigt in / originaire de: Corfù (Italia)

dimorante a / Wohnhaft in / domicilié à: Biella (…) via / Strasse / rue:

Professione / Beruf / profession: Impiegato

celibe / ledig / célibataire | ammogliato con / verheiratet mit / marié avec: celibe

Incorporazione militare / Militäreinteilung / Incorporation militaire: Passato il 15. 12. 43 a Brugnella
Ha valori da depositare,
Ha parenti già internati qui.

Data: 16. 12. 43

Ammesso dalla Dogana di Brugnella

Firma del dichiarante: [signature]

Declaration of admission

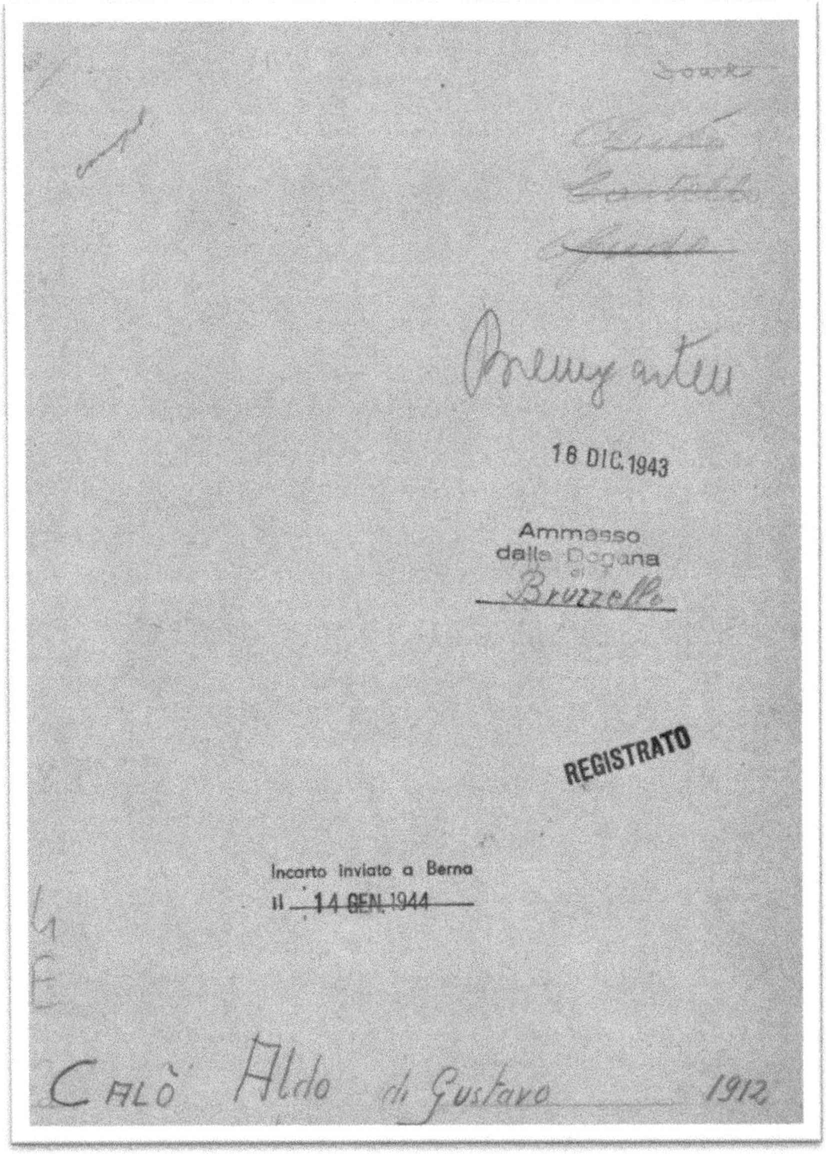
18 DIC. 1943

Ammesso dalla Dogana di Bruzzella

REGISTRATO

Incarto inviato a Berna il 14 GEN. 1944

CALÒ Aldo di Gustavo 1912

17. Ort und Zeit des Grenzübertrittes:
Lieu et date du passage de la frontière:
Località, data e ora dello sconfinamento: Al POsto Guardie Federali di Bruzzella, il 14.12.43. a,lle ore 17.30

18. Gesundheitszustand:
Etat de santé:
Condizioni di salute: buone

19. Verwandte und Bekannte in der Schweiz:
Parents et connaissances en Suisse:
Parenti e conoscenze nella Svizzera: nessuno

20. Allfällige Garanten in der Schweiz:
Répondants éventuels en Suisse:
Eventuali garanti nella Svizzera:

21. Genaue Zusammenstellung der Vermögensmittel im In- und Ausland:
Liste exacte des ressources à l'étranger et en Suisse:
Specificazione esatta dei beni patrimoniali in Svizzera e all'estero: Non posseggo beni patrimoniali nè in Isvizzera nè all'Estero.Ho portato con me 50 marenghi oro e Lire it. 10,000-

22. Vermerk ob Mitteilung über Verhalten der Flüchtlinge bekanntgegeben:
L'« avis au réfugié » a-t-il été porté à la connaissance du réfugié?
La « Communicazione ai rifugiati » è stata portata a conoscenza dell'interessato? si.

Einvernommen durch:
Interrogé par:
Interrogato da:

Der Flüchtling:
Le réfugié:
Il rifugiato:

Alba Milla Caló

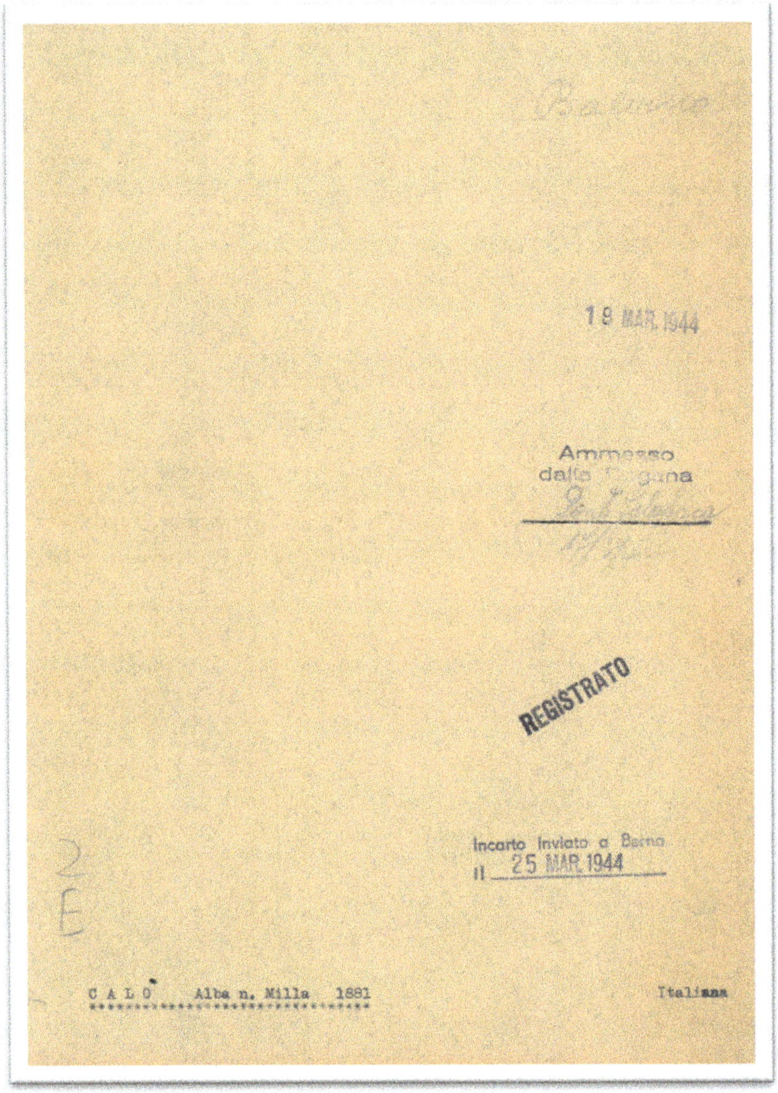
18 MAR. 1944

Ammesso
dalla Dogana

REGISTRATO

Incarto inviato a Berna
il 25 MAR. 1944

C A L O Alba n. Milla 1881 Italiana

Eidgenössisches Justiz- und Polizeidepartement
Polizeiabteilung
Département fédéral de justice et police
Division de police
Dipartimento federale di giustizia e polizia
Divisione della polizia

Einvernahmeprotokoll
Procès-verbal d'interrogatoire
Verbale d'interrogatoio

B ellinzona, den / le / li 19.3.1944

1. Name: / Nom: / Cognome: C a l ò - Milla
2. Vorname: / Prénom: / Nome: Alba
3. Staatszugehörigkeit: / Nationalité: / Nazionalità: italienne
4. Bei Staatenlosigkeit frühere Staatszugehörigkeit: / Ancienne nationalité (en cas d'apatridie): / Precedente nazionalità (per apolidi):
5. Vorname des Vaters: / Prénom du père: / Nome del padre: Raffaele +
6. Vor- und Geburtsname der Mutter: / Prénom et nom de famille de la mère: / Nome e cognome di nascita della madre: Elisa Bassani +
7. Geburtsdatum: / Date de naissance: / Data di nascita: 11.11.1881
8. Geburtsort: / Lieu de naissance: / Luogo di nascita: Verona
9. Früherer Wohnort: / Ancien domicile: / Domicilio precedente: Mantova, Via G.Govi, 9
10. Beruf: / Profession: / Professione: ménagère
11. Zivilstand: / Etat-civil: / Stato civile: mariée
12. Konfession: / Confession: / Religione: israelite
13. Begleitende Familienangehörige: / Membres de la famille accompagnant l'intéressé: / Congiunti che accompagnano l'interessato:
    Mari : Calò Gustavo, 1879, Firenze
    Nièce : Vitale Nora, 1939, Biella
    Nièce : " Silvia,1941, Biella
    Neveu: Schlesinger Lodovico, 1940, Mantova
14. Ausweispapiere: / Papiers d'identité: / Documenti di legittimazione: Carte d'identité No. 0.112.641 Mantova 28.5.1941
15. Militärische Einteilung: / Incorporation militaire: / Incorporazione militare: aucune.
16. Grund und Umstände der Flucht sowie eingeschlagener Weg: / Motifs et circonstances de la fuite ainsi que route suivie: / Motivi e circostanze della fuga come pure percorso seguito:

Motif de la fuite: Persécution raciale.
Circonstances de la fuite: J'ai fait mes études à l'école publique de Verona, obtenant le diplôme d'institutrice. J'ai exercé ma profession quelques années à Verona et en 1909 je me suis mariée, suivant ainsi mon mari qui était rabbin-chef, à Corfù(Grèce). En 1919 nous partîmes pour Bengasi(Lybie); nous rentrâmes en 1922 en Italie prenant domicile à Pitigliano xxxxxxxxxxx en 1925 à Parma, puis finalement à Mantova. Je n'ai jamais eu des ennuis avec la police, même après la loi raciale de 1938. Mais avec l'arrivée des allemands à Mantoue, commencèrent les perquisitions dans la maison. En effet au début du mois d'octobre j'ai eu la visite des allemands qui m'ont demandé si j'avais des armes. J'en avais pas et ils sont alorsrepartis, emportant la montre en or de mon mari, ainsi que les vivres que j'avais dans la cuisine. Le lendemain deux autres allemands se sont présentés à nouveau à mon domicile, mettant les mains partout. Ils n'ont rien emporté cette fois; par contre ils m'ont demandé une quantité de renseignements sur le compte de mes enfants, et notamment de mon beau-fils Schlesinger, mettant la maison sous séquestre. Il était évident, que ma liberté ne pouvait être de longue durée. Ainsi nous avons décidé de nous éclipser. Je suis partie pour Biella chez ma fille et comme là aussi on n'était pas en sureté, je suis partie pour Gattinara et ensuite à Formigliana(Vercelli) dans une étable de propriété de ma fille. Le locataire, devant dénoncer à la prefecture ma présence, en application de la loi sur le recensement, j'ai dû me décider de prendre la fuite vers la Suisse. Route suivie: Le mercredi 15.3.4 je suis partie avec mon mari et les enfants pour Novara et Olgiate Comasco, où je suis déscendue à la Trattoria della Stazione, où nous avons été reçus par un inconnu, qui nous a conduit chez lui.

F 115/685

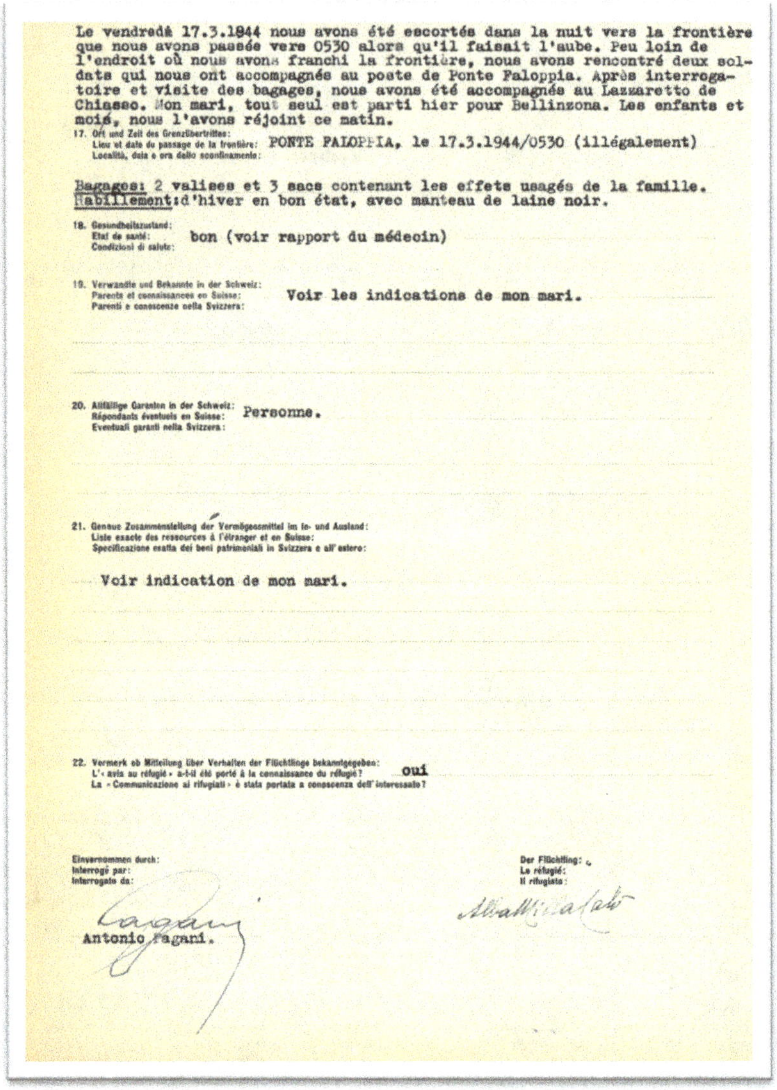

Le vendredâ 17.3.1944 nous avons été escortés dans la nuit vers la frontière que nous avons passée vers 0530 alors qu'il faisait l'aube. Peu loin de l'endroit où nous avons franchi la frontière, nous avons rencontré deux soldats qui nous ont accompagnés au poste de Ponte Faloppia. Après interrogatoire et visite des bagages, nous avons été accompagnés au Lazzaretto de Chiasso. Mon mari, tout seul est parti hier pour Bellinzona. Les enfants et moié, nous l'avons réjoint ce matin.

17. Ort und Zeit des Grenzübertrittes:
Lieu et date du passage de la frontière: PONTE FALOPPIA, le 17.3.1944/0530 (illégalement)
Località, data e ora dello sconfinamento:

Bagages: 2 valises et 3 sacs contenant les effets usagés de la famille.
Habillement: d'hiver en bon état, avec manteau de laine noir.

18. Gesundheitszustand:
Etat de santé: bon (voir rapport du médecin)
Condizioni di salute:

19. Verwandte und Bekannte in der Schweiz:
Parents et connaissances en Suisse: Voir les indications de mon mari.
Parenti e conoscenze nella Svizzera:

20. Allfällige Garanten in der Schweiz:
Répondants éventuels en Suisse: Personne.
Eventuali garanti nella Svizzera:

21. Genaue Zusammenstellung der Vermögensmittel im In- und Ausland:
Liste exacte des ressources à l'étranger et en Suisse:
Specificazione esatta dei beni patrimoniali in Svizzera e all'estero:

Voir indication de mon mari.

22. Vermerk ob Mitteilung über Verhalten der Flüchtlinge bekanntgegeben:
L'« avis au réfugié » a-t-il été porté à la connaissance du réfugié? oui
La « Comunicazione ai rifugiati » è stata portata a conoscenza dell'interessato?

Einvernommen durch:
Interrogé par:
Interrogato da:

Antonio Pagani.

Der Flüchtling:
Le réfugié:
Il rifugiato:

Interrogation report issued by the Police at Bellinzona

Reason for fleeing: racial persecutions.

Fleeing circumstances: I graduated a public school in Verona and received a teaching certificate; I worked as a teacher in Verona and in 1909 I married and followed my husband that was a chief Rabbi to Corfu' (Greece). In 1919 we moved to Bengazi (Lybia) and in 1923 we returned to Italy, to Pitigliano. In 1925 we moved to Parma and finally to Mantova. I never had any problems with the police, not even after the racial laws of 1938 but with the arrival of the Germans to Mantova they started conducting searches in our house. Actually, in the beginning of October Germans came and asked if we had weapons. As we did not have any they took my husband's gold watch and some food from the kitchen and left. The next day two other Germans came back to our house and went around touching everything. This time they didn't take anything but on the other hand they asked a lot about my kids and particularily my daughter in law Schlesinger, placing the house under supervision. It was obvious that my freedom would not last. Thus we decided to leave. I left with my daughter for Biella but since we weren't safe even there we left for Gattinara and then Formigliana (Vercelli) to a barn that belonged to my daughter. Due to the recent census, the tenant had to report our presence. I therefore decided to escape to Switzerland.

Route taken: Wednesday March 15, 1944 I left with my husband and children towards Novara and Olgate Commasco where I stopped at the "Trattoria della stazione" where we met a stranger that took us to his place. Friday, March 17, 1944 we were escorted towards the border which we crossed at 05:30, at dawn. Not far from the point where we crossed the border we came upon two soldiers that took us to the station at Ponte Faloppia. After an interrogation and perusal of our bags we were taken to Lazzaretto de Chiasso. My husband, went by himself to Bellinzona. The children and I joined him in the morning.

DIPARTIMENTO CANTONALE DI POLIZIA

Bellinzona.

UFFICIO CANTONALE STRANIERI

Alla Gendarmeria cantonale

No. 1947.-

Orselina

Vi trasmettiamo annesso il decreto d'internamento emanato dalla Divisione di Polizia del Dipartimento Federale di Giustizia e Polizia nei confronti dell'attinente italiano

C A L O' Alba, nata il 11 novembre 1881,

Lo stesso è autorizzato a dimorare in Orselina

presso

sino nuovo avviso, ed alle seguenti condizioni:

1. Astensione da qualsiasi attività politica di atto e contegno contrario alla neutralità della Svizzera.
2. Divieto di esercitare qualsiasi attività lucrativa o anche di accettare un impiego non retribuito.
3. Divieto di esercitare una pubblica attività (Conferenze, scritti per giornali, pubblicazioni, collaborazioni alla radio, al teatro, ai cinema).
4. Divieto di abbandonare la località di residenza fissata e di cambiare residenza nella località di soggiorno.
5. Deposito presso la Banca Popolare Svizzera a Berna di tutti i mezzi liquidi e degli oggetti di valore posseduti in Svizzera o che possono loro pervenire dall'estero.
6.

Il rifugiato rimane sottoposto al controllo della Divisione Federale di Polizia del Dipartimento Federale di Giustizia e Polizia.

Non è necessario che vengano regolate le condizioni della sua dimora.

TESSERA DI RAZIONAMENTO - Per la sussistenza ogni interessato riceverà per ogni 15 giorni, dall'Ufficio cant. Forestieri, una dichiarazione di sussistenza (Modulo UGV AF 1) che dovrà essere consegnata all'Ufficio dell'Economia di Guerra del Comune di dimora per ottenere le corrispondenti tessere di razionamento, qualora non fosse ancora in possesso del Libretto per rifugiati.

UFFICIO CANTONALE DEGLI STRANIERI

COMUNICAZIONE:

all'interessato per il tramite della Polizia cant. di Orselina

alla Polizia cant. di Orselina

alla Municipalità di Orselina

all'Ufficio comunale dell'Economia di Guerra di Orselina

Al Comando Terr. 9b. - Uff. di polizia - Posta da Campo.

Allegato menzionato.

44 603 2000

The local police advise the police of Orselina that Alba Caló has been granted permission to stay in Orselina with the following restrictions:

Forbidden to take part in any political activity contrary to the neutrality of Switzerland.

1. Forbidden to exercise any payable activity or even non payable activity

2. Forbidden to exercise any public activity (Conferences, write to newspapers, participate in radio, theatre and cinema)

3. Forbidden to leave her assigned place of residence for a different one.

Deposit with Banca Popolare Svizzera in Bern all liquid assets or valuables in her possession in Switzerland or others assets that may come into her possession from outside Switzerland.

Eidgenössisches Justiz- und Polizeidepartement
Polizeiabteilung
Département fédéral de justice et police
Division de police
Dipartimento federale di giustizia e polizia
Divisione della polizia

Einvernahmeprotokoll
Procès-verbal d'interrogatoire
Verbale d'interrogatoio

Bellinzona, den / le / il 18.3.1944

1. Name: / Nom: / Cognome: C a l ò
2. Vorname: / Prénom: / Nome: Gustavo
3. Staatszugehörigkeit: / Nationalité: / Nazionalità: italienne
4. Bei Staatenlosigkeit frühere Staatszugehörigkeit: / Ancienne nationalité (en cas d'apatridie): / Precedente nazionalità (per apolidi):
5. Vorname des Vaters: / Prénom du père: / Nome del padre: Giuseppe +
6. Vor- und Geburtsname der Mutter: / Prénom et nom de famille de la mère: / Nome e cognome di nascita della madre: Enrichetta Chiron +
7. Geburtsdatum: / Date de naissance: / Data di nascita: 29.8.1879
8. Geburtsort: / Lieu de naissance: / Luogo di nascita: Firenze
9. Früherer Wohnort: / Ancien domicile: / Domicilio precedente: Mantova, Via Gilberto Govi, 9
10. Beruf: / Profession: / Professione: Rabbin-chef
11. Zivilstand: / Etat-civil: / Stato civile: marié
12. Konfession: / Confession: / Religione: israelite
13. Begleitende Familienangehörige: / Membres de la famille accompagnant l'intéressé: / Congiunti che accompagnano l'interessato:
    Femme: Calò-Milla Alta, 1881, Verona
    Nièce: Vitale Nora, 1939, Biella
    Nièce: " Silvia, 1941, Biella
    Neveu : Schlesinger Lodovico, 1940, Mantova.
14. Ausweispapiere: / Papiers d'identité: / Documenti di legittimazione: Carte d'identité No. 11.548.845 Mantova 7.10.1943
    Certificat de naissance No. 1879/14469 Florence 13.10.1936.
15. Militärische Einteilung: / Incorporation militaire: / Incorporazione militare: Aucune.
16. Grund und Umstände der Flucht sowie eingeschlagener Weg: / Motifs et circonstances de la fuite ainsi que route suivie: / Motivi e circostanze della fuga come pure percorso seguito:
    Motif de la fuite: Persécution raciale.
    Circonstances de la fuite: J'ai fait mes études au Collège pour Rabbins et à l'Université de Florence. En 1907 j'ai été nommé rabbin de Verona, en 1909 à Corfù, 1920 à Bongani, en 1922 à Pitigliano(Grosseto) en 1925 à Parma et finalement en 1927 à Mantova. Je suis resté dans cette ville jusqu'au mois d'octobre 1943, alors que je me suis éclipsé pour ne pas être arrêté. En ma qualité de rabbin, je n'ai jamais eu des difficultés avec les autorités italiennes, même après l'entrée en vigueur de la loi raciale de 1938. En effet, c'est seulement à la suite de l'arrivée des allemands, que j'ai été importuné par eux. Au début du mois d'octobre 1943, alors que j'étais tout seul à la maison, deux soldats allemands se sont présentés à mon domicile, qui a été perquisitionné. Ils ont emporté ma montre avec la chaîne en or qui était sur la table, ainsi que des vivres et ils sont ensuite repartis, sans m'arrêter, après avoir demandé si j'avais des armes. Le lendemain se sont présentés deux allemands, pour le même but. Ils ont mis la maison sous séquestre, mais ils ne m'ont pas arrêté. Dans ces conditions il était trop évident que mon arrestation n'était plus lointaine. et ainsi je me suis éclipsé avec ma femme. Je me suis réfugié d'abord à Brescia, dans un hôtel et ensuite à Gattinara(Vercelli) chez mon ami Pagliardi, passant ensuite à Formigliana(Vercelli) dans une étable. C'était le 17.11.1943 alors que j'arrivais dans ce hameau. Le propriétaire devant dénoncer ma présence à la suite d'un ordre analogue du Préfet de la Province, j'ai du me décider à fuir en Suisse. Route suivie: Le mercredi 15.3.1944 je suis parti avec ma femme et mes neveux pour Olgiate Comasco, où je suis descendu à la Trattoria della Stazione. Les guides (5) m'ont accompagné avec ma famille à la frontière que j'ai passée le 16.3.1944/0530 dans les environs de Ponte Faloppia. Peu loin de l'endroit

F 115/555

deux

où j' ai franchi la frontière, j'ai rencontré ~~xx~~ soldats qui m'ont accompagné au poste. Après interrogatoire et visite des bagages, j'ai été a compagné en auto au Lazzaretto de Chiasso, où a eu lieu la visite sanitaire. Ce matin je sui parti tout seul pour Bellinzona. Ma femme avec ses noveux est restée à Chiasso pour la désinfection et suivrant dans deux ou trois jours.

17. Ort und Zeit des Grenzübertrittes:
Lieu et date du passage de la frontière:
Località, data e ora dello sconfinamento: PONTE FALOPPIA, le 17.3.1944/0530 (illégalement)

B agages: 2 valises et 3 sacs contenant leseffets personnels usagés de toute la famille.

Habillement: d'hiver en bon état, avec manteau de laine noir.

18. Gesundheitszustand:
Etat de santé:
Condizioni di salute: bon (voir rapport du médecin).

19. Verwandte und Bekannte in der Schweiz:
Parents et connaissances en Suisse:
Parenti e conoscenze nella Svizzera: Fille: Elsa Vitale-Calò, 1916, avec son mari Alberto, Villa Les Hirondelles, LOCARNO-ORSELINA. (Réfugiés Civils libérés)

Fille: Enrichetta Schlesinger-Calò, avec le mari Guido et les deux filles, Réfugiés civils, atuellement au camp "MAJESTIC" de Lugano.

Fils: Raffaele Calò, avec sa femme Matilde Vita-Levi, réfugiés civils en Suisse, depuis une quinzaine(adresse inconnue)

Fils: Aldo Calò, 1912, Réfugié civil depuis décembre 1943 (adresse inconnue)

20. Allfällige Garanten in der Schweiz:
Répondants éventuels en Suisse:
Eventuali garanti nella Svizzera: Personne.

21. Genaue Zusammenstellung der Vermögensmittel im In- und Ausland:
Liste exacte des ressources à l'étranger et en Suisse:
Specificazione esatta dei beni patrimoniali in Svizzera e all'estero:

En Suisse: Les bijoux que j'ai déposé à Bellinzona, selon quittance.

En Italie: Rien.Je vivais de mon maigre salaire.

22. Vermerk ob Mitteilung über Verhalten der Flüchtlinge bekanntgegeben:
L'« avis au réfugié » a-t-il été porté à la connaissance du réfugié? oui.
La « Communicazione ai rifugiati » è stata portata a conoscenza dell'interessato?

Einvernommen durch:
Interrogé par:
Interrogato da:

Antonio Pagani.

Der Flüchtling:
Le réfugié:
Il rifugiato:

Report of interrogation (issued by the Police of Bellinzona):

Reason for fleeing: Racial persecutions.

Fleeing circumstances: I graduated the College for Rabbis and University in Florence. In 1907 I was nominated Rabbi of Verona, in 1909 Rabbi of Corfu', 1920 of Bengasi, 1922 Pitigliano (Grosseto), 1925 Parma, and finally 1927 Mantova. I stayed there until October 1943 when I was afraid of being arrested and had to flee. As a Rabbi I never had any problem with the Italian authorities, not even after the implementation of the racial laws in 1938. As a matter of fact it was only after the arrival of the Germans that I was bothered at all. At the beginning of October 1943, as I was by myself in the apartment, two soldiers showed up and searched the place. They took my gold watch with the gold chain that was on the table , some food, asked me if I had any weapons and left without arresting me. The next day they came back to do the same without arresting me. Under these circumstances it was evident that my arrest was imminent and I fled with my wife. First I found refuge in a hotel in Brescia, then in Gattinara (Vercelli) at my friend's Pagliardi house, then on November 1, 1943 onto Formigliana (Vercelli) in a barn. The owner of the barn, had to denounce me so I decided to flee to Switzerland.

Route taken: Wednesday March 15, 1944 I left with my wife, children and my nephew towards Olgate Commasco where I stopped at the "Trattoria della stazione". The guides (5) escorted us on March 16, 1944 towards the border which we crossed at 05:30 near Ponte Faloppia. Not far from the point where we crossed I came upon some soldiers that took us to the station. After an interrogation and perusal of our bags we were taken by car to Lazzaretto de Chiasso where we had a medical exam. That morning I left by myself for Bellinzona. My wife and our nephew stayed behind for the medical exam and followed me after two or three days.

Acquaintances in Switzerland:

Daughters: Elsa Vitale-Caló with her husband Alberto, Villa les Hirondelles, Locarno/Orselina, released civil refugees.

Enrichetta Schlesinger Caló with her husband Guido and two daughters, civil refugees, currently at the Majestic camp, Lugano.

Son: Raffaele Caló with his wife Matilde Vita/Levi, civil refugees in Switzerland, address unknown.

Aldo Caló 1912, civil refugee since December 1943, address unknown.

Assets in Switzerland: Jewelry which I deposited in Bellinzona, as per receipt.

Abroad: nothing, I lived of my modest income.

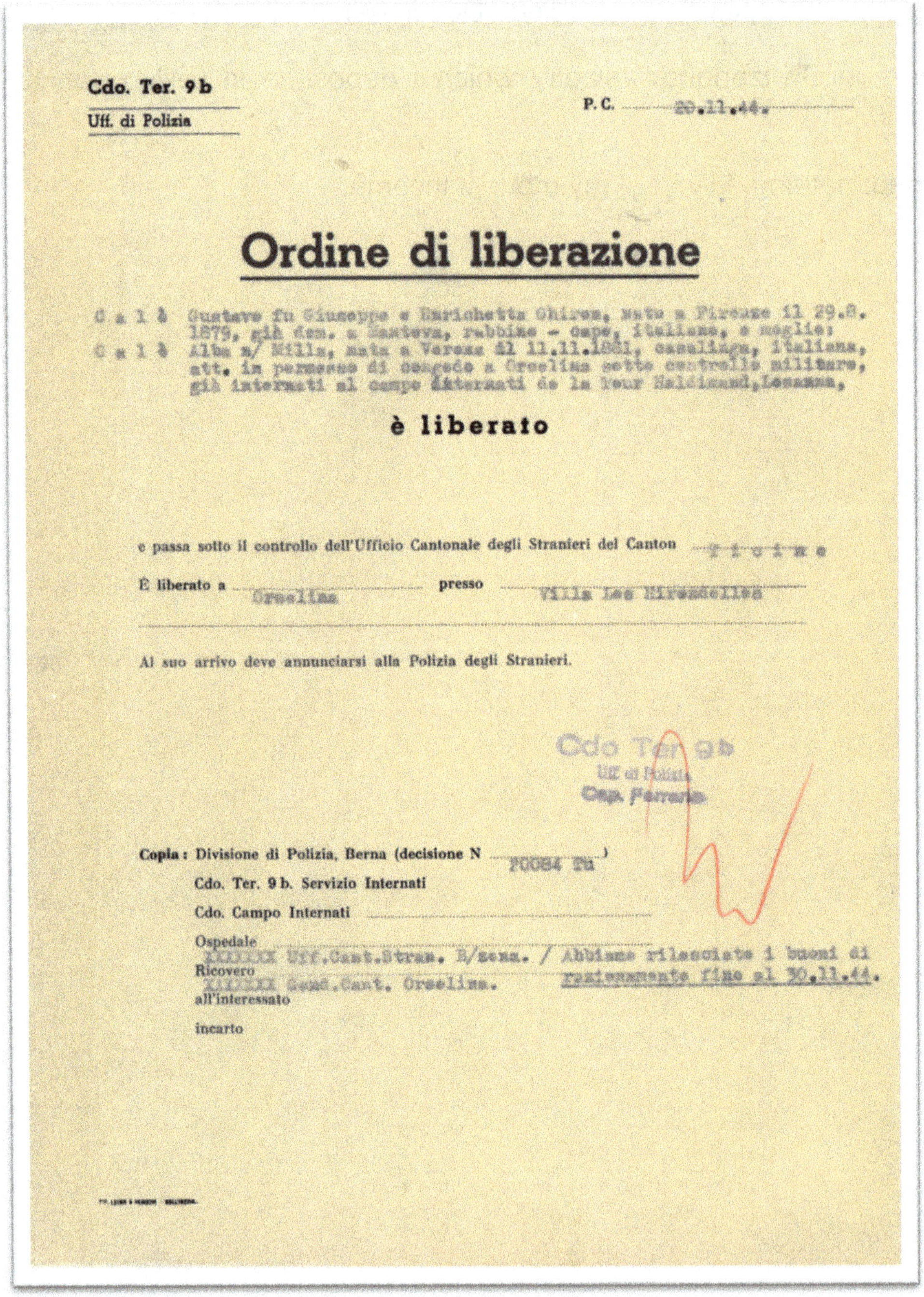

Cdo. Ter. 9 b

Uff. di Polizia

P. C. 20.11.44.

Ordine di liberazione

Calò Gustavo fu Giuseppe e Enrichetta Ghiron, nato a Firenze il 29.8.1879, già dom. a Genova, rabbino - capo, italiano, e moglie:
Calò Alba n/ Milla, nata a Varese il 11.11.1881, casalinga, italiana, att. in permesso di congedo a Orselina sotto controllo militare, già internati al campo internati de la Tour Haldimand, Losanna,

è liberato

e passa sotto il controllo dell'Ufficio Cantonale degli Stranieri del Canton Ticino

È liberato a Orselina presso Villa Les Hirondelles

Al suo arrivo deve annunciarsi alla Polizia degli Stranieri.

Cdo Ter 9b
Uff di Polizia
Cap. Ferraris

Copia: Divisione di Polizia, Berna (decisione N F0084 Fu)
Cdo. Ter. 9 b. Servizio Internati
Cdo. Campo Internati
Ospedale XXXXXX Uff.Cant.Stran. B/zona. / Abbiamo rilasciato i buoni di
Ricovero XXXXXX Gend.Cant. Orselina. razionamento fino al 30.11.44.
all'interessato
incarto

Eidgenössisches Justiz- und Polizeidepartement
Polizeiabteilung

Département fédéral de justice et police
Division de police

Dipartimento federale di giustizia e polizia
Divisione della polizia

No. N 20084 Kü

Bitte in der Antwort angeben
A indiquer dans la réponse
Pregasi ripeterlo nella risposta

Berna, 11 9 gennaio 1945.

Signor Gustavo Calò,
Villa les hirondelles,
Orselina, TI.

Ci riferiamo alla vostra lettera del 15 dicembre 1944 e vi comunichiamo che i due libretti per rifugiati di Gustavo C a l ò, nato il 29 agosto 1879, e di Alba C a l ò, nata l'11 novembre 1881, sono stati inoltrati in data 25 aprile 1944 all'Uff. di Polizia del Cdo. Ter. 9 b, poichè a quell'epoca eravate ambedue sottoposti al controllo di detto ufficio militare. Se nel frattempo non siete venuto in possesso dei due libretti, vi preghiamo di volar entrare direttamente in comunicazione con tale Istanza. Non appena avrete ottenuto i libretti, vogliate farceli pervenire, affinchè possiamo registrarvi il cambiamento d'indirizzo.

Con distinta stima:

IL CAPO DELLA DIVISIONE DELLA POLIZIA.

p.o.

i. A. sig. Tschäppät

Copia a:

Cdo. Ter. 9 b, Uff. di Polizia, Posta da campo, con preghiera di esaminare se i libretti dei rifugiati suddetti si trovano ancora in vostro possesso. In tal caso, vi preghiamo di spedirceli, affinchè possiamo registrarvi il cambiamento di indirizzo e trasmetterli all'Ufficio competente.

Kü

3 D 9646

18 MAR. 1944
Ammesso
dalla Dogana
di
17-3-44
REGISTRATO
Incarto inviato a Berna
il 25 MAR. 1944
C A L O'' Gustavo fu' Giuseppe 1879

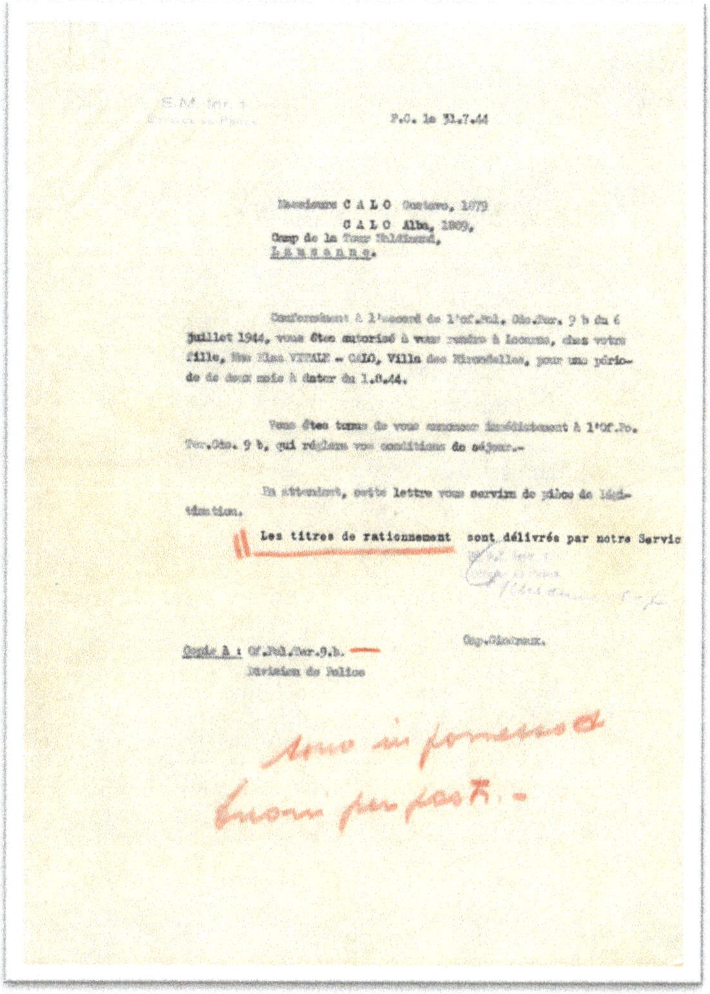

P.C. le 31.7.44

Messieurs C A L O Gustavo, 1879
C A L O Alba, 1889,
Camp de la Tour Haldimand,
Lausanne.

Conformément à l'accord de l'Of.Pol. Cdo.Ter. 9 b du 6 juillet 1944, vous êtes autorisé à vous rendre à Locarno, chez votre fille, Mme [illegible] VITALE – CALO, Villa des Hirondelles, pour une période de deux mois à dater du 1.8.44.

Vous êtes tenus de vous annoncer immédiatement à l'Of.Po. Ter.Cdo. 9 b, qui réglera vos conditions de séjour.-

En attendant, cette lettre vous servira de pièce de légitimation.

Les titres de rationnement sont délivrés par notre Servic

Cap. [illegible]

Copie à : Of.Pol.Ter.9.b.
Division de Police

The Police at Camp de la Tour Halimand in Lausanne grants Gustavo Caló and Alba Caló permission to go to Locarno and stay with their daughter for a period of two months. They are given food stamps

Cdo. Ter. 9 b

Uff. di Polizia

P. C. 8.8.44.

Liberazione sotto controllo militare

C a l o' Gustavo, fu Giuseppe e Enrichetta Ghiron, nato a Firenze il 29.8.1879, già dom. a Mantova, sposato, Capo-Rabbino, citt. ital., e moglie
C a l o' Alba, fu Raffaele e Elisa Bassani, nata a Verona il 11.11.1881, sposata, casalinga, att. al campo de la Tour Haldimand, Losanna,

è liberato

dal campo di internamento e autorizzato a risiedere provvisoriamente a Locarno-Orselina presso la figlia Sig.ra Elsa Vita la-Calo'; Villa des Hirondelles.-

sotto controllo militare. dal 1.8.44. al 30.9.44.-

Il rifugiato si impegna a sottostare alle seguenti condizioni:

a) Astensione da qualsiasi attività politica di atto e contegno contrario alla neutralità della Svizzera. Stretta osservanza delle leggi ed ordinanze e delle prescrizioni vigenti nella Svizzera.

b) Divieto di esercitare qualsiasi attività lucrativa o anche di accettare un impiego non retribuito.

c) Divieto di esercitare una pubblica attività (conferenze, scritti per giornali, pubblicazioni, collaborazione con la Radio, al teatro, ai cinema).

d) Divieto di abbandonare la località di residenza fissata e di cambiare residenza nella località di soggiorno.

e) Deposito presso la Banca Popolare Svizzera a Berna di tutti i mezzi liquidi e degli oggetti di valore posseduti in Svizzera o che possono loro pervenire dall'estero.

f) In caso di malattia darne immediato avviso all'Ufficiale di Polizia il quale provvederà per l'assistenza o l'eventuale ospitalizzazione.

g) Presentarsi alla Gendarmeria Cantonale del luogo di residenza **il primo, il dieci e il venti di ogni mese.**

Divieto di abbandonare il domicilio assegnato dalle ore 2200 alle 0700.

Cdo Ter 9b
Uff. di Polizia

Copia: Divisione di Polizia, Berna
Cdo. Ter. 9 b. Servizio Internati
Cdo. Campo Internati
Ospedale
Ricovero E.M. Ter. 1 Service de Police.
Gendarmeria Cantonale di Orselina.
All'interessato (unita dichiarazione di sussistenza)
incarto

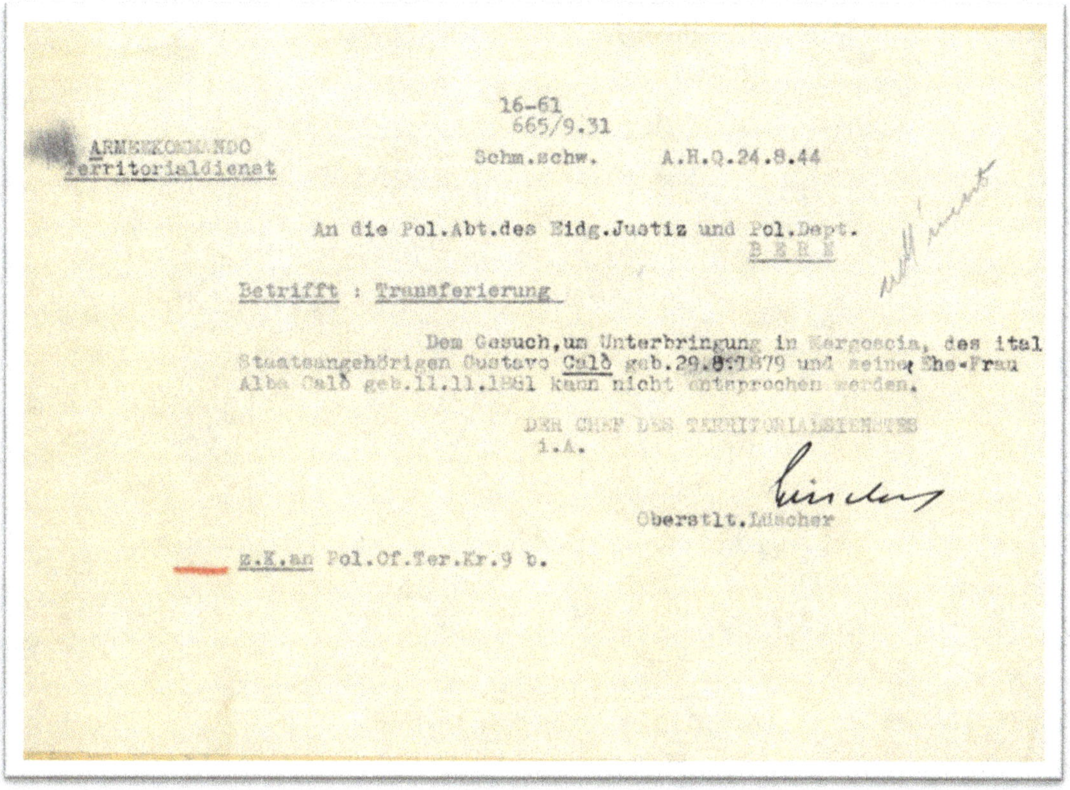

ARMEEKOMMANDO
Territorialdienst

16-61
665/9.31

Schm.schw. A.H.Q.24.8.44

An die Pol.Abt.des Eidg.Justiz und Pol.Dept.
B E R N

Betrifft : Transferierung

Dem Gesuch,um Unterbringung in Mergoscia, des ital Staatsangehörigen Gustavo Calò geb.29.8.1879 und seiner Ehe-Frau Alba Calò geb.11.11.1881 kann nicht entsprochen werden.

DER CHEF DES TERRITORIALDIENSTES
i.A.

Oberstlt.Lüscher

z.K.an Pol.Of.Ter.Kr.9 b.

The local Police advise Bern authorities that Gustavo Caló is forbidden to leave his assigned place of residence from 10 p.m. until 7 a.m.

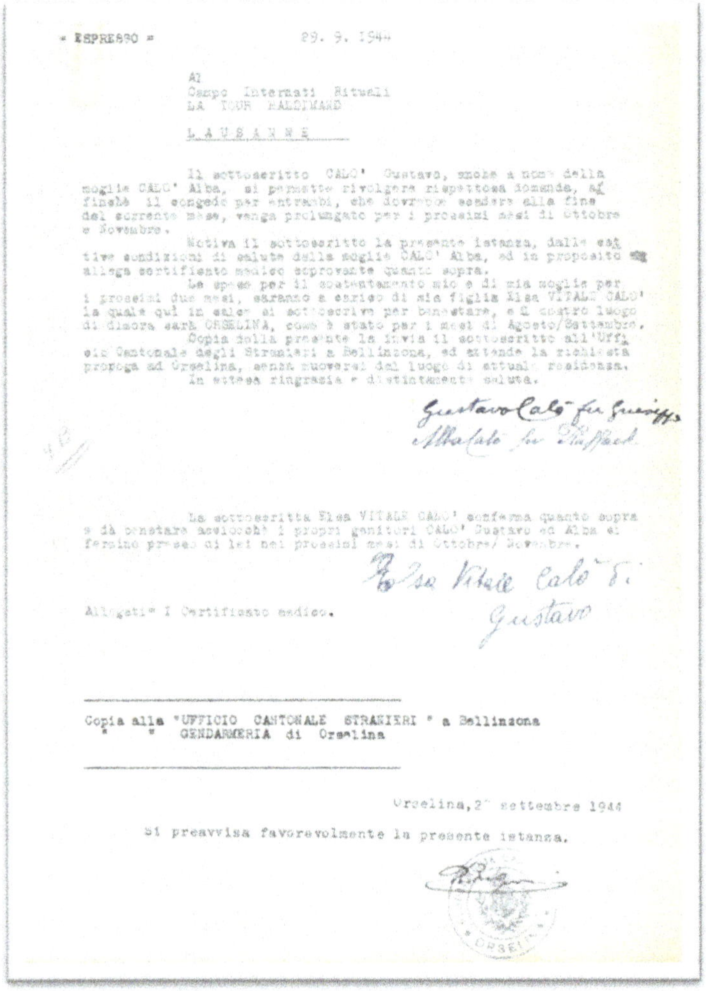

* ESPRESSO *   29. 9. 1944

Al
Campo Internati Rituali
LA TOUR HALDIMAND

LAUSANNE

Il sottoscritto CALO' Gustavo, anche a nome della moglie CALO' Alba, si permette rivolgere rispettosa domanda, affinchè il congedo per entrambi, che dovrebbe scadere alla fine del corrente mese, venga prolungato per i prossimi mesi di Ottobre e Novembre.

Motiva il sottoscritto la presente istanza, dalle cattive condizioni di salute della moglie CALO' Alba, ed in proposito allega certificato medico comprovante quanto sopra.

Le spese per il sostentamento mio e di mia moglie per i prossimi due mesi, saranno a carico di mia figlia Elsa VITALE CALO' la quale qui in calce si sottoscrive per benestare, e il nostro luogo di dimora sarà ORSELINA, come è stato per i mesi di Agosto/Settembre.

Copia della presente la invia il sottoscritto all'Ufficio Cantonale degli Stranieri a Bellinzona, ed attende la richiesta proroga ad Orselina, senza muoversi dal luogo di attuale residenza.

In attesa ringrazia e distintamente saluta.

Gustavo Calò fu Giuseppe
Alba Calò fu Raffael

La sottoscritta Elsa VITALE CALO' conferma quanto sopra e dà benestare acciocchè i propri genitori CALO' Gustavo ed Alba si fermino presso di lei nei prossimi mesi di Ottobre/Novembre.

Elsa Vitale Calò fu Gustavo

Allegati: 1 Certificato medico.

Copia alla "UFFICIO CANTONALE STRANIERI" a Bellinzona
" " GENDARMERIA di Orselina

Orselina, 2[illegible] settembre 1944

Si preavvisa favorevolmente la presente istanza.

ORSELINA

The Police of Orselina advise the camp de la Tour Haldimand in Lausanne that Gustavo Caló asks to extend his stay with his daughterfor two months due to his wife medical condition; he attachemedical certificate in the matter

Schweizerische Armee - Armée suisse - Esercito svizzero

Stab oder Einheit: - Etat-major ou unité: - Stato maggiore o unità: CAMP TOUR HALDIMAND

No.

Ort und Datum: - Lieu et date: - Luogo e data: Losanna, li 30 settembre 1944

AS/eb

Sig. Gustavo Calò
Villa "Les Hirondelles"
O R S E L I N A (Locarno)

In possesso della sua lettera espresso del 29 sett., nella quale ella mi domanda, per lei e per sua moglie, una prolongazione di 2 mesi del congedo accordatole, mi affretto a comunicarle che deve indirizzare tale domanda all'

Ufficiale di Polizia Ter. 9 b
B E L L I N Z O N A

che è l'Autorità competente per concedere tale prolungazione.

Le rinvio pertanto, accluse alla presente, la sua domanda e la dichiarazione medica.

Tanto le dovevo e distintamente la saluto.

Camp de réfugiés
La Tour Haldimand
Le Commandant
PLT. A. SOUTTER

2 allegati

P.S. - Per sua norma, lei, e così pure la sua signora, non dipende più da noi, ma esclusivamente dal suddetto Ufficiale di Polizia di Bellinzona.

627/79120

Dr. med. L. BACILIERI
LOCARNO
Tel. 4.21

DICHIARAZIONE MEDICA

Dal mese di agosto 1944, la Sig.ra Calo' Alba 1881, cittadina Italiana, è in mia cura causa attacchi asmatici, unitamente a debolezza cardiaca, di guisa che si è dovuto intrapprendere una cura molto energica e con iniezioni del caso. Essa deve essere assistita da una persona.

Lo stato attuale è alquanto migliorato, non però in modo tale da potere fare senza del trattamento medico, il quale dovrebbe continuare almeno per altri due/tre mesi.

Dal punto di vista medico sarebbe molto arrischiato di inviare la sopra nominata in un campo di internamento, specialmente se questo si trovasse al di là del Gottardo.

Locarno 29. Settembre. 1944

(Dott. Bacilieri)

Dr. Bacilieri of the Swiss Army Medical declaration:

From the month of August 1944 Mrs. Alba Caló … is in my care for asthmatic attacks as well as heart weakness. …From the medical point of view it would be very risky to send the above mentioned to an internment camp, especially if it were on the other side of the St. Gotthard Pass.

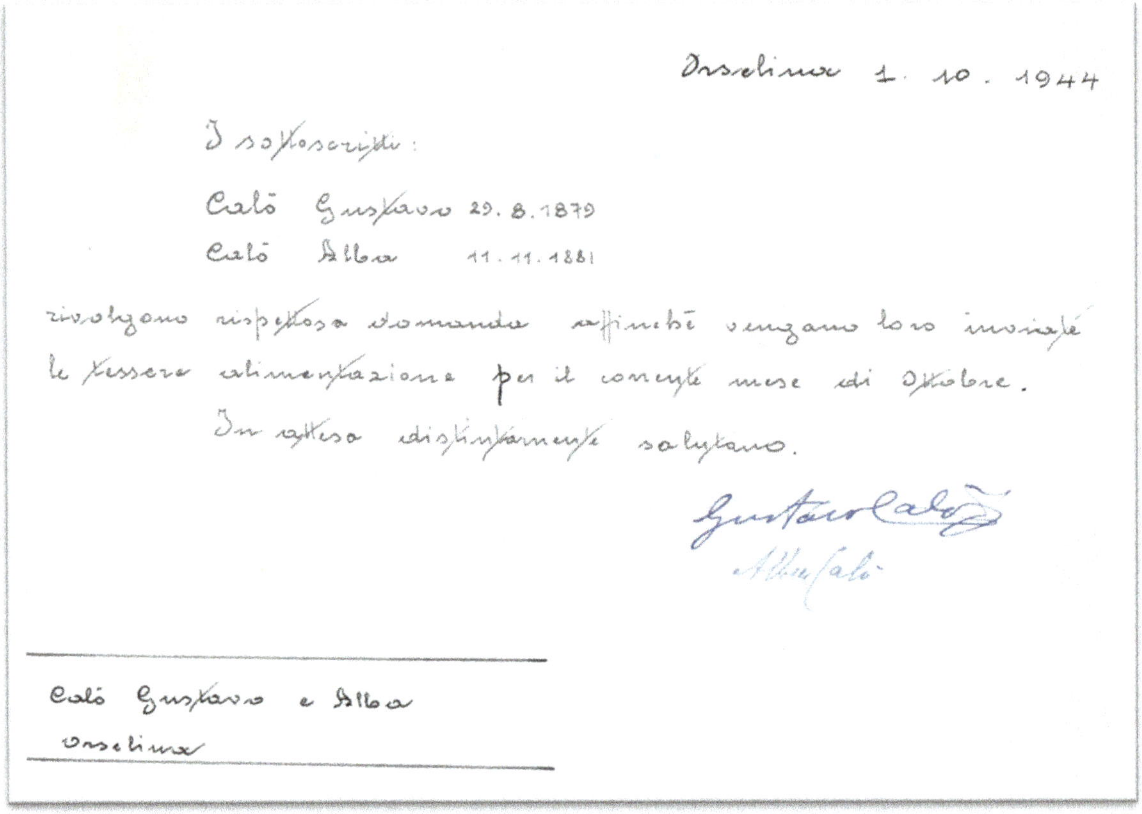

Orselina 1. 10. 1944

I sottoscritti:

Calò Gustavo 29. 8. 1879
Calò Alba 11. 11. 1881

rivolgono rispettosa domanda affinchè vengano loro inviate le tessere alimentazione per il corrente mese di Ottobre.

In attesa distintamente salutano.

Gustavo Calò
Alba Calò

Calò Gustavo e Alba
Orselina

CALO' GUSTAVO
O R S E L I N A

Orselina 4. 10. 1944

Al Lod.
COMANDO TERRITORIALE 9= b.
Uff. di Polizia
B E L L I N Z O N A

Faccio seguito alla mia lettera del 29.9. u.s., diretta all'Ufficio Cantonale Stranieri a Bellinzona, per comunicarVi che il Comando del Campo "La Tour Haldimand" a Losanna, mi ha risposto in data del 30.9. u.s., come la richiesta di rinnovo del congedo per i mesi di Ottobre e Novembre, per me stesso e per mia moglie CALO' Alba, io la debba rivolgere direttamente a codesto lod. Comando 9b.

Mi permetto pertanto con la presente, anche a nome di mia moglie CALO' Alba, rivolgerVi rispettosa domanda, affinchè la nostra liberazione sotto Controllo Militare, emessa da codesto Uff. di Polizia in data 8.8.44., venga rinnovata per altri due mesi, in attesa di ottenere la liberazione definitiva sotto controllo civile, per la quale si renderà garante il Verband Schweirescher Jüdischer Flüchtlingshil, di Zurigo - Lavatestrasse 57 - e per ottenere la quale attendo mi inviate gli stampati necessari.

Motiva il sottoscritto la richiesta di rinnovo, dalle cattive condizioni di salute della moglie, ed in proposito allega certificato medico.

Allega il sottoscritto la primitiva domanda inviata in data 29.9.u.s. a Losanna, unitamente alla risposta del Comando del Campo di colà.

Le spese per il sostentamento mio e di mia moglie, per i mesi di Ottobre/Novembre saranno a carico di mia figlia VITALE CALO' Elsa, la quale quì in calce firma per benestare.

Resta in attesa di benestare, e distintamente saluta.

Gustavo Calò fu Giuseppe
Alba Calò fu Raffaele

3 allegati.

La sottoscritta Elsa VITALE CALO', conforma quanto sopra, e dà benestare acciocchè i propri genitori CALO' Gustavo ed Alba si fermino presso di Lei nei prossimi mesi di Ottobre/Novembre.

Elsa Vitale Calò di Gustavo

Orselina, 4 ottobre 1944

Vi preghiamo di volerci rimettere
il formulario bianco UGV/AF1 onde
poter consegnare agli interessati
i documenti di razionamento.

UFFICIO COMUNALE
dell ECONOMIA di GUERRA
ORSELINA

össisches Justiz- und Polizeidepartement
Polizeiabteilung
Département fédéral de justice et police
Division de police
Dipartimento federale di giustizia e polizia
Divisione della polizia

N 20084 Tu

Bern, den
Berne, le
Berna, il 17 novembre 1944.

Cdo. Terr. 9 b,
Uff. di Polizia,
Posta da Campo.

Betrifft:	**Objet:**	**Oggetto:**
Entlassung aus der militärischen Kontrolle und private Unterbringung (Internierung)	Libération du contrôle militaire et internement en résidence privée	Liberazione dal controllo militare ed internamento sotto controllo civile
von	de	di

Gustavo C a l ò, nato il 29 agosto 1879; Alba C a l ò, nata l'11 novembre 1881, cittadini italiani, attualmente a Orselina,

nach / à / a

Orselina, sopra Locarno.

Die Polizeiabteilung verzichtet vorläufig auf die Einweisung in ein Arbeitslager oder Interniertenheim. Sie behält sich ausdrücklich vor, bei Änderung der Sachlage auf diesen Entscheid zurückzukommen.	La Division de police renonce provisoirement à un placement dans un camp de travail ou dans un home d'internés. Elle se réserve cependant de modifier, suivant les circonstances, la présente décision.	La Divisione della polizia rinuncia provvisoriamente ad un collocamento in un campo di lavoro o in un asilo d'internati. Tuttavia essa si riserva, secondo le circostanze, di modificare la presente decisione.

Beilage/Annexe/Allegato:
2 decreti d'internamento.

DER CHEF DER POLIZEIABTEILUNG
LE CHEF DE LA DIVISION DE POLICE
IL CAPO DELLA DIVISIONE DELLA POLIZIA
p.o.

Kopie an / Copie à / Copia a:
Signor Gustavo Calò;
Kantonale Fremdenpolizei
Police cantonale des étrangers
Polizia cantonale degli stranieri Bellinzona;
Gemeinde
Commune
Comune Orselina;
Ter. Kdo.
Cdmt. ter.
Cdo. terr. 9b, Uff. dei rifugiati, P. da C.;
Schweiz. Bundesanwaltschaft, Bern
Verband Schweiz. Jüdischer Flüchtlingshilfen, Lavaterstr.57, Zürich, ad: GO/ES/NFI;
Statistik
Direzione centrale dei campi di lavoro, Zurigo;

Wichtige Mitteilung auf der Rückseite.
Remarque importante au verso.
Osservazione importante a tergo.

GO F. 22 48 3354

Cdo. Terr. 9 b.
Uff.di Polizia.   P.C. 5 ottobre 1944

Sig. CALO `Gustavo e moglie
<u>O r s e l i n a.</u>

Vi comunichiamo che vi accordiamo un prolungo di congedo di 2 mesi e cioè fino al 30.11.44 ad Orselina, presso la figlia sig.ra Vitale Elsa. Continuerete a presentarvi alla Gendarmeria di Orselina per il controllo.

Cdo Ter 9 b
Uff. di Polizia
Cap. Ferrario

Copia: Cdo. Terr. 1 Off. Pol.
Gendarmeria Cantonale, Orselina
interessati (a mezzo gendarmeria)
incarto

Cdo. Terr. 9 b.
Uff.di Polizia.   P.C. 5 ottobre 1944

Sig. CALO `Gustavo e moglie
<u>O r s e l i n a.</u>

Vi comunichiamo che vi accordiamo un prolungo di congedo di 2 mesi e cioè fino al 30.11.44 ad Orselina, presso la figlia sig.ra Vitale Elsa. Continuerete a presentarvi alla Gendarmeria di Orselina per il controllo.

Cdo Ter 9 b
Uff. di Polizia
Cap. Ferrario

Copia: Cdo. Terr. 1 Off. Pol.
Gendarmeria Cantonale, Orselina
interessati (a mezzo gendarmeria)
incarto

DIPARTIMENTO CANTONALE
DI POLIZIA
UFFICIO CANTONALE STRANIERI

Bellinzona, 25 ottobre 1944

PERMESSO PROVVISORIO DI RESIDENZA

COGNOME E NOME: G A L O' Gustavo, e moglie Alba-1881

DATA DI NASCITA:

NAZIONALITÀ: italiana

LUOGO D'INTERNAMENTO PRIVATO: --

O DEL CAMPO D'INTERNAMENTO: Losanna al Campo Int. Rituali, La Tour Haldimand

LOCALITÀ DI RESIDENZA PROVVISORIA: Orselina

INDIRIZZO ESATTO: (presso chi): figlia Vitale Galo' Elsa, Villa Les Hirondelles

DURATA DELLA RESIDENZA: dal al 30.11.1944

MOTIVO: Cura medica .-

CONDIZIONI: Il rifugiato deve annunciare l'arrivo e la partenza alla Gendarmeria cantonale competente.

La decisione del permesso di residenza dovrà essere timbrato dall'autorità di polizia cantonale competente.

Il rifugiato è personalmente responsabile dell'osservanza di queste condizioni.

Alla scadenza del permesso di residenza provvisoria, il permesso dovrà essere ritornato, munito del timbro di arrivo e partenza, all'Ufficio cantonale degli stranieri in Bellinzona.

UFFICIO CANTONALE STRANIERI

COMUNICAZIONI:

all'interessato a ½ Gend. Cant. di Orselina

alla Gendarmeria cant. di Orselina

alla Municipalità di Orselina

al C.do Terr. 9b., Posta da Campo

all'Ufficio cantonale stranieri di --

alla Divisione federale di Polizia, Berna - No. di rif.

alla Direzione del Campo Internati di xx Rituali, La Tour Haldimand Losanna

44 1292 2000

Wichtige Mitteilung.
Remarque importante.
Osservazione importante.

Für den Lagerkommandanten oder Ter. Pol. Of.:

Vor der Entlassung ist dem Flüchtling der Internierungsbeschluss zu eröffnen und der Polizeiabteilung, versehen mit der unterschriftlichen Bestätigung, dass er davon Kenntnis genommen habe, wieder zuzustellen.

Für den Flüchtling:

Sie haben sich sofort bei der Ortspolizeibehörde des Bestimmungsortes anzumelden, die der kantonalen Fremdenpolizei Meldung erstattet. Diese wird Ihnen die nähern Bedingungen des Internierungsvollzuges bekannt geben.
Falls noch kein Signalementsblatt und keine Photographien erstellt worden sind, die zur Ausstellung des Flüchtlingsausweises benötigt werden, ist dies bei der Anmeldung der Ortspolizei mitzuteilen; diese wird dafür sorgen, dass es nachgeholt wird.

Pour le commandant du camp ou l'officier de police de l'arrondissement territorial:

Avant la libération, la décision d'internement est notifiée au réfugié qui la signera en attestant qu'il en a pris connaissance. Elle sera ensuite renvoyée à la Division de police.

Pour le réfugié:

Vous avez l'obligation de vous annoncer à la police de votre nouveau lieu de résidence qui fera part de votre arrivée à l'autorité de police cantonale des étrangers. Celle-ci vous donnera connaissance des conditions de l'internement.
Si la feuille de signalement et les photographies requises pour l'établissement du livret de réfugié font encore défaut, le réfugié en fera part en s'annonçant à la police locale qui fera en sorte que le nécessaire soit fait.

Per il commandante del campo o l'ufficiale di polizia del circondario territoriale:

Prima della liberazione la decisione d'internamento sarà notificata al rifugiato che la firmerà attestando di averne preso conoscenza. Essa sarà poi rispedita alla Divisione della polizia

Per il rifugiato:

Voi avete l'obbligo di annunciarvi alla polizia del vostro nuovo luogo di residenza che comunicherà il vostro arrivo all'autorità della polizia cantonale degli stranieri. Questa vi metterà a conoscenza delle condizioni d'internamento.
Se il foglio di segnalazione e le fotografie richieste per la creazione del libretto di rifugiato dovessero mancare, il rifugiato ne avviserà la polizia locale, la quale provvederà a fare il necessario.

...Terr. 9 b.
...di Polizia. N 20084 Kü P.C. 12 gennaio 1945

Divisione Federale di Polizia
B e r n a.

In merito alla vostra lettera concernente i libretti per rifugiati di:
C a l ò Gustavo 1879
C a l ò Alba 1881
vi facciamo sapere quanto segue.
Questi 2 internati sono entrati in Isvizzera il 18.3.44 e dopo essere passati per diversi campi del Cdo. Terr. 9 b. sono partiti il giorno 17.4.44 da Balerna xxxxxx al campo di Girenbad/Hinwil.
In data 25.4.44 abbiamo ricevuti i due libretti che sono stati spediti in data 26.4.44 al Cdo. del Campo di Girenbad/Hinwil. Questi libretti sono forse in possesso di quel Cdo.

p.o. App. Bottani Fausto

Copia: sig. Calò Gustavo, Orselina

Eidgenössisches Justiz- und Polizeidepartement
Polizeiabteilung
Département fédéral de justice et police
Division de police
Dipartimento federale di giustizia e polizia
Divisione della polizia

N 20084 Kl
No.
Bitte in der Antwort angeben
A indiquer dans la réponse
Pregasi ripeterlo nella risposta

Berna, il 26 giugno 1945

Signor
Gustavo C a l ò,
rabbino,
Villa "Les Hirondelles"
Orselina-Locarno.

Ci riferiamo alla vostra lettera del 23 maggio 1945 indirizzata alla Gendarmeria cantonale di Orselina e ci pregiamo comunicarvi, che dopo aver preso contatto con le autorità competenti, vi autorizziamo d'occuparvi dell'insegnamento religioso ai bambini rifugiati ebrei residenti nel Cantone Ticino.

Il permesso è provvisoriamente valido fino al 31 agosto 1945.

Nel caso che vi si presenti l'occasione di rimpatrio dovrete interrompere la vostra attività e lasciare la Svizzera.

Per potere effettuare viaggi al di fuori del vostro luogo di dimora, dovete chiedere il permesso alla polizia cantonale degli stranieri a Bellinzona.

Con distinta stima :

IL CAPO DELLA DIVISIONE DELLA POLIZIA

p.o.

p.o. sig. Rod

Copia a :

Polizia cantonale degli stranieri, Bellinzona;
Cdo. Ter. Uff. di Pol. Postada Campo;
N 42/44/15

3 D 19933

cl

The Bern Police authorizes Gustavo Caló to teach children refugees in the Ticino Canton until August 31, 1945. If he needs to travel outside his place of residence he needs to apply for permission from the Canton Police for foreigners in Bellinzona .

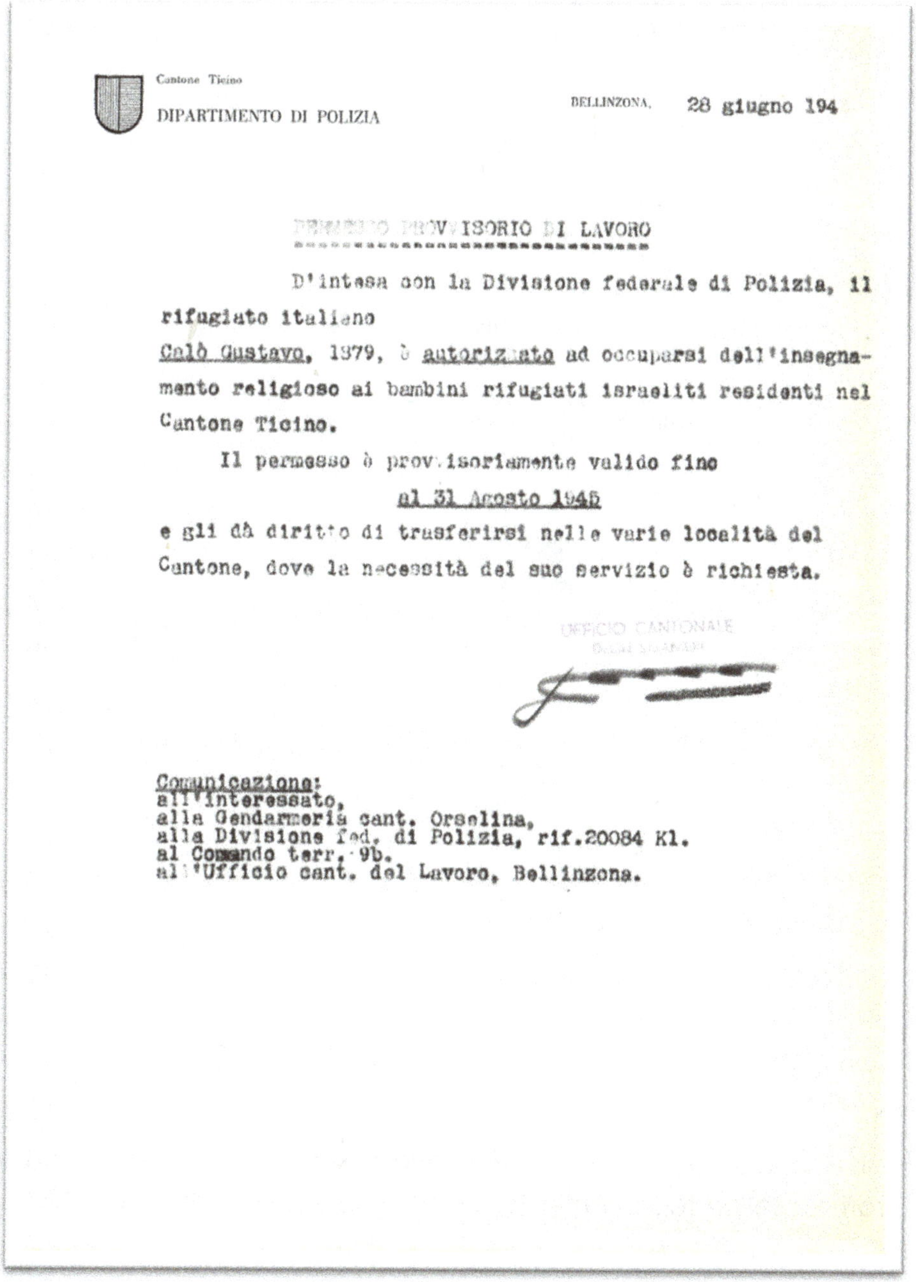

Cantone Ticino
DIPARTIMENTO DI POLIZIA

BELLINZONA, 28 giugno 194

PERMESSO PROVVISORIO DI LAVORO

D'intesa con la Divisione federale di Polizia, il rifugiato italiano Calò Gustavo, 1879, è autorizzato ad occuparsi dell'insegnamento religioso ai bambini rifugiati israeliti residenti nel Cantone Ticino.

Il permesso è provvisoriamente valido fino al 31 Agosto 1945 e gli dà diritto di trasferirsi nelle varie località del Cantone, dove la necessità del suo servizio è richiesta.

UFFICIO CANTONALE

Comunicazione:
all'interessato,
alla Gendarmeria cant. Orselina,
alla Divisione fed. di Polizia, rif.20084 Kl.
al Comando terr. 9b.
all'Ufficio cant. del Lavoro, Bellinzona.

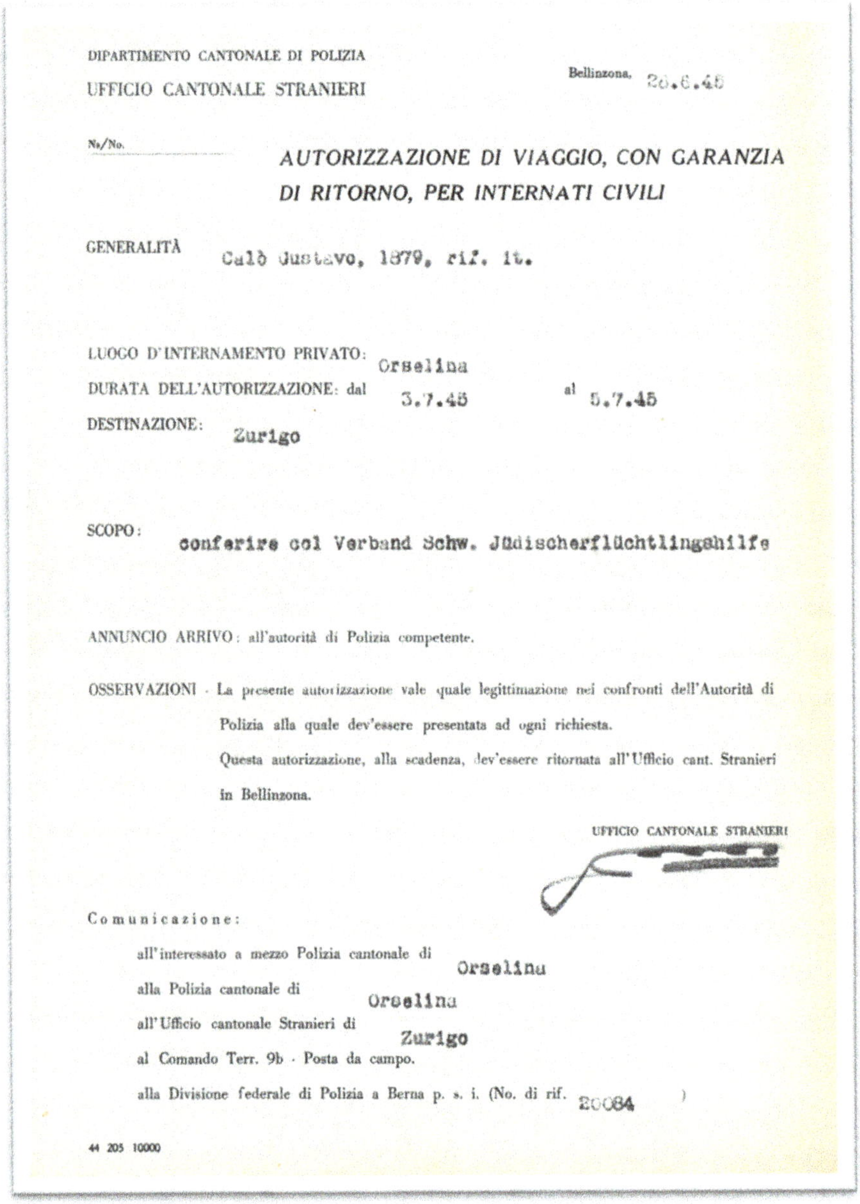
DIPARTIMENTO CANTONALE DI POLIZIA
UFFICIO CANTONALE STRANIERI

Bellinzona, 26.6.45

Nr./No.

AUTORIZZAZIONE DI VIAGGIO, CON GARANZIA DI RITORNO, PER INTERNATI CIVILI

GENERALITÀ Calò Gustavo, 1879, rif. it.

LUOGO D'INTERNAMENTO PRIVATO: Orselina

DURATA DELL'AUTORIZZAZIONE: dal 3.7.45 al 5.7.45

DESTINAZIONE: Zurigo

SCOPO: conferire col Verband Schw. Jüdischerflüchtlingshilfe

ANNUNCIO ARRIVO: all'autorità di Polizia competente.

OSSERVAZIONI - La presente autorizzazione vale quale legittimazione nei confronti dell'Autorità di Polizia alla quale dev'essere presentata ad ogni richiesta.
Questa autorizzazione, alla scadenza, dev'essere ritornata all'Ufficio cant. Stranieri in Bellinzona.

UFFICIO CANTONALE STRANIERI

Comunicazione:

all'interessato a mezzo Polizia cantonale di Orselina
alla Polizia cantonale di Orselina
all'Ufficio cantonale Stranieri di Zurigo
al Comando Terr. 9b - Posta da campo.
alla Divisione federale di Polizia a Berna p. s. i. (No. di rif. 20084)

44 205 10000

The Police of Bellinzona grants Gustavo Caló a two days permission to travel from Orselina to Zurich.

Eidgenössisches Justiz- und Polizeidepartement
Polizeiabteilung

Département fédéral de justice et police
Division de police

Dipartimento federale di giustizia e polizia
Divisione della polizia

Einvernahmeprotokoll
Procès-verbal d'interrogatoire
Verbale d'interrogatoio

Bellinzona den / le / li 24.3.1944

1. Name: / Nom: / Cognome: Calo, geb. Vita-Levi
2. Vorname: / Prénom: / Nome: Matilde
3. Staatszugehörigkeit: / Nationalité: / Nazionalità: italienisch
4. Bei Staatenlosigkeit frühere Staatszugehörigkeit: / Ancienne nationalité (en cas d'apatridie): / Precedente nazionalità (per apolidi):
5. Vorname des Vaters: / Prénom du père: / Nome del padre: Guido, gest.
6. Vor- und Geburtsname der Mutter: / Prénom et nom de famille de la mère: / Nome e cognome di nascita della madre: Amalia Diena
7. Geburtsdatum: / Date de naissance: / Data di nascita: 15.6.1914.
8. Geburtsort: / Lieu de naissance: / Luogo di nascita: Turin
9. Früherer Wohnort: / Ancien domicile: / Domicilio precedente: Biella, via Torino 55
10. Beruf: / Profession: / Professione: Hausfrau
11. Zivilstand: / Etat-civil: / Stato civile: Verh. mit Raffaele Calo
12. Konfession: / Confession: / Religione: Jüdin
13. Begleitende Familienangehörige: / Membres de la famille accompagnant l'intéressé: / Congiunti che accompagnano l'interessato: Ehemann
14. Ausweispapiere: / Papiers d'identité: / Documenti di legitimazione: Eheschein der israelit. Gemeinde Turin n 146.
15. Militärische Einteilung: / Incorporation militaire: / Incorporazione militare:
16. Grund und Umstände der Flucht sowie eingeschlagener Weg: / Motifs et circonstances de la fuite ainsi que route suivie: / Motivi e circostanze della fuga come pure percorso seguito:

Am Nachmittag des 20.9.43 wurde mein Mann informiert, dass die Judenverfolgungen auch in Biella angefangen hatten. Wir verliessen die Stadt sofort und versteckten uns in der Umgebung. Am 19.1.44 fuhren wir nach Intra, wo wir übernachteten. Am 20.1. begaben wir uns in Begleitung eines Führers im Auto nach Scareno und zu Fuss nach Piaggio. Wir übernachteten in einer Hütte und am nächsten Tag gingen wir weiter nach Socraggio. In der Nacht setzten wir die Reise fort. An einem gewissen Punkt behaupteten die Führer, wir seien auf Schweizergebiet angekommen und verliessen uns. Da ~~mxxxxx~~ Frau sehr erschöpft war, blieb ich zurück während mein Mann sich auf die Suche nach den Grenzwächtern machte. Nachdem ich lange vergebens auf ihn gewartet hatte, ging ich allein weiter bis nach Cortaccio. Inzwischen war auch er dort angekommen. Nachmittag begleitete uns ein Soldat nach Brissago und Locarno. Am 24.1.44 wurden wir nach Bellinzona gebracht.

F 115 / 82868

Document issued by the Police of Bellinzona:

Reason and circumstances of the escape and the route taken:

In the afternoon of September 20, 1943 we left Biella and hid in the area. On the 19th of January, 1943 we drove to Intra, where we stayed overnight; on January 20th a guide took us to Scareno, then on to Piaggia, where we spent the night in a hut and the next day we continued to Socraggio.

I was exhausted. ...My husband went in search for the.... ...After waiting for him in vain for a long time, I continued on my own to Cortaccio. In the meantime he got back and at noon a soldier accompanied him to Brissago and Locarno. On January 24th, 1944 we were taken to Bellinzona.

17. Ort und Zeit des Grenzübertrittes:
Lieu et date du passage de la frontière:
Località, data e ora dello sconfinamento: Cortaccio, 23.1.1944, 10.30

18. Gesundheitszustand:
Etat de santé:
Condizioni di salute: gut

19. Verwandte und Bekannte in der Schweiz:
Parents et connaissances en Suisse:
Parenti e conoscenze nella Svizzera: In der Schweiz in einem Lager interniert.

Amaliàia Vita-Levi, geb. Diena, Mutter

Elda Saceruotti, geb. Vita-Levi, Schwester

20. Allfällige Garanten in der Schweiz:
Répondants éventuels en Suisse:
Eventuali garanti nella Svizzera:

21. Genaue Zusammenstellung der Vermögensmittel im In- und Ausland:
Liste exacte des ressources à l'étranger et en Suisse:
Specificazione esatta dei beni patrimoniali in Svizzera e all'estero: Ich besitze in Turin, via Carlo Giordana in Gemeinschaft mit meiner Schwester, eine Wohnung von 5 Zimmern nebst Zubehör.- Ich brachte mit mir (zusammen mit meinem Mann) :

22 englische Pfund, Gold, sowie andere Metalmünzen und etwas Schmuck, in Bellinzona abgegeben.

22. Vermerk ob Mitteilung über Verhalten der Flüchtlinge bekanntgegeben:
L'« avis au réfugié » a-t-il été porté à la connaissance du réfugié?
La « Communicazione ai rifugiati » è stata portata a conoscenza dell'interessato? Ja

Einvernommen durch:
Interrogé par:
Interrogato da:

Der Flüchtling:
Le réfugié:
Il rifugiato:

Eidgenössisches Justiz- und Polizeidepartement
Polizeiabteilung

Département fédéral de justice et police
Division de police

Dipartimento federale di giustizia e polizia
Divisione della polizia

N 17857
Be/Kl.

Berna, il 5 luglio 1945.

Sign.
C a l ò Matylde,
Home Morcote,
M o r c o t e .

Le autorità di occupazione alleate in Italia permettono il vostro ritorno in patria.

V'invitiamo a volervi presentare il

giorno 16 luglio 1945

a Chiasso alle ore 16.30 al più tardi. In ogni caso siete tenuto a presentarvi all'Ufficio della Polizia Militare alla stazione di convocazione subito dopo l'arrivo del vostro treno. Non vi sarà nessuna possibilità di rinvio della data di partenza. Non vi sarà modo di essere spostati da una lista sull'altra, perchè le liste sono state verificate ed approvate dagli alleati secondo un ordine determinato e perciò, nostro malgrado, non potremo apportare modificazione alcuna agli ordini di partenza. Ugualmente è inutile vi presentiate prima della data fissata, perchè non vi sarà la possibilità di partire e l'Ufficiale di Polizia dovrà arrestarvi e punirvi.

Vi facciamo noto che, se il vostro ritorno in Isvizzera si rendesse necessario, potrete presentare una domanda di entrata regolare ai nostri Consolati in Italia; la vostra domanda sarà trattata dalla Polizia Federale degli Stranieri.

I vostri documenti vi sono già stati spediti. Per disposizione delle autorità di occupazione alleate vi facciamo noto che i rifugiati celibi od isolati potranno portare seco un bagaglio del peso che sono capaci loro stessi di trasportare. Le famiglie dei rifugiati, invece, potranno portare con loro bagagli del peso massimo di 45 kg per persona. Per tutte le altre disposizioni da parte svizzera, concernenti le merci o i quantitativi esportabili, vi invitiamo ad attenervi alle istruzioni impartite al riguardo alle autorità di polizia ed alle direzioni dei campi e delle case per rifugiati, con nostra circolare del 25 maggio 1945. (Vi rendiamo tuttavia attenti al fatto che, mentre da parte svizzera si permette l'esportazione di 5 orologi per persona, da parte italiana, si autorizza ad ogni rifugiato l'importazione di un solo orologio.)

La Svizzera ha avuto il privilegio di potervi accogliere nel momento in cui vi siete trovato in difficoltà. Non è stato possibile, nostro malgrado, offrire ad ognuno, quanto avremmo voluto offrire; abbiamo tuttavia fatto del nostro meglio per darvi tutto quanto ci era possibile in relazione ai nostri mezzi limitati. Abbiamo grata questa occasione per formularvi i migliori auguri per il vostro rimpatrio e ci permettiamo di esprimere i migliori voti per l'avvenire del vostro Paese.

Il capo della divisione della polizia
p. o.

Copia a:

~~Polizia cantonale degli stranieri;~~
Direzione centrale dei campi di lavoro, Zurigo;
~~Ufficio comunale di razionamento;~~
Campo od home di Morcote
Statistica;

F. 199 - 23340

EIDGENÖSSISCHES
JUSTIZ- UND POLIZEIDEPARTEMENT
POLIZEIABTEILUNG
Zentralleitung der Arbeitslager

DEPARTEMENT FEDERAL DE JUSTICE ET POLICE
DIVISION DE POLICE
Direction centrale des camps de travail

DIPARTEMENTO FEDERALE DI GIUSTIZIA E POLIZIA
DIVISIONE DELLA POLIZIA
Direzione centrale dei campi di lavoro

Zurigo, 8 maggio 1944.

Uff. Pol. Com. Terr. 9 b,

Posta di Campo 5394.

Ihr Zeichen / V. réf. / V. ref.:

Unser Zeichen / N. réf. / N. ref.: Dä/ku
Bitte in der Antwort anzugeben.
A rappeler dans la réponse s. v. p.
Da richiamare nella risposta p. f.

ZL 18471 C a l ò Matilde, 15. 6. 1914, PA 17857.

Secondo le istruzioni della Divisione di Polizia a Berna vi preghiamo di liberare questa rifugiata dal vostro controllo, coll' effetto del 15 maggio, affinchè ella possa raggiungere, lo stesso giorno e prima delle ore 18.00, la casa per internati Brissago. Vi accludiamo i buoni di trasporto occorrenti.

DIREZIONE CENTRALE DEI CAMPI DI LAVORO
Il capo p.o.:
Valay

2 buoni di trasport no.93994/95.

Copia:
Divisione di Polizia, Berna
Direzione della casa per internati Brissago

32

Zentralleitung der Arbeitslager, Zürich 2
Direction centrale des camps de travail, Zurich 2,
Direzione centrale dei campi di lavoro, Zurigo 2,
Beethovenstrasse 11, Telefon 7 38 50

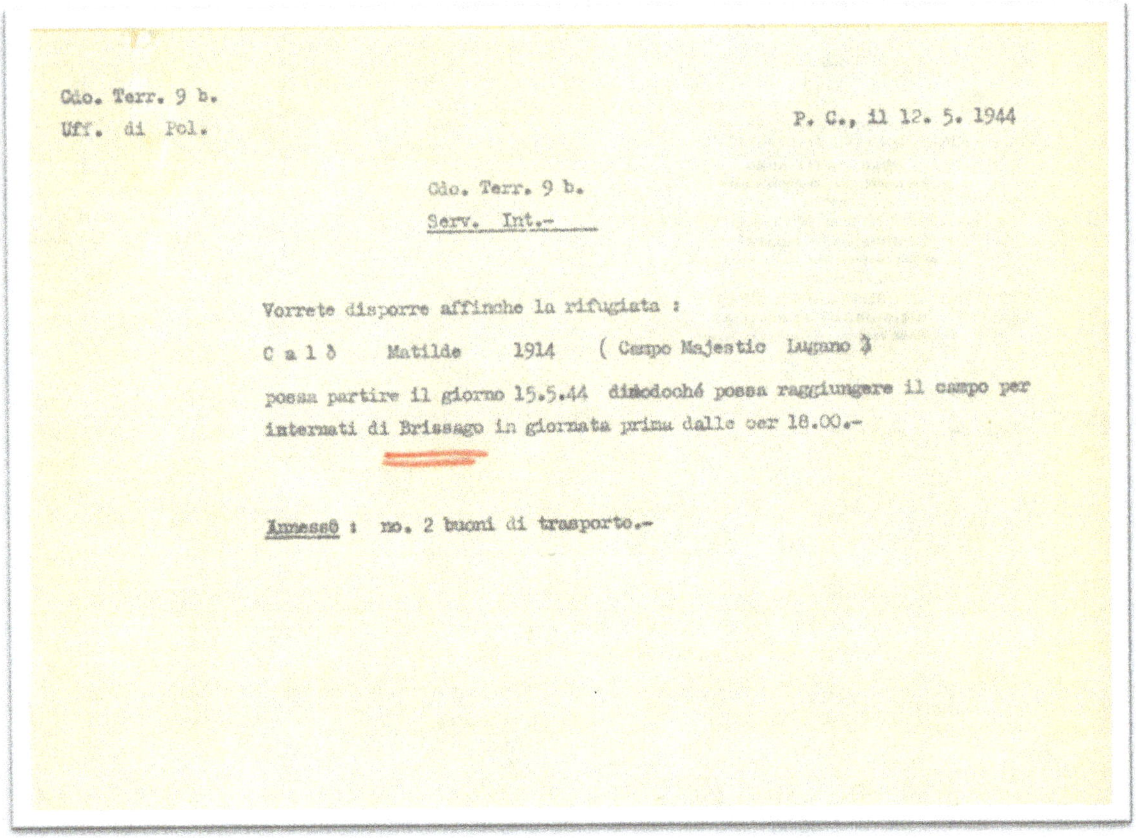
Cdo. Terr. 9 b.
Uff. di Pol.

P. C., il 12. 5. 1944

Cdo. Terr. 9 b.
Serv. Int.-

Vorrete disporre affinche la rifugiata :

C a l ò   Matilde   1914   (Campo Majestic Lugano)

possa partire il giorno 15.5.44 dimodoché possa raggiungere il campo per internati di Brissago in giornata prima dalle oer 18.00.-

Annessi : no. 2 buoni di trasporto.-

Matilde was taken to a refugees house in Brissago

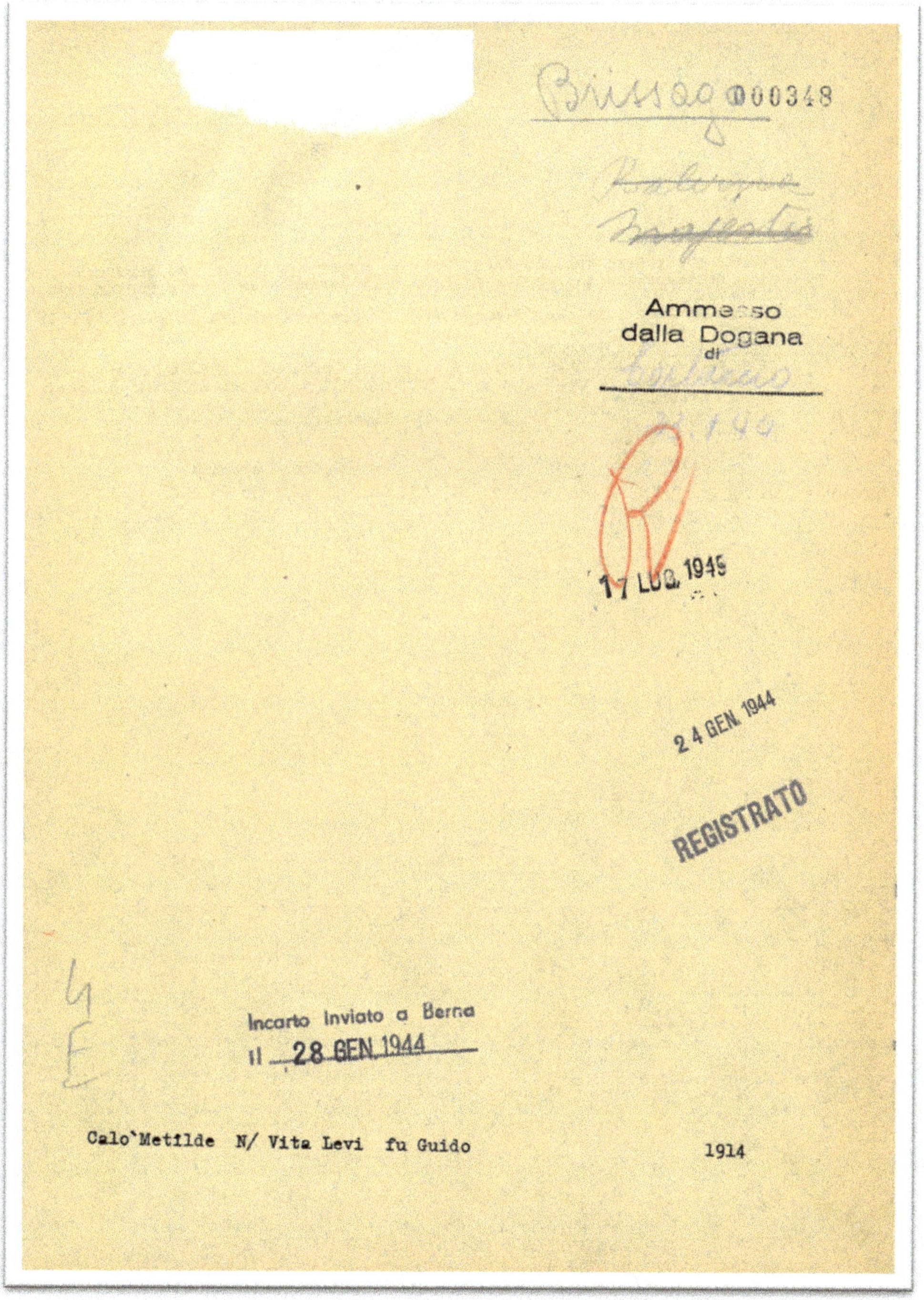

Brissago 000348

Ammesso
dalla Dogana
di

17 LUG. 1945

24 GEN. 1944

REGISTRATO

Incarto inviato a Berna
il 28 GEN. 1944

Calo`Metilde N/ Vita Levi fu Guido 1914

Cimdo che questo comando faccia il neccessario a fin quando Questa Guar
sia rintracciata e di poter rientrare in possesso delle mie ginque ster
ne oro.
Ci garantisco pure che riconoscerei la Guardia Federale la quale ci die
queste sterline oro.-
<u>Connotati della Guardia:</u>
età circa 35 anni, tipo alto snello bruno, parȁava Italiano, e cosi pur
tedesco perche lo udii quando ci ha dato gli ordine ai militari di cond
ci a Brissago.-

Null'altro daggiungere.

I.F.

Letto e approvato

… the custom control of Cortaccio (one of the Federal Guards) asked me for a gratuity that would be given to the soldier that would take us to Brissago. I asked him how much it would be in Italian Lire and he started laughing, saying that we have to pay in gold. I offered half a sterling and he said that was not enough. Since I did not know what else I could offer he said I have to give him five pieces of gold sterling which I gave him. … we were taken to Brissago… and then to Bellinzona. Here, in the camp Casa Italia … everybody said they never paid a guard… for their transport.

Here I started to suspect that this Federal Guard had robbed me. I ask this command post to do whatever is necessary …so I can repossess my five gold sterling. I … will recognise the Federal Guard. … about 35 years of age, very tall and slim, brown hair, spoke Italian and German because I heard him when he gave the orders to take us to Brissago.

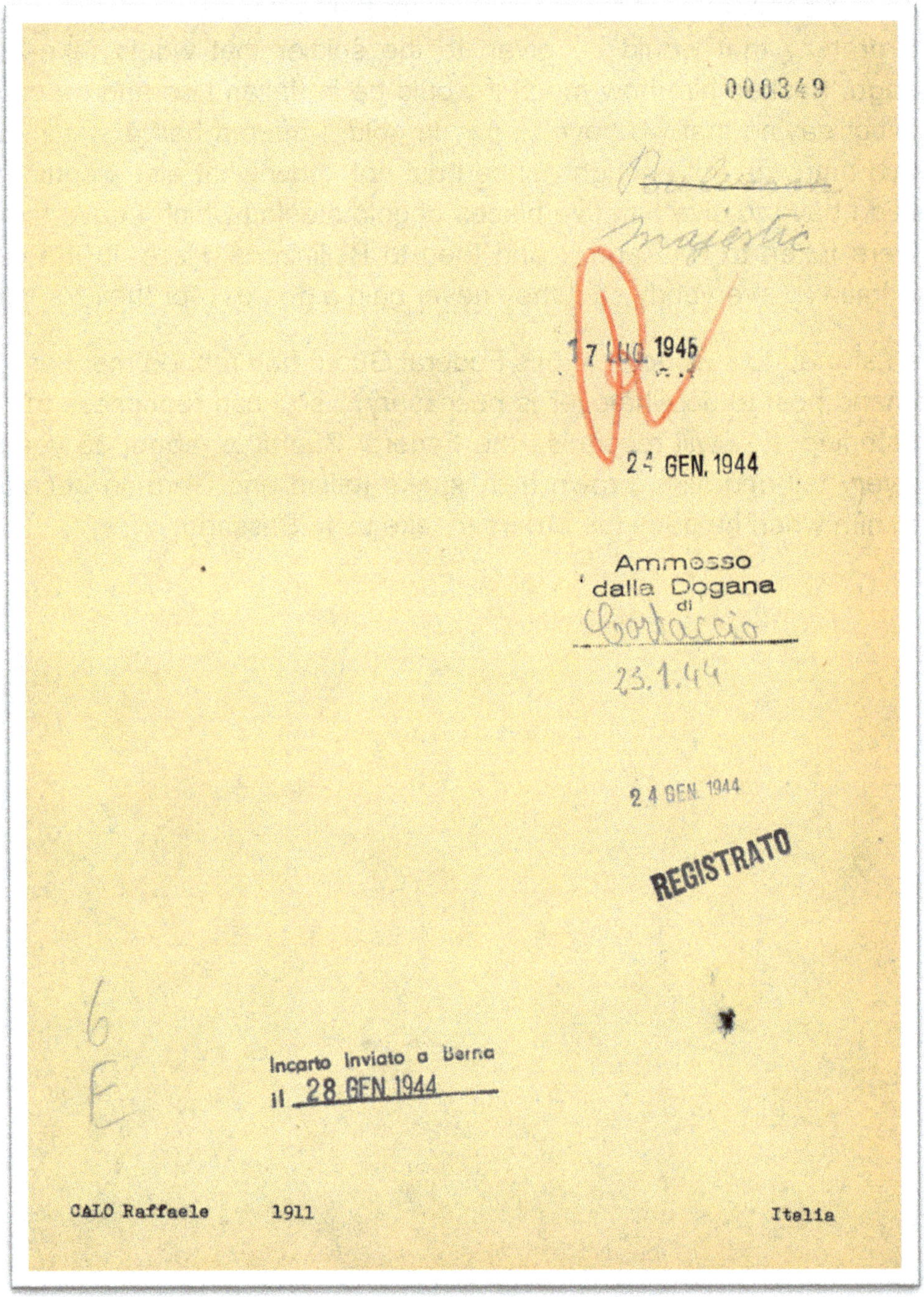

000349

majestic

17 LUG. 1945

24 GEN. 1944

Ammesso dalla Dogana di Cortaccio

23.1.44

24 GEN. 1944

REGISTRATO

6 E

Incarto inviato a Berna il 28 GEN. 1944

CALO Raffaele 1911 Italia

Eidgenössisches Justiz- und Polizeidepartement
Polizeiabteilung

Département fédéral de justice et police
Division de police

Dipartimento federale di giustizia e polizia
Divisione della polizia

Einvernahmeprotokoll
Procès-verbal d'interrogatoire
Verbale d'interrogatoio

Bellinzona den / le / li 24.1.1944.

1. Name / Nom / Cognome: Calò
2. Vorname / Prénom / Nome: Raffaele
3. Staatszugehörigkeit / Nationalité / Nazionalità: italiana
4. Bei Staatenlosigkeit frühere Staatszugehörigkeit / Ancienne nationalité (en cas d'apatridie) / Precedente nazionalità (per apolidi):
5. Vorname des Vaters / Prénom du père / Nome del padre: Gustav
6. Vor- und Geburtsname der Mutter / Prénom et nom de famille de la mère / Nome e cognome di nascita della madre: Alba Milla
7. Geburtsdatum / Date de naissance / Data di nascita: 3.1.1911
8. Geburtsort / Lieu de naissance / Luogo di nascita: Corfu
9. Früherer Wohnort / Ancien domicile / Domicilio precedente: Biella, via Torino 55
10. Beruf / Profession / Professione: (impiegato) Angestellter bei Flli. Vitale
11. Zivilstand / Etat-civil / Stato civile: verh. mit Vita Levi Metilde
12. Konfession / Confession / Religione: Jude
13. Begleitende Familienangehörige / Membres de la famille accompagnant l'intéressé / Congiunti che accompagnano l'interessato: Ehefrau

14. Ausweispapiere / Papiers d'identité / Documenti di legittimazione: Kennkarte N 4,726,500 Biella, 18.8.42.
Entlassungsschein aus dem ital. Heer, Mantua, 6.8.40.

15. Militärische Einteilung / Incorporation militaire / Incorporazione militare: Infolge Rassengesetz entlassen

16. Grund und Umstände der Flucht sowie eingeschlagener Weg / Motifs et circonstances de la fuite ainsi que route suivie / Motivi e circostanze della fuga come pure percorso seguito: Am Nachmittag des 20.9.43 wude ich auf dem Bureau gewarnt, dass die Judenverfolgungen auch in Biella angefangen hatten. Ich verliess mit meiner Frau sofort die Stadt und versteckte mich in der Umgebung bis zum 19.1.44. An diesem Tag fuhren wir nach Intra, wo wir übernachteten. Am 2o.1. begaben wir uns in Begleitung eines Führers im Auto nach Scareno und zu Fuss nach Piaggia, wo wir in einer Hütte über - nachteten. Tags darauf gingen wir weiter nach Socraggio und warteten bis 3 Uhr Nachts, um die Reise in den Bergen fortzusetzen. An einem gewissen Punkt angekommen, behaupteten die Führer, wir seien auf Schweizergebiet ~~angekommen~~ und verliessen uns. Da meine Frau sehr erschöpft war, blieb sie zurück und ich machte mich auf die Suche nach der Grenzwache. Dort erfuhr ich, dass sie sich noch in Italien befand und kehrte zurück. Es war inzwischen Nacht geworden und meine Frau hatte sich auch auf den Weg gemacht. Da ich sie nicht fand, kehrte ich nach Cortaccio zurück, wo eine halbe Stunde auch sie eintraf. Nachmittags begleitete uns ein Soldat nach Brissago und später wurden wir mit dem Autobus nach Locarno gebracht. Am 24.1. 44 langten wir in Bellinzona an.

F 115 / 82868

Document issued by the Police of Bellinzona:

In September 1943 ... the persecution of the Jews had started in Biella as well. I immediately left the city with my wife and went into hiding in the area, until the 19th of January 1944. That day we drove to Intra where we were stayed until the 20th of January. Accompanied by a guide we went by car to Scareno and on foot to Piaggia, where we spent the night. The next day we went on to Socraggio and waited ... until 3 a.m. to continue the route in the mountains. At ... a sticky point, the guides claimed we were on Swiss territory and left. Since my wife was exhausted, she stayed behind while I went in search of the border guard. (In the meantime) I found out that she was still in Italy, night had fallen and (I could not find her). I returned to Cortaccio and she arrived in half an hour. In the afternoon a soldier accompanied us to Brissago and later we were taken to Locarno by bus. We arrived in Bellinzona on January 24, 1944.

17. Ort und Zeit des Grenzübertrittes:
Lieu et date du passage de la frontière:
Località, data e ora dello sconfinamento: Cotaccio, 23.1.1944, 10.30

18. Gesundheitszustand:
Etat de santé:
Condizioni di salute: Von der Flucht sehr erschöpft, sonst gesund.

19. Verwandte und Bekannte in der Schweiz:
Parents et connaissances en Suisse:
Parenti e conoscenze nella Svizzera: Adv. Aldo Calo, Bruder. Elsa Vitale geb.Calo,

Schwester mit deren Mann Alberto Vitale. Andere Schwester Enrichetta Schlesinger mit deren Mann Guido

Alle in der Schweiz interniert.

20. Allfällige Garanten in der Schweiz:
Répondants éventuels en Suisse:
Eventuali garanti nella Svizzera:

21. Genaue Zusammenstellung der Vermögensmittel im In- und Ausland:
Liste exacte des ressources à l'étranger et en Suisse:
Specificazione esatta dei beni patrimoniali in Svizzera e all'estero: [illegible]

Keine Mittel weder in Italien noch in der Schweiz.

22. Vermerk ob Mitteilung über Verhalten der Flüchtlinge bekanntgegeben:
L'« avis au réfugié » a-t-il été porté à la connaissance du réfugié?
La « Communicazione ai rifugiati » è stata portata a conoscenza dell'interessato? si

Einvernommen durch:
Interrogé par:
Interrogato da:

Der Flüchtling:
Le réfugié:
Il rifugiato:

Raffaele Calo

ARMÉE SUISSE
GENDARMERIE DE L'ARMÉE

SCHWEIZERISCHE ARMEE
HEERESPOLIZEI

ESERCITO SVIZZERO
GENDARMERIA DELL'ESERCITO

Gendarmeria dell'Esercito
No. Cdo. Terr. 9b
DISTACCAMENTO CHIASSO

DET. Terr. 9b   Chiasso, 23 febbraio 1944.-

All'Ufficiale di Polizia Cdo. Terr. 9b
Posta da Campo.-

CONCERNE: Scorta da Balerna Campo Internati a Chiasso dal Sigr. Avv. Pedrolini e viceversa di due internati.-

Come da ordine ricevuto dal locale Capo Posto, questa mattina ho scortato da Balerna a Chiasso e viceversa i sottonominati internati:

C A L Ò Raffaele di Gustavo nato il 3.1.1911, impiegato, domiciliato a Biella, Italiano , Ebreo e la moglie

C A L Ò Matilde n/ Vitaleli nata il 15.6.1914 domiciliata a Biella, Italiana , Ebrea.-

Detti internati ebrei sono stati da me presi in consegna al Campo Internati di Balerna e condotti all'Avv. Pedrolini a Chiasso per interrogatorio, in riguardo alla loro intrata in Svizzera.-Indi sono stati di nuovo ritornati al Campo di Balerna.
Il trasporto é avvenuto a mezzo tram.-

Con stima:

Cpl. R. Regazzoni.-

Kanzlei A. St.

Eidgenössisches Justiz- und Polizeidepartement
Polizeiabteilung

Département fédéral de justice et police
Division de police

Dipartimento federale di giustizia e polizia
Divisione della polizia

N 17857 Bia

Berna, il 6 luglio 1945

Signor
Raffaele Calò, 3.1.11,
Casa per rifugiati,
M o r c o t e.

Le autorità di occupazione alleate in Italia permettono il vostro ritorno in patria.
V'invitiamo a volervi presentare il

giorno 16 luglio 1945

a Chiasso alle ore 16.30 al più tardi. In ogni caso siete tenuto a presentarvi all'Ufficio della Polizia Militare alla stazione di convocazione subito dopo l'arrivo del vostro treno. Non vi sarà nessuna possibilità di rinvio della data di partenza. Non vi sarà modo di essere spostati da una lista sull'altra, perchè le liste sono state verificate ed approvate dagli alleati secondo un ordine determinato e perciò, nostro malgrado, non potremo apportare modificazione alcuna agli ordini di partenza. Ugualmente è inutile vi presentiate prima della data fissata, perchè non vi sarà la possibilità di partire e l'Ufficiale di Polizia dovrà arrestarvi e punirvi.

V'invitiamo a presentarvi alla data sopracitata, alle ore 10.30 alla Società di banca svizzera Chiasso, per il ritiro dei valori depositati presso il nostro ufficio fiduciario. La Banca Popolare Svizzera a Berna è stata già incaricata dell'invio dei vostri averi alla suddetta banca. E perciò inutile inviare lettere a noi o alla Banca Popolare svizzera a Berna. Come documento di legittimazione potete presentare il libretto di rifugiato. Dopo il ritiro dei vostri averi vi ripresenterete all'Ufficiale di Polizia.

Vi facciamo noto che, se il vostro ritorno in Isvizzera si rendesse necessario, potrete presentare una domanda di entrata regolare ai nostri Consolati in Italia; la vostra domanda sarà trattata dalla Polizia Federale degli Stranieri.

I vostri documenti vi sono già stati spediti. Per disposizione delle autorità di occupazione alleate vi facciamo noto che i rifugiati celibi od isolati potranno portare seco un bagaglio del peso che sono capaci loro stessi di trasportare. Le famiglie dei rifugiati, invece, potranno portare con loro bagagli del peso massimo di 45 Kg. per persona. Per tutte le altre disposizioni da parte svizzera, concernenti le merci e i quantitativi esportabili, vi invitiamo ad attenervi alle istruzioni impartite al riguardo alle autorità di polizia ed alle direzioni dei campi e delle case per rifugiati, con nostra circolare del 25 maggio 1945. (Vi rendiamo tuttavia attenti al fatto che, mentre da parte svizzera si permette l'esportazione di 5 orologi per persona, da parte italiana, si autorizza ad ogni rifugiato l'importazione di un solo orologio.)

La Svizzera ha avuto il privilegio di potervi accogliere nel momento in cui vi siete trovato in difficoltà. Non è stato possibile, nostro malgrado, offrire ad ognuno, quanto avremmo voluto offrire; abbiamo tuttavia fatto del nostro meglio per darvi tutto quanto ci era possibile in relazione ai nostri mezzi limitati. Abbiamo grata questa occasione per formularvi i migliori auguri per il vostro rimpatrio e ci permettiamo di esprimere i migliori voti per l'avvenire del vostro Paese.

IL CAPO DELLA DIVISIONE DELLA POLIZIA.

p.o.

Copia a: Società di banca svizzera (1 lettera)

Polizia ~~cantonale degli stranieri,~~
Direzione centrale dei campi di lavoro, Zurigo;
~~Ufficio comunale di razionamento,~~
~~Campo od~~ home di Morcote;
Banca Popolare Svizzera, Berna; allegata 1 lettera;
~~Ufficio federale delle imposte, Berna, all'intenzione del Dr. Kradolfer;~~
Direzione generale delle dogane, Berna;
Statistica.
Contabilità 1 lettera;

Nr. 4 cycl.* 1600 PS

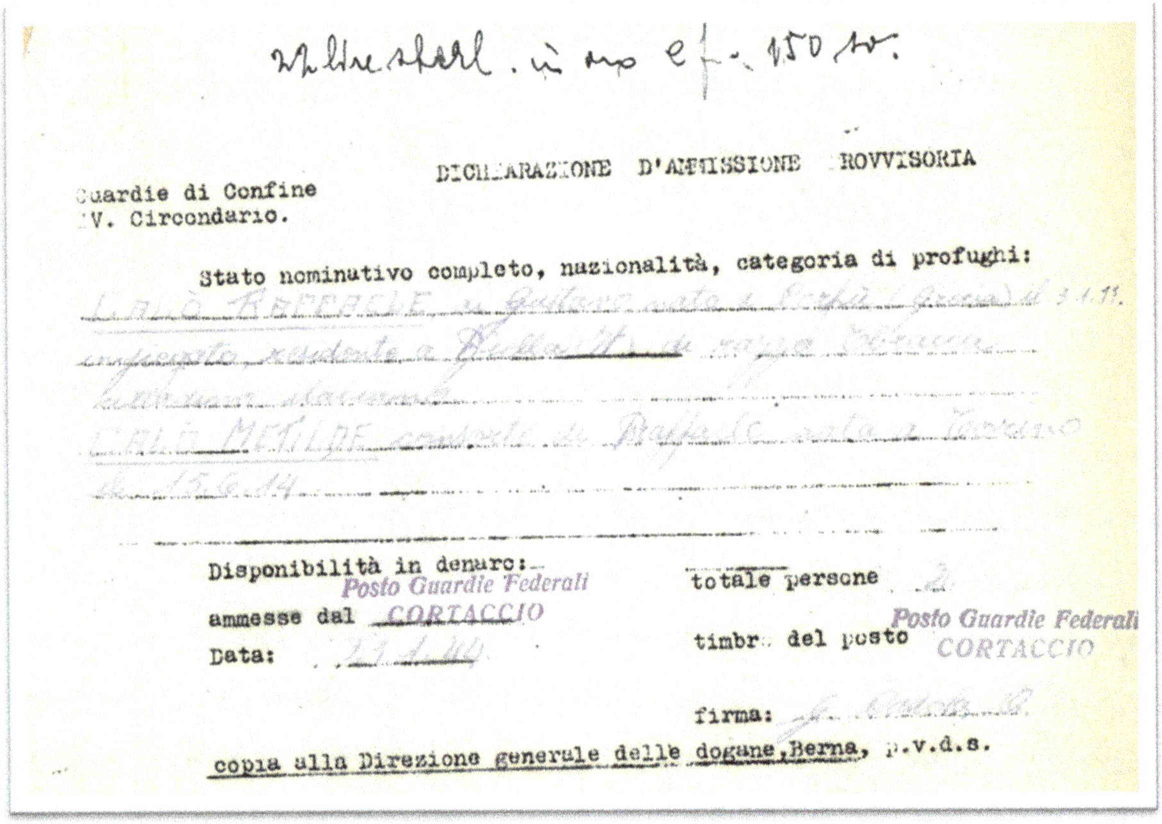

DICHIARAZIONE D'AMMISSIONE PROVVISORIA

Guardie di Confine
IV. Circondario.

Stato nominativo completo, nazionalità, categoria di profughi:

CALÒ RAFFAELE di Gustavo nato a Corfù (Grecia) il 3.1.11. impiegato residente a Biella (It.) di razza ebraica cittadino italiano

CALÒ MATILDE consorte di Raffaele nata a Torino il 15.6.14

Disponibilità in denaro: [illegible] totale persone 2

ammesse dal Posto Guardie Federali CORTACCIO

Data: 23.1.44

timbro del posto Posto Guardie Federali CORTACCIO

firma: [illegible]

copia alla Direzione generale delle dogane, Berna, p.v.d.s.

Anna Schlesinger, 11 years old, was taken under the auspices of the Red Cross.

Cdo. Terr. 9 b.
Uff.di Polizia.

P.C. 7 giugno 1944

O R D I N E   D I   L I B E R A Z I O N E

S C H L E S I N G E R Anna di Guido e di Calò Enrichetta,nata a Brescia il 28.9.1935,scolara,domiciliata a Mantova,italiana,

E ' L I B E R A T A

dal controllo militare e passa sotto il controllo della Croce Rossa Svizzera,Soccorso ai Fanciulli,Berna.
E 'liberata a Flims(Grigioni)presso il Kinderheim Dr. Schoch.
La Bambina sarà ritirata dagli addetti della Croce Rossa,sezione Ticino.

Copia:Divisione di Polizia(decisione N 20046 Kl)
Cdo. Terr. 9 b.Servizio Internati
Cdo. Campo Internati,albergo Mayestic,Lugano
all'interessata
incarto
Croce Rossa Svizzera,sezione Ticino.

DICHIARAZIONE D'AMMISSIONE.

Cognome. Ottolenghi Giuseppina in Vitale fu Maurizio
~~Nome.~~ 26.7.85 ad Acqui dom. Biella
ebrea italiana
figlio Vitale Alberto fu Samuele dom. Biella
ebreo ital.
moglie Elsa di Gustavo 9.5.16 dom. Biella
ebrea ital.

Ammesso dal l'Uff. Cs. Mendrisio

Data: 10 - 12 . 43 timbro del posto Posto Guardie Federali BRUZELLA

(Scrivere a macchina o lapis copiativo)

Firma: [illegible]

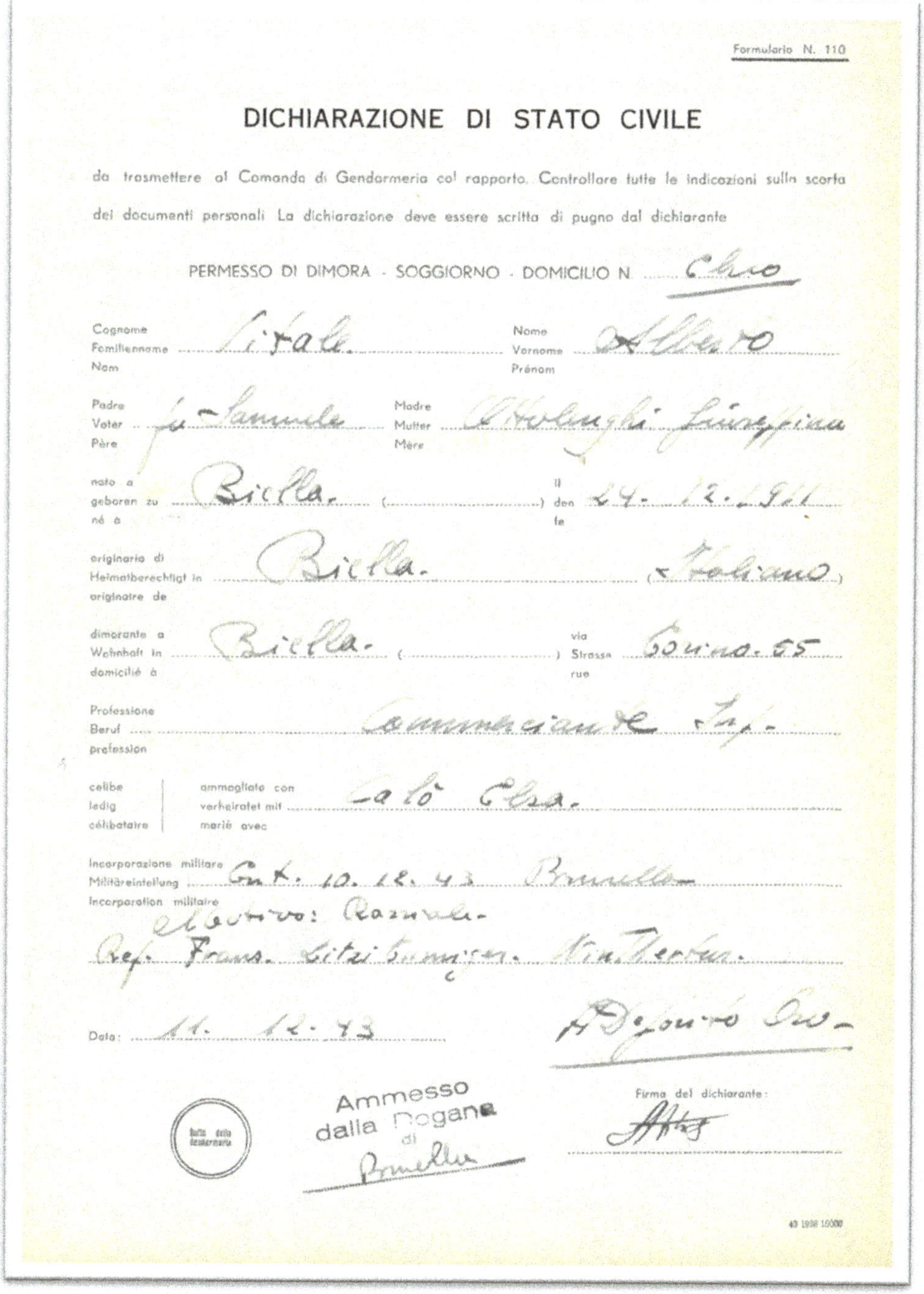

Formulario N. 110

DICHIARAZIONE DI STATO CIVILE

da trasmettere al Comando di Gendarmeria col rapporto. Controllare tutte le indicazioni sulla scorta dei documenti personali. La dichiarazione deve essere scritta di pugno dal dichiarante

PERMESSO DI DIMORA - SOGGIORNO - DOMICILIO N. Chur

Cognome / Familienname / Nom: Vitale.
Nome / Vorname / Prénom: Alberto

Padre / Vater / Père: fu Samuele
Madre / Mutter / Mère: Ottolenghi Giuseppina

nato a / geboren zu / né à: Biella. ( )
il / den / le: 24.12.1911

originario di / Heimatberechtigt in / originaire de: Biella. (Italiano)

dimorante a / Wohnhaft in / domicilié à: Biella. ( )
via / Strasse / rue: Torino 55

Professione / Beruf / profession: Commerciante Ing.

celibe / ledig / célibataire
ammogliato con / verheiratet mit / marié avec: Calò Elsa.

Incorporazione militare / Militäreinteilung / Incorporation militaire: Ent. 10.12.43 Brusella
Motivo: Razziale.
Ref. Franz. [illegible]

Data: 11.12.43

[illegible signature]

Firma del dichiarante: [signature]

Ammesso dalla Dogana di Brusella

43 1938 10000

DIPARTIMENTO CANTONALE DI POLIZIA — Bellinzona, 1 febbraio 1944

Ufficio cant. Stranieri

Alla Gendarmeria cantonale

No. 864,.- — Orselina

Vi trasmettiamo annesso il decreto d'internamento emanato dalla Divisione di Polizia del Dip.to fed. di Giustizia e Polizia nei confronti dell'attinente italiano v i t a l e Alberto, nato il 24 dicembre 1911

Lo stesso è autorizzato a dimorare in xxxxxx Orselina presso sig. ra Vollet Olga, Villa hirondelles sino a nuovo avviso, ed alle seguenti condizioni :

1. Obbligo di tenere la sua effettiva residenza nel Comune quì sopra indicato. -
2. Divieto di cambiare alloggio senza autorizzazione.
3. Divieto di esercitare un'attività lucrativa.-
4.-Astenersi da qualsiasi atteggiamento contrario alla neutralità svizzera.
5. ....
6. ....

Il rifugiato rimane sottoposto al controllo della Divisione fed. di Polizia del Dipartimento fed. di Giustizia e Polizia .-

Non è necessario che vengano regolate le condizioni della sua dimora.-

TESSERE DI RAZIONAMENTO.- Per la sussistenza fino al 30 novembre 1943, l'internato potrà ritirare i documenti di razionamento presso l'ufficio dell'Economia di Guerra del Comune dove risiede.

A partire dal 1 dicembre 1943 ogni internato riceverà, per ogni 15 giorni, dall'Ufficio cantonale degli Stranieri, una dichiarazione di sussistenza (Modulo UGV AF 1) che dovrà essere consegnata all'ufficio dell'Economia di Guerra del Comune di dimora per ottenere le corrispondenti tessere di razionamento, qualora non fosse ancora in possesso del Libretto per rifugiati.-

UFFICIO CANTONALE DEGLI STRANIERI,

Comunicazione :

a l'interessato per il tramite della Gendarmeria cant. di Orselina
alla Gendarmeria cantonale di Orselina
alla Municipalità di Orselina
all'Ufficio comunale dell'Economia di Guerra di Orselina
al Comando della Gendarmeria cantonale in Bellinzona -
alla Divisione fed. di polizia Berna No. 19225 Wb P.S.I.

Allegato menzionato -

DIPARTIMENTO CANTONALE DI POLIZIA

UFFICIO CANTONALE STRANIERI

Bellinzona, 8 settembre 1944

No/No. 864

AUTORIZZAZIONE DI VIAGGIO, CON GARANZIA DI RITORNO, PER INTERNATI CIVILI

GENERALITÀ: VITALE Alberto, nato il 24 dicembre 1911, Giuseppina nata il 26 agosto 1885, Elsa, nata il 9.5.1916 - rifugiati italiani -

LUOGO D'INTERNAMENTO PRIVATO: ORSELINA - Villa Les Hirondelles

DURATA DELL'AUTORIZZAZIONE: dal 9 settembre al 10 settembre 1944

DESTINAZIONE: ROVEREDO (Gr.)

SCOPO: visitare la zia sig.ra Morlenghi Colomba, presso il Ricovero Immacolata e gravemente ammalata .-

ANNUNCIO ARRIVO: all'autorità di Polizia competente.

OSSERVAZIONI - La presente autorizzazione vale quale legittimazione nei confronti dell'Autorità di Polizia alla quale dev'essere presentata ad ogni richiesta.

Questa autorizzazione, alla scadenza, dev'essere ritornata all'Ufficio cant. Stranieri in Bellinzona.

UFFICIO CANTONALE STRANIERI

Comunicazione:

all'interessato a mezzo Polizia cantonale di Orselina

alla Polizia cantonale di Orselina

all'Ufficio cantonale Stranieri di Coira

al Comando Terr. 9b - Posta da campo.

alla Divisione federale di Polizia a Berna p. s. i. (No. di rif. 19225 WB)

44 756 10000

DIPARTIMENTO CANTONALE
DI POLIZIA

N. ______ Bellinzona, 18 aprile 1944

UFFICIO CENTRALE FORESTIERI

Ns/N° ______

GARANZIA DI RITORNO

per

V I T A L E Alberto , nato il 24 dicembre 1911, rifugiato italiano, presentemente a Orselina, presso Villa Hirondelles.-

valevole sino al 22.2.1944

Al suddetto è assicurato il ritorno nel Canton Ticino.

Questa garanzia di ritorno non dà però diritto all'occupazione di un posto di lavoro, nè al permesso di dimora o di tolleranza.

Lo straniero prima della sua partenza deve chiedere, all'Ufficio cantonale degli Stranieri del Cantone ove intende trasferirsi, l'autorizzazione di lavoro, di dimora o di tolleranza.

Dovrà inoltre notificare l'arrivo alle Autorità di Polizia competenti del nuovo luogo di dimora.

Scopo :

Visita ad un amico a Winterthur ed al prorpio fratello Maurizio internato a Ringlikon.-

POLIZIA CANTONALE TICINESE
UFFICIO CENTRALE FORESTIERI

COMUNICAZIONE:

all'interessato per il tramite della Polizia Cantonale,

alla Polizia cantonale in Orselina,

alla Municipalità di Orselina,

alla Divisione fed. di polizia Berna

~~alla Polizia federale degli Stranieri a~~ Berna

alCdo. Ter. 9b (N. di rif. 19225 Wb)

RTIMENTO CANTONALE DI POLIZIA

ICIO CANTONALE STRANIERI

Bellinzona, 13 aprile 194[illegible]

. 864 - 865.-

AUTORIZZAZIONE DI VIAGGIO, CON GARANZIA DI RITORNO, PER INTERNATI CIVILI

ERALITÀ: V I T A L E Alberto, nato il 1911 e Giuseppina, nata il 1885, rifugiati italiani.

GO D'INTERNAMENTO PRIVATO: Orselina, Villa Les Hirondelles.

ATA DELL'AUTORIZZAZIONE: dal 15.4. al 16.4.1944

TINAZIONE: Roveredo (Grigioni) e Bellinzona

PO: Recarsi a Roveredo per visita alla zia Norlenghi Colomba.
a Bellinzona, per visitare il nipotino Schlesinger Lodovico, residente al Ricovero Von Mentlen.-

UNCIO ARRIVO: all'autorità di Polizia competente.

RVAZIONI - La presente autorizzazione vale quale legittimazione nei confronti dell'Autorità di Polizia alla quale dev'essere presentata ad ogni richiesta.

Questa autorizzazione, alla scadenza, dev'essere ritornata all'Ufficio cant. Stranieri in Bellinzona.

UFFICIO CANTONALE STRANIERI:

unicazione:

all'interessato a mezzo Polizia cantonale di Orselina

alla Polizia cantonale di Orselina

all'Ufficio cantonale Stranieri di Coira

al Comando Terr. 9b - Posta da campo.

alla Divisione federale di Polizia a Berna - p. s. i. (No. di rif. 19225 [illegible])

44 282 2000

DIPARTIMENTO CANTONALE DI POLIZIA

UFFICIO CANTONALE STRANIERI

Bellinzona, 31 ottobre 1944

Ns/No. __________

AUTORIZZAZIONE DI VIAGGIO, CON GARANZIA DI RITORNO, PER INTERNATI CIVILI

GENERALITÀ: V I T A L E Alberto, nato il 24 dicembre 1911, rifugiato italiano.-

LUOGO D'INTERNAMENTO PRIVATO: Orselina, Villa "Les Hirondelles"

DURATA DELL'AUTORIZZAZIONE: dal 1.11. al 7.11.1944

DESTINAZIONE: Berna-Zurigo-Winterthur-Roveredo (Gr)

SCOPO: Recarsi a Berna, per conferire con la Div. fed. di Polizia. A Zurigo, per conferire con il Verband Schweiz. Jüdischer Flüchtlingshilfen.- A Winterthur, per visita al fratello Vitale Maurizio.- A Roveredo (Gr.), per visita alla zia Morlenghi Colomba, Ricovero Immacolata.-

ANNUNCIO ARRIVO: all'autorità di Polizia competente.

OSSERVAZIONI - La presente autorizzazione vale quale legittimazione nei confronti dell'Autorità di Polizia alla quale dev'essere presentata ad ogni richiesta.

Questa autorizzazione, alla scadenza, dev'essere ritornata all'Ufficio cant. Stranieri in Bellinzona.

UFFICIO CANTONALE STRANIERI

Comunicazione:

all'interessato a mezzo Polizia cantonale di ~~xxxxxxxxxxxxxxxxx~~

alla Polizia cantonale di Orselina

all'Ufficio cantonale Stranieri di Berna-Zurigo-Coira

al Comando Terr. 9b - Posta da campo.

alla Divisione federale di Polizia a Berna p. s. i. (No. di rif. 19285 Vb)

44 756 10000

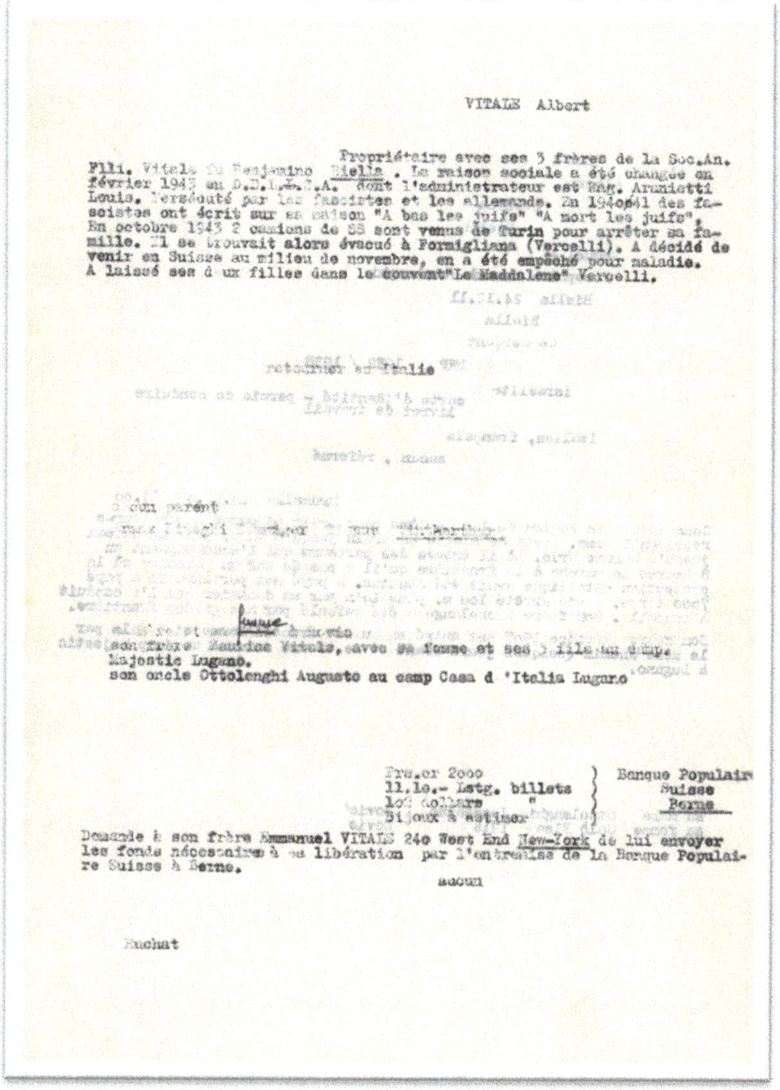

VITALE Albert

Propriétaire avec ses 3 frères de la Soc.An. Flli. Vitale fu Benjamino Biella . La maison sociale a été changée en février 1943 en D.D.L.A.S.A. dont l'administrateur est Ing. Arunietti Louis. Persécuté par les fascistes et les allemands. En 1940ø41 des fascistes ont écrit sur sa maison "A bas les juifs" "A mort les juifs". En octobre 1943 2 camions de SS sont venus de Turin pour arrêter sa famille. Il se trouvait alors évacué à Formigliana (Vercelli). A décidé de venir en Suisse au milieu de novembre, en a été empêché pour maladie. A laissé ses d ux filles dans le couvent"Le Maddalene" Vercelli.

retourner en Italie

à son parent

son frère Maurice Vitale, avec sa femme et ses 3 fils au camp. Majestic Lugano.
son oncle Ottolenghi Augusto au camp Casa d 'Italia Lugano

Frs.or 2000 11.10.- Lstg. billets 102 dollars " Bijoux à estimer	}	Banque Populaire Suisse Berne

Demande à son frère Emmanuel VITALE 240 West End New-York de lui envoyer les fonds nécessaires à sa libération par l'entremise de la Banque Populaire Suisse à Berne.

aucun

Buchat

Document issued by the Police of Bellinzona:

...On the 1st of April 1940 fascists wrote on his house "Down with the Jews". In October 1943 2 SS trucks came from Turin to arrest his family. He then left for Formigliana (Vercelli) and decided to come to Switzerland in the middle of November. He was prevented from doing so because of illness. He left his daughters in the convent "Le Maddalene" in Vercelli.

...2000 gold francs

102 dollars

Jewelry, Banque Populaire Suisse, Berne.

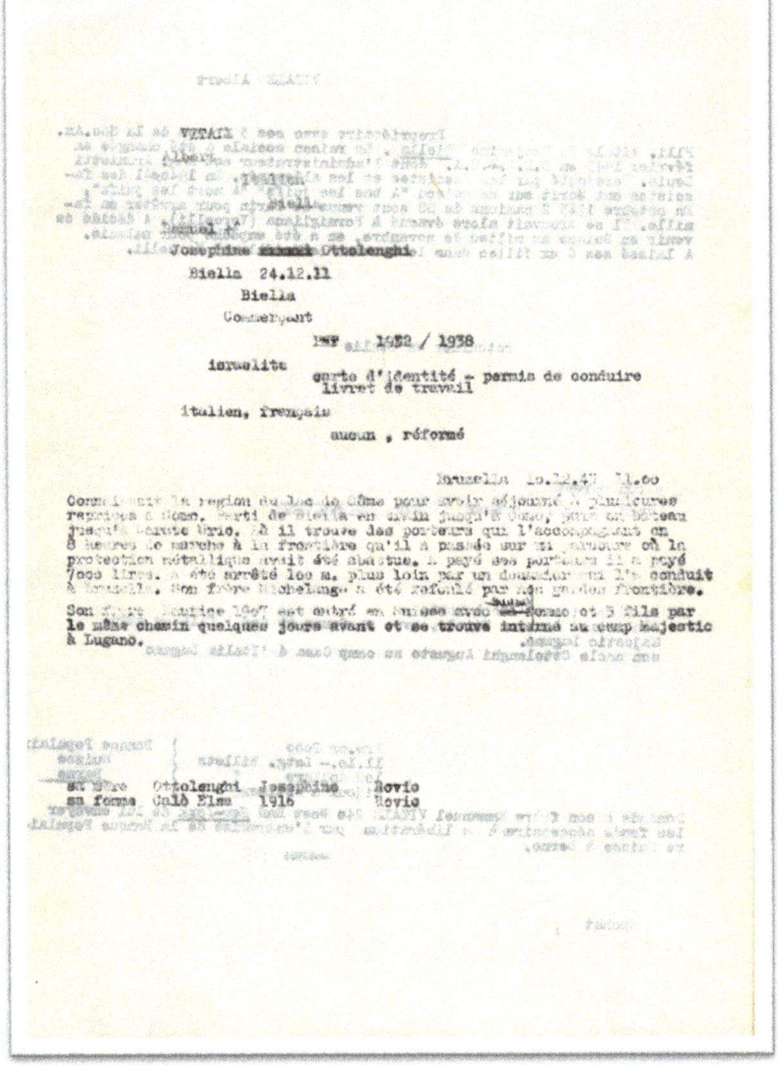

VITALI
Albert
Italien
Biella
Josephine Ottolenghi

Biella 24.12.11

Biella

Commerçant

PNF 1932 / 1938

israelite

carte d'identité - permis de conduire
livret de travail

italien, français

aucun , réformé

Bruzella 19.12.43 11.00

Connaît [illegible] la region du lac de Côme pour avoir séjourné [illegible] plusieures reprises à Como. Parti de Biella en train jusqu'à Como, puis en bâteau jusqu'à Carate Urio. Là il trouve des porteurs qui l'accompagnent en 8 heures de marche à la frontière qu'il a passée sur un [illegible] où la protection métallique avait été abattue. A payé ses porteurs il a payé 7000 lires. A été arrêté 100 m. plus loin par un douanier qui l'a conduit à Bruzella. Son frère Michelangelo a été refoulé par nos gardes frontière.

Son frère Maurice 1907 est entré en Suisse avec sa femme et 3 fils par le même chemin quelques jours avant et se trouve interné au camp Majestic à Lugano.

sa mère Ottolenghi Josephine Rovio
sa femme Calò Elsa 1916 Rovio

He went by train from Biella to Como and then by boat to Carate Urie where he found guides who accompanied him for 8 hours to the border which he crossed where the metal fence had been knocked down. He paid the guides 7000 lire and was arrested 100 meters further by a custom officer that took him to Bruzella.

Eidg. Justiz- und Polizeidepartement
POLIZEIABTEILUNG

Bern, den 14. Februar 1944

S 20046 Kl

DIE POLIZEIABTEILUNG
des
Eidg. Justiz- und Polizeidepartements
stellt

im Rahmen der Bemühungen zur Unterbringung von Flüchtlingskindern
fest.

Die italienische Staatsangehörige Anna Schlesinger, geb. 28. September 1935
hat am **18. Januar 1944** illegal die Schweizergenze überschritten. Dieses Flüchtlingskind hat zurzeit keine Möglichkeit, die Schweiz zu verlassen. Es erscheint als angezeigt und dringlich, das Kind an einem Freiplatz in einem privaten Haushalt unterzubringen. Bis zur fremdenpolizeilichen Regelung des Aufenthaltsverhältnisses in einem Kanton muss das Kind im Sinne des Kreisschreibens des eidgenössischen Justiz- und Polizeidepartements vom 3. Dezember 1942 formell als interniert behandelt werden.

Deshalb hat die Polizeiabteilung des eidgenössischen Justiz- und Polizeidepartements in Anwendung der Art. 14, Abs.2, und Art. 15, Abs. 4, des Bundesgesetzes über Aufenthalt und Niederlassung der Ausländer vom 26. März 1931 sowie Art. 7 des Bundesratsbeschlusses vom 17. Oktober 1939 über Aenderungen der fremdenpolizeilichen Regelung

e r k a n n t :

1. Das obgenannte Kind wird in diesem Sinne bis auf weiteres interniert.
2. Mitteilung an. **z.Zt. Casa d'Italia, Bellinzona**
   a) Schweizer. Emigrantenkinderhilfswerk, Zürich, im Doppel,
   b) Eidgenössische Fremdenpolizei,
   c) Statistik.
   d) Pol.Of.Ter.Kdo. 9b

DER CHEF DER POLIZEIABTEILUNG
i.... sig. Jäggi.

F 26 d.

Guido Schlesinger

Eidgenössisches Justiz- und Polizeidepartement
Polizeiabteilung

Département fédéral de justice et police
Division de police

Dipartimento federale di giustizia e polizia
Divisione della polizia

Einvernahmeprotokoll
Procès-verbal d'interrogatoire
Verbale d'interrogatoio

Bellinzona den / le / li 19.1.1944

1. Name: / Nom: / Cognome: Schlesinger
2. Vorname: / Prénom: / Nome: Guido
3. Staatszugehörigkeit: / Nationalité: / Nazionalità: Staatenlos
4. Bei Staatenlosigkeit frühere Staatszugehörigkeit: / Ancienne nationalité (en cas d'apatridie): / Precedente nazionalità (per apolidi): ex -Italiener
5. Vorname des Vaters: / Prénom du père: / Nome del padre: Ludwig, gest.
6. Vor- und Geburtsname der Mutter: / Prénom et nom de famille de la mère: / Nome e cognome di nascita della madre: Laura Hammermüller
7. Geburtsdatum: / Date de naissance: / Data di nascita: 18.3.1909
8. Geburtsort: / Lieu de naissance: / Luogo di nascita: Catania
9. Früherer Wohnort: / Ancien domicile: / Domicilio precedente: Mantova
10. Beruf: / Profession: / Professione: Angestellter
11. Zivilstand: / Etat-civil: / Stato civile: Verh.mit Enrichetta Calo
12. Konfession: / Confession: / Religione: israelit.
13. Begleitende Familienangehörige: / Membres de la famille accompagnant l'intéressé: / Congiunti che accompagnano l'interessato:

Dichiarazione di riforma, consiglio di leva di Brescia 14.3.1934.

14. Ausweispapiere: / Papiers d'identité: / Documenti di legittimazione: carta d'identità N 5,273,747, Mantova,1.5.43.
Aufenthaltsbewilligung Mantova, 15.3.1940

15. Militärische Einteilung: / Incorporation militaire: / Incorporazione militare: untauglich

16. Grund und Umstände der Flucht sowie eingeschlagener Weg: / Motifs et circonstances de la fuite ainsi que route suivie: / Motivi e circostanze della fuga come pure percorso seguito: Nach dem in Kraft-treten des Rassengesetzes vom 1.12.43, wornach alle Juden verhaftet wurden, versteckte ich mich mit meiner Mutter, meiner Frau und zwei Kindern in der Nähe von Vercelli. Am 14.1.44 fuhren wir über Biella nach Intra und Scareno. Von dort begaben wir uns mit Führern in die Berge und übernachteten vom 15/16 in einer Hütte bei Piaggio di Valmara. Am 17. kamen wir nach Cavaglio und gegen Mittag verliessen uns die Führer indem sie angaben, wir befänden uns in der Schweiz. Wir waren alle sehr erschöpft; nach kurzer Rast machte ich mich auf die Suche nach den Grenzwächtern. Es war schon dunkel geworden und ich entschloss mich zurückzukehren, um die Meinen in einem Stall unterzubringen. Auf dem Weg glitt ich aus und verletzte mich am Kopf, wobei ich viel Blut verlor. Die Nacht verbrachte ich in einem Abgrund und am nächsten Tag irrte ich in den Bergen herum, bis ich mit Hilfe von zwei Waldarbeitern den Grenzposten von Cortacco erreichte.. Erst da erfuhr ich, dass sich meine Familie noch auf italienischem Gebiet befand. Die Soldaten versuchten von der Grenze aus meine Leute zu veranlassen zu ihnen zu kommen, ein vereister steiler Abhang verhinderte jedoch die Annäherung. Ich übernachtete in Cortaccio und am 19.1.44 wurde ich über Brissago und Locarno nach Bellinzona gebracht.

F 115 / 82868

r

Document issued by the Police of Bellinzona:

Reason and circumstances of the escape and the route taken:

...I hid with my mother, my wife and two children near Vercelli. On January 14th, 1944 we drove via Biella to Intra and Scareno. From there we went onto the mountains with guides and stayed in a hut at Piaggio di Valmara until the 16th. On the 17th we arrived at Cavaglio and around noon the guides left us saying we were in Switzerland. We were all exhausted; after a short rest I went in search of the border guards. It was already dark and I decided to go back to the stable where I left my family. On the way, I slipped and hit my head, losing a lot of blood. I spent the night in a ravine, the next day I wandered around in the mountains until, with the help of two forest workers I reached the Cortaccio border post. Only then I found out that my family was still on Italian territory. The soldiers tried to help my family... but a steep, icy slope prevented the approach. I spent the night in Cortaccio and on January 19, 1944 I was taken to Bellinzona via Brissago and Locarno......

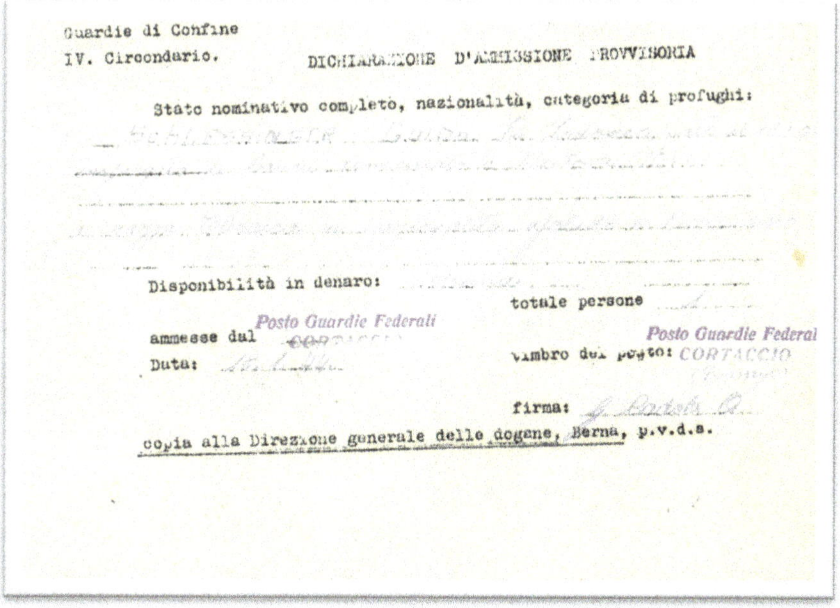
Guardie di Confine
IV. Circondario.

DICHIARAZIONE D'AMMISSIONE PROVVISORIA

Stato nominativo completo, nazionalità, categoria di profughi:

Disponibilità in denaro:

totale persone

ammesse dal

Data:

timbro del posto: Posto Guardie Federali CORTACCIO

firma:

copia alla Direzione generale delle dogane, Berna, p.v.d.s.

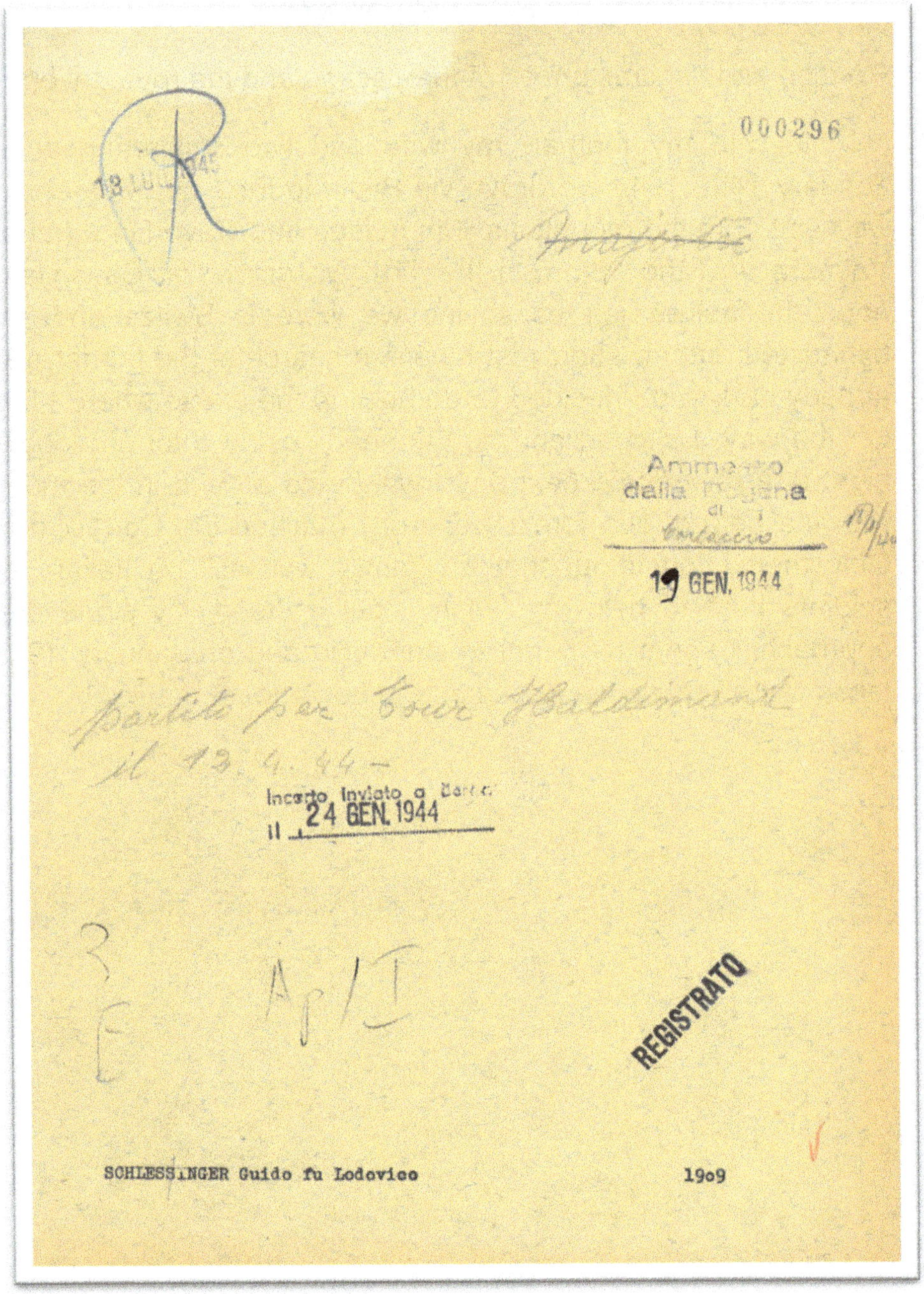
000296

Ammesso
dalla Dogana
di
19 GEN. 1944

partiti per Tour Haldimand
il 12. 4. 44-

Incarto inviato a
il 24 GEN. 1944

REGISTRATO

SCHLESSINGER Guido fu Lodovico 1909

Eidgenössisches Justiz- und Polizeidepartement
Polizeiabteilung

Département fédéral de justice et police
Division de police

Dipartimento federale di giustizia e polizia
Divisione della polizia

N 20046 Be

Berna, il 4 luglio 1945

Sig. Guido SCHLESINGER
con Lea
Home Schweizerhof
Beatenberg. (BE)

Le autorità di occupazione alleate in Italia permettono il vostro ritorno in patria.

V'invitiamo a volervi presentare il

giorno 12 luglio 1945

a Chiasso alle ore 16.30 al più tardi. In ogni caso siete tenuto a presentarvi all'Ufficio della Polizia Militare alla stazione di convocazione subito dopo l'arrivo del vostro treno. Non vi sarà nessuna possibilità di rinvio della data di partenza. Non vi sarà modo di essere spostati da una lista sull'altra, perchè le liste sono state verificate ed approvate dagli alleati secondo un ordine determinato e perciò, nostro malgrado, non potremo apportare modificazione alcuna agli ordini di partenza. Ugualmente è inutile vi presentiate prima della data fissata, perchè non vi sarà la possibilità di partire e l'Ufficiale di Polizia dovrà arrestarvi e punirvi.

Vi facciamo noto che, se il vostro ritorno in Isvizzera si rendesse necessario, potrete presentare una domanda di entrata regolare ai nostri Consolati in Italia; la vostra domanda sarà trattata dalla Polizia Federale degli Stranieri.

I vostri documenti vi sono già stati spediti. Per disposizione delle autorità di occupazione alleate vi facciamo noto che i rifugiati celibi od isolati potranno portare seco un bagaglio del peso che sono capaci loro stessi di trasportare. Le famiglie dei rifugiati, invece, potranno portare con loro bagagli del peso massimo di 45 kg per persona. Per tutte le altre disposizioni da parte svizzera, concernenti le merci o i quantitativi esportabili, vi invitiamo ad attenervi alle istruzioni impartite al riguardo alle autorità di polizia ed alle direzioni dei campi e delle case per rifugiati, con nostra circolare del 25 maggio 1945. (Vi rendiamo tuttavia attenti al fatto che, mentre da parte svizzera si permette l'esportazione di 5 orologi per persona, da parte italiana, si autorizza ad ogni rifugiato l'importazione di un solo orologio.)

La Svizzera ha avuto il privilegio di potervi accogliere nel momento in cui vi siete trovato in difficoltà. Non è stato possibile, nostro malgrado, offrire ad ognuno, quanto avremmo voluto offrire; abbiamo tuttavia fatto del nostro meglio per darvi tutto quanto ci era possibile in relazione ai nostri mezzi limitati. Abbiamo grata questa occasione per formularvi i migliori auguri per il vostro rimpatrio e ci permettiamo di esprimere i migliori voti per l'avvenire del vostro Paese.

Il capo della divisione della polizia
p. o.

Copia a:
~~Polizia cantonale~~ degli stranieri,
Direzione centrale dei campi di lavoro, Zurigo;
~~Ufficio comunale di razionamento,~~
Campo od home di Schweizerhof, Beatenberg, BE
Statistica;

F.189 - 23340 fc

17. Ort und Zeit des Grenzübertrittes: Lieu et date du passage de la frontière: Località, data e ora dello sconfinamento: Cortaccio, 18.1.44 , 18 Uhr.

18. Gesundheitszustand: Etat de santé: Condizioni di salute: chronische Colecistitis, gegenwärtig Kopfverletzung und sehr erschöpft.

19. Verwandte und Bekannte in der Schweiz: Parents et connaissances en Suisse: Parenti e conoscenze nella Svizzera: In der Schweiz interniert: meine Schwäger Alberto Vitale und Dr. Aldo ~~Elm.~~ Calò
Herr Lory, Generaldirektor der Banca della Svizzera italiana, Lugano

20. Allfällige Garanten in der Schweiz: Répondants éventuels en Suisse: Eventuali garanti nella Svizzera:

21. Genaue Zusammenstellung der Vermögensmittel im In- und Ausland: Liste exacte des ressources à l'étranger et en Suisse: Specificazione esatta dei beni patrimoniali in Svizzera e all'estero: Meine Möbel in Mantua wurden unter Sequester gestellt, Vermögen habe ich weder im Ausland noch in der Schweiz.

22. Vermerk ob Mitteilung über Verhalten der Flüchtlinge bekanntgegeben: L'« avis au réfugié » a-t-il été porté à la connaissance du réfugié? La « Communicazione ai rifugiati » è stata portata a conoscenza dell'interessato? si

Einvernommen durch:
Interrogé par:
Interrogato da:

Der Flüchtling:
Le réfugié:
Il rifugiato:

Enrichetta Schlesinger

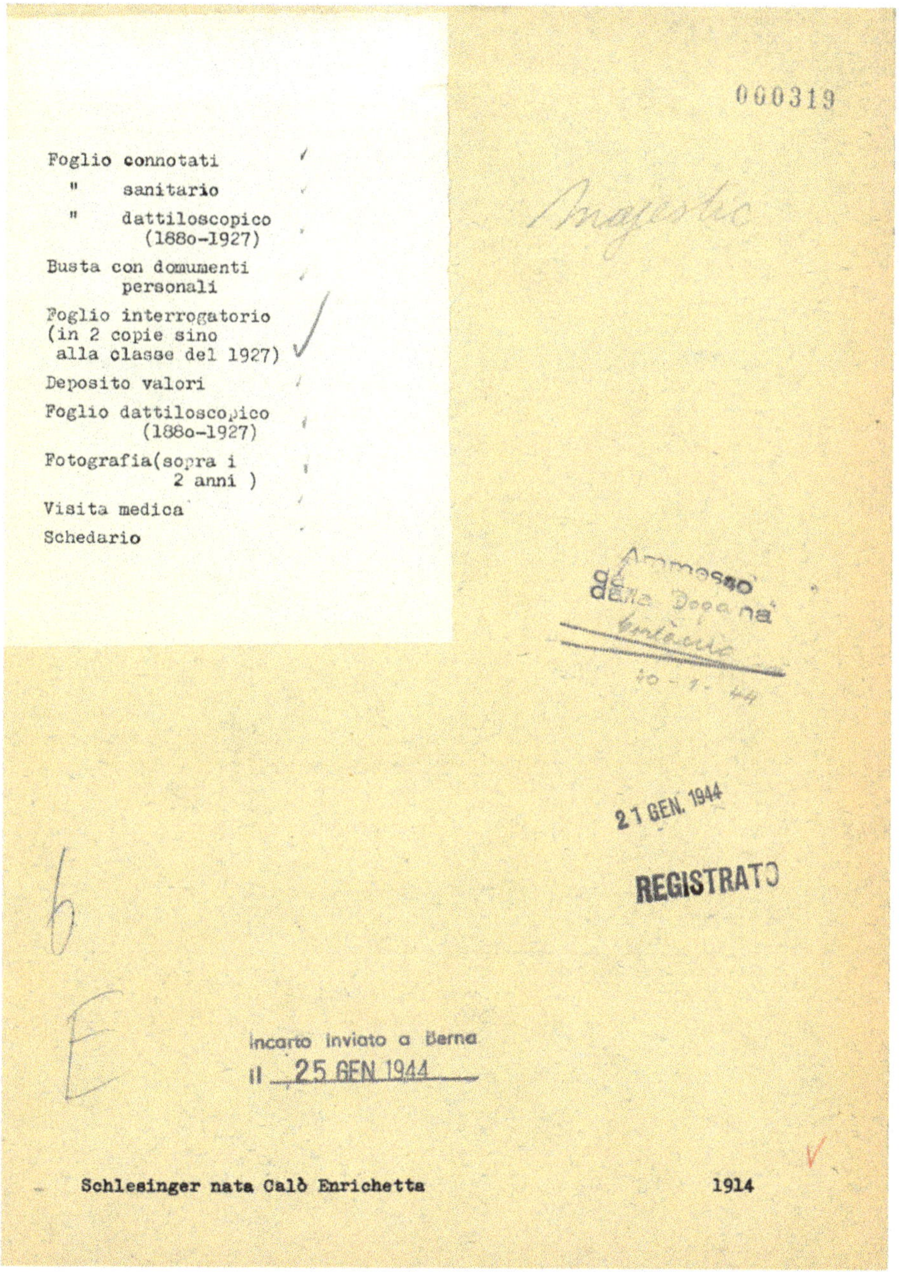

000319

Foglio connotati ✓
" sanitario ✓
" dattiloscopico (1880-1927) ✓
Busta con documenti personali ✓
Foglio interrogatorio (in 2 copie sino alla classe del 1927) ✓
Deposito valori ✓
Foglio dattiloscopico (1880-1927) ✓
Fotografia(sopra i 2 anni) ✓
Visita medica ✓
Schedario ✓

Majestic

Ammesso dalla Dogana
Ponte Tresa
10 - 1 - 44

21 GEN. 1944

REGISTRATO

6

E

Incarto inviato a Berna
il 25 GEN 1944

Schlesinger nata Calò Enrichetta 1914

Eidgenössisches Justiz- und Polizeidepartement
Polizeiabteilung

Département fédéral de justice et police
Division de police

Dipartimento federale di giustizia e polizia
Divisione della polizia

N 20046 Bia/Be

Berna, il 3 luglio 1945

Signore
Enrichetta Schlesinger, 13.9.14
e Laura 17.4.84,
Home "Schweizerhof"

B e a t e n b e r g.

Le autorità di occupazione alleate in Italia permettono il vostro ritorno in patria. V'invitiamo a volervi presentare il

giorno 12 luglio 1945

a Chiasso alle ore 16.30 al più tardi. In ogni caso siete tenuto a presentarvi all'Ufficio della Polizia Militare alla stazione di convocazione subito dopo l'arrivo del vostro treno. Non vi sarà nessuna possibilità di rinvio della data di partenza. Non vi sarà modo di essere spostati da una lista sull'altra, perchè le liste sono state verificate ed approvate dagli alleati secondo un ordine determinato e perciò, nostro malgrado, non potremo apportare modificazione alcuna agli ordini di partenza. Ugualmente è inutile vi presentiate prima della data fissata, perciò non vi sarà la possibilità di partire e l'Ufficiale di Polizia dovrà arrestarvi e punirvi.

V'invitiamo a presentarvi alla data sopracitata, alle ore 14.00 alla Società di banca svizzera Chiasso, per il ritiro dei valori depositati presso il nostro ufficio fiduciario. La Banca Popolare Svizzera a Berna è stata già incaricata dell'invio dei vostri averi alla suddetta banca. È perciò inutile inviare lettere a noi o alla Banca Popolare svizzera a Berna. Come documento di legittimazione potete presentare il libretto di rifugiato. Dopo il ritiro dei vostri averi vi ripresenterete all'Ufficiale di Polizia.

Vi facciamo noto che, se il vostro ritorno in Isvizzera si rendesse necessario, potrete presentare una domanda di entrata regolare ai nostri Consolati in Italia; la vostra domanda sarà trattata dalla Polizia Federale degli Stranieri.

I vostri documenti vi sono già stati spediti. Per disposizione delle autorità di occupazione alleate vi facciamo noto che i rifugiati celibi ed isolati potranno portare seco un bagaglio del peso che sono capaci loro stessi di trasportare. Le famiglie dei rifugiati, invece, potranno portare con loro bagagli del peso massimo di 45 Kg. per persona. Per tutte le altre disposizioni da parte svizzera, concernenti le merci o i quantitativi esportabili, vi invitiamo ad attenervi alle istruzioni impartite al riguardo alle autorità di polizia ed alle direzioni dei campi e delle case per rifugiati, con nostra circolare del 25 maggio 1945. (Vi rendiamo tuttavia attenti al fatto che, mentre da parte svizzera si permette l'esportazione di 5 orologi per persona, da parte italiana, si autorizza ad ogni rifugiato l'importazione di un solo orologio.)

La Svizzera ha avuto il privilegio di potervi accogliere nel momento in cui vi siete trovato in difficoltà. Non è stato possibile, nostro malgrado, offrire ad ognuno, quanto avremmo voluto offrire; abbiamo tuttavia fatto del nostro meglio per darvi tutto quanto ci era possibile in relazione ai nostri mezzi limitati. Abbiamo grata questa occasione per formularvi i migliori auguri per il vostro rimpatrio e ci permettiamo di esprimere i migliori voti per l'avvenire del vostro Paese. La convocazione dei vostri famigliari per la stessa data, seguirà.

IL CAPO DELLA DIVISIONE DELLA POLIZIA

p.o.

Copia a: Società di banca svizzera Chiasso;
~~Polizia centrale degli stranieri~~,
Direzione centrale dei campi di lavoro, Zurigo;
~~Ufficio centrale di razionamento~~, Beatenberg;
~~Campo ed~~ sono di
Banca Popolare Svizzera, Berna;
~~Ufficio federale delle imposte, Berna, all'attenzione del Dr. Kradolfer;~~
Direzione generale delle dogane, Berna;
Statistica.

„Nr. 4 cycl." 1693

3096

Zürich, den 17. März 1945

Express.

Fräulein
Enrichetta Schlesinger
Villino Clara

O r s e l i n a b/Locarno

M/il ZL 18557, geb. 1914

Auf Grund des uns zugestellten Zeugnisses von Herrn Dr. Alfonso Franzoni, Locarno-Muralto, vom 1. März 1945 haben wir uns einverstanden erklärt, Ihren ausserordentlichen Urlaub bis 19. März 1945 zu verlängern.

Unerklärlicherweise haben Sie uns bis heute die Bewilligung des Ter.-Kommandos 9B immer noch nicht zugestellt, trotzdem Sie genau wissen, welche Unterlagen für die Verbringung eines ausserordentlichen Urlaubes ausserhalb des zuständigen Flüchtlingsheimes, erforderlich sind. Der Ordnung halber machen wir Sie darauf aufmerksam, dass wir Ihren Urlaub nicht mehr verlängern können und Sie deshalb am 19. März 1945 ins Flüchtlingsheim Beatenberg einzurücken haben.

Die zuständigen fremdenpolizeilichen und militärischen Instanzen werden mit gleicher Post von unserem Entscheid in Kenntnis gesetzt.

ZENTRALLEITUNG DER ARBEITSLAGER
Flüchtlingskontrolle

Rösch

Kopie an: Fremdenpolizei des Kantons Tessin, Bellinzona
Ter.-Kommando, 9B, Feldpost
Flüchtlingsheim "Schweizerhof" Beatenberg.

2677

DIPARTIMENTO CANTONALE
DI POLIZIA
UFFICIO CANTONALE STRANIERI

c r Zürich

Bellinzona, 9 marzo 1945

Proroga del

PERMESSO PROVVISORIO DI RESIDENZA del 16.1.1945

COGNOME E NOME: S C H L E S I N G E R -Calo' Enrichetta

DATA DI NASCITA: 13.9.1914

NAZIONALITÀ: italiana

LUOGO D'INTERNAMENTO PRIVATO: --

O DEL CAMPO D'INTERNAMENTO: Casa per rifugiati "Schweizerhof" Beatenberg (Berna

LOCALITÀ DI RESIDENZA PROVVISORIA: Orselina

INDIRIZZO ESATTO: (presso chi): i genitori Prof. Gustavo Calo', Villino Clara

DURATA DELLA RESIDENZA: dal al 19.3.1945

MOTIVO: Cura e convalescenza.-

CONDIZIONI: Il rifugiato deve annunciare l'arrivo e la partenza alla Gendarmeria cantonale competente.

La decisione del permesso di residenza dovrà essere timbrato dall'autorità di polizia cantonale competente.

Il rifugiato è personalmente responsabile dell'osservanza di queste condizioni.

Alla scadenza del permesso di residenza provvisoria, il permesso dovrà essere ritornato, munito del timbro di arrivo e partenza, all'Ufficio cantonale degli stranieri in Bellinzona.

UFFICIO CANTONALE STRANIERI

COMUNICAZIONI:

all'interessato a V2 Gend.Cant. Orselina

alla Gendarmeria cant. di Orselina

alla Municipalità di Orselina

al C.do Terr. 9b., Posta da Campo

all'Ufficio cantonale stranieri di --

alla Divisione federale di Polizia, Berna - No. di rif.

alla Direzione del Campo Internati di Beatenberg (Berna)

44 1801 3000

Document issued by the Police of Bellinzona:

Reasons of escape and route taken:
Since September 25, 1943 I had been hiding with my family in the area of Vercelli and Biella because we feared of being persecuted for racial reasons. On January 15th, 1944 we left Biella and went via Intra and Scarena to Piaggio Valmara, where we spent the night. We went on to Cavaglio Port and walked all night until the guides told us we were in Switzerland. On January 17th my husband went on alone to search for the Swiss border guard because we were exhausted. Since he didn't come back and I didn't dare to go down the steep slope with my elderly mother and the little children, we spent two more nights outdoors. At about noon on the 19th of January, 1944 I decided to go down alone and I walked for 2 hours until I came onto a patrol that took me back to the border and helped me bring across those who stayed behind. We were taken to Cortaccio, where we arrived at midnight. On January 20th we arrived to Brissago and on the 21st to Bellinzona.

17. Ort und Zeit des Grenzübertrittes:
Lieu et date du passage de la frontière:
Località, data e ora dello sconfinamento: Cotaccio , 19.1.1944 Mitternacht.

18. Gesundheitszustand:
Etat de santé:
Condizioni di salute: gut

19. Verwandte und Bekannte in der Schweiz:
Parents et connaissances en Suisse:
Parenti e conoscenze nella Svizzera: Dr. Aldo Calo, Bruder, Mitte Dezember43 in die Schweiz geflüchtet, Adresse unbekannt.

20. Allfällige Garanten in der Schweiz:
Répondants éventuels en Suisse:
Eventuali garanti nella Svizzera:

21. Genaue Zusammenstellung der Vermögensmittel im In- und Ausland:
Liste exacte des ressources à l'étranger et en Suisse:
Specificazione esatta dei beni patrimoniali in Svizzera e all'estero: Möbel und persönliche Effekten in Mantua von den Deutschen beschlagnamt.

Ich habe Lire 2,000.- und etwas Schmuck mitgebracht.

22. Vermerk ob Mitteilung über Verhalten der Flüchtlinge bekanntgegeben: Ja.
L'« avis au réfugié » a-t-il été porté à la connaissance du réfugié?
La « Communicazione ai rifugiati » è stata portata a conoscenza dell'interessato?

Einvernommen durch:
Interrogé par:
Interrogato da:

Max Casparis

Der Flüchtling:
Le réfugié:
Il rifugiato:

Enrichetta Schlesinger

DIPARTIMENTO CANTONALE
DI POLIZIA
UFFICIO CANTONALE STRANIERI

Bellinzona, [illegible]

PERMESSO PROVVISORIO DI RESIDENZA

COGNOME E NOME: S C H L E S I N G E R -Calo' Enrichetta

DATA DI NASCITA: 13.9.1914

NAZIONALITÀ: Italiana

LUOGO D'INTERNAMENTO PRIVATO: —

O DEL CAMPO D'INTERNAMENTO: Casa per rifugiati "Schwizerhof" Beatenberg (Berna)

LOCALITÀ DI RESIDENZA PROVVISORIA: Orselina,

INDIRIZZO ESATTO: (presso chi): i genitori Prof. Gustavo Calo', Villino Clara

DURATA DELLA RESIDENZA: dal 4 settimane al

MOTIVO: Cura e convalescenza .

CONDIZIONI: Il rifugiato deve annunciare l'arrivo e la partenza alla Gendarmeria cantonale competente.

La decisione del permesso di residenza dovrà essere timbrato dall'autorità di polizia cantonale competente.

Il rifugiato è personalmente responsabile dell'osservanza di queste condizioni.

Alla scadenza del permesso di residenza provvisoria, il permesso dovrà essere ritornato, munito del timbro di arrivo e partenza, all'Ufficio cantonale degli stranieri in Bellinzona.

UFFICIO CANTONALE STRANIERI

COMUNICAZIONI:

all'interessato a V2 Casa per rifugiati "Schweizerhof" Beatenberg

alla Gendarmeria cant. di Orselina

alla Municipalità di Orselina

al C.do Terr. 9b., Posta da Campo

all'Ufficio cantonale stranieri di —

alla Divisione federale di Polizia, Berna - No. di rif.

alla Direzione del Campo Internati di Beatenberg (Berna)

44 1801 3000

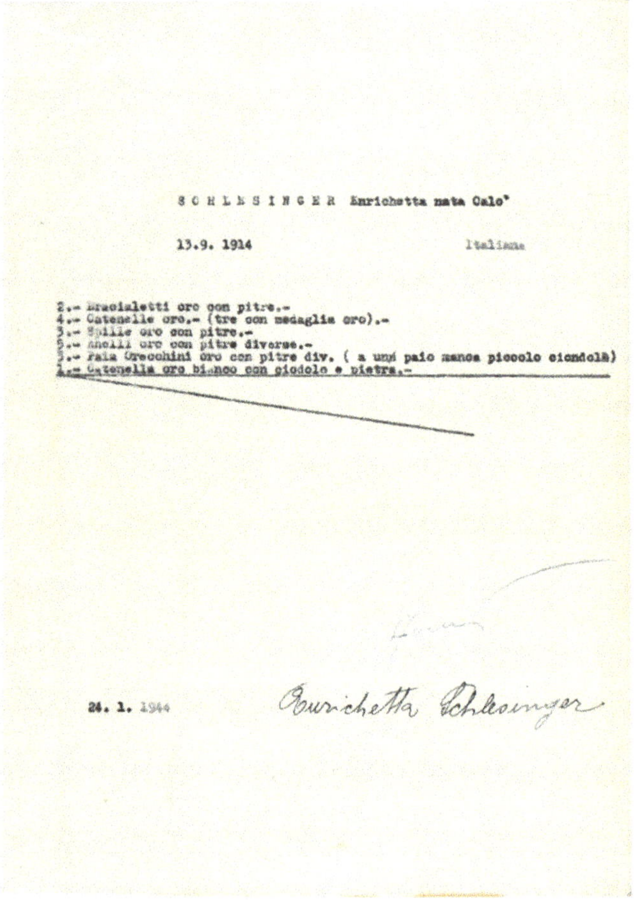

S C H L E S I N G E R Enrichetta nata Calo'

13.9. 1914 Italiana

2.- Braccialetti oro con pitre.-
4.- Catenelle oro.- (tre con medaglia oro).-
3.- Spille oro con pitre.-
5.- Anelli oro con pitre diverse.-
3.- Paia Orecchini oro con pitre div. (a unó paio manca piccolo ciondolà)
1.- Catenella oro bianco con ciodolo e pietra.-

24. 1. 1944 Enrichetta Schlesinger

I had 2000 lire and jewelry.
2 gold bracelets with stones
4 gold chains,
3 with a gold pendant
3 gold pins with stones
5 gold rings with various stones
3 pairs of gold earrings with stones

(one pair is missing a small pendant)
1 small white gold chain with a pendant and a stone

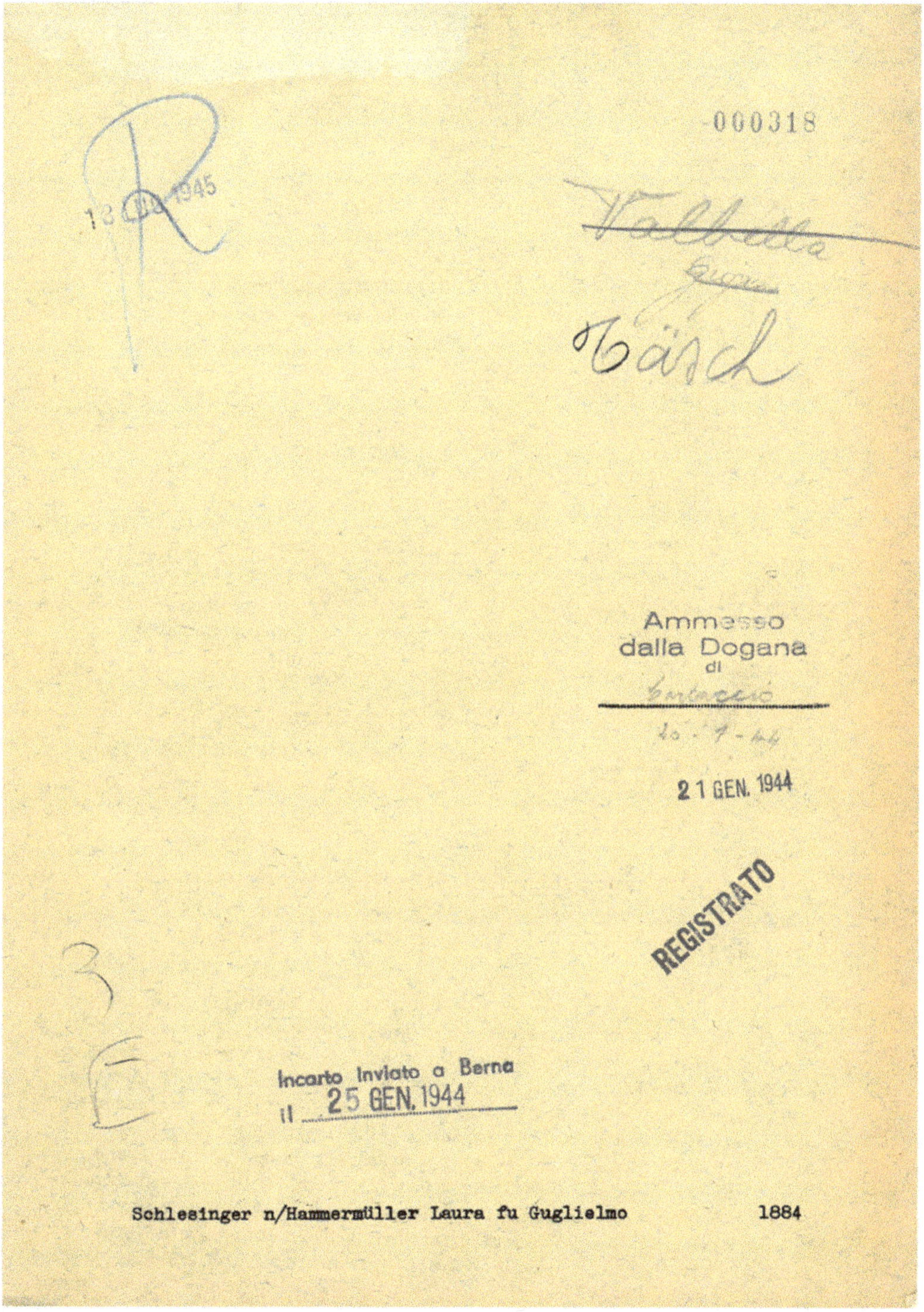
000318

Ammesso
dalla Dogana
di

20-1-44

21 GEN. 1944

REGISTRATO

Incarto Inviato a Berna
il 25 GEN. 1944

Schlesinger n/Hammermüller Laura fu Guglielmo 1884

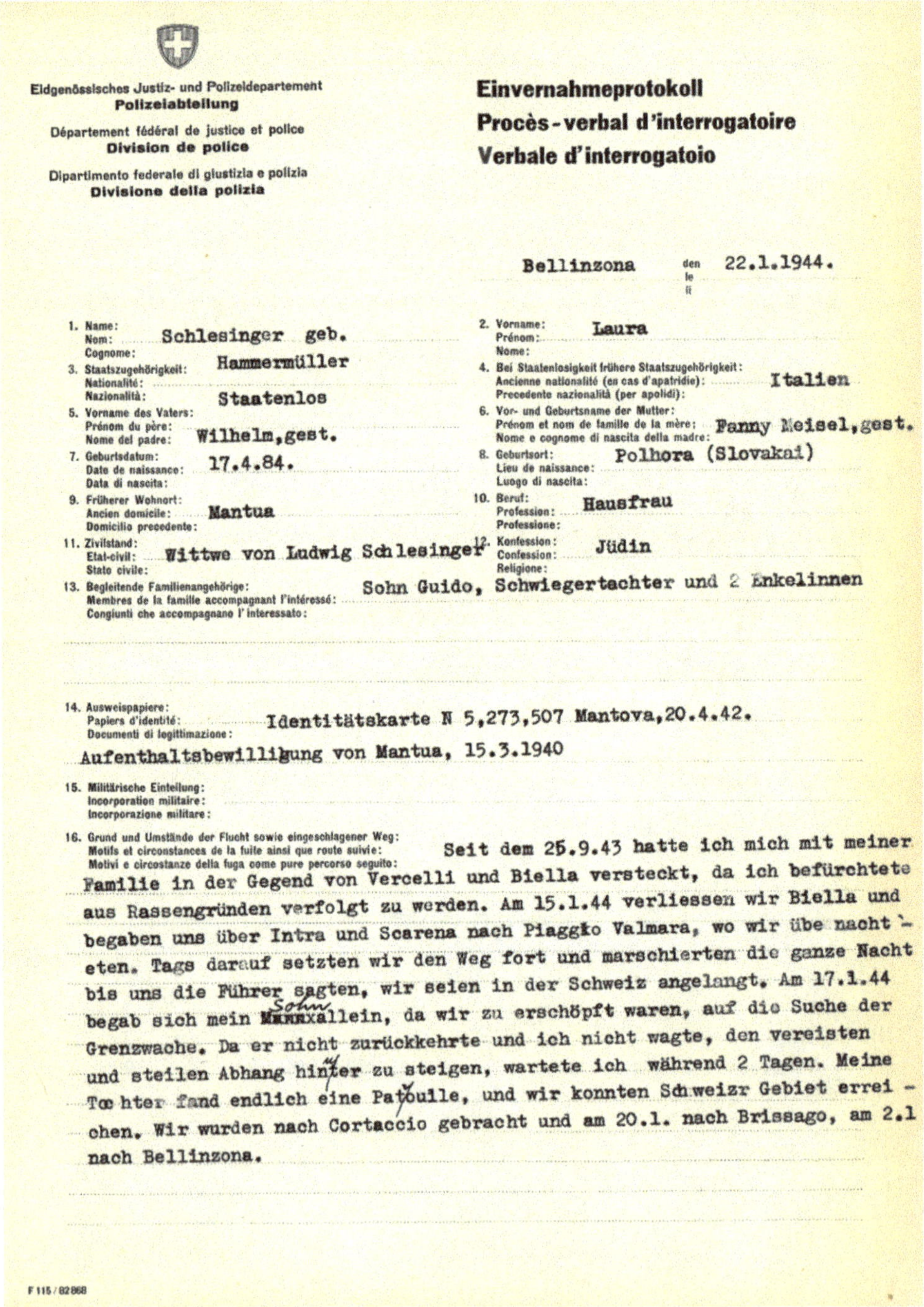

Eidgenössisches Justiz- und Polizeidepartement
Polizeiabteilung

Département fédéral de justice et police
Division de police

Dipartimento federale di giustizia e polizia
Divisione della polizia

Einvernahmeprotokoll
Procès-verbal d'interrogatoire
Verbale d'interrogatoio

Bellinzona den / le / il 22.1.1944.

1. Name: / Nom: / Cognome: Schlesinger geb. Hammermüller
2. Vorname: / Prénom: / Nome: Laura
3. Staatszugehörigkeit: / Nationalité: / Nazionalità: Staatenlos
4. Bei Staatenlosigkeit frühere Staatszugehörigkeit: / Ancienne nationalité (en cas d'apatridie): / Precedente nazionalità (per apolidi): Italien
5. Vorname des Vaters: / Prénom du père: / Nome del padre: Wilhelm,gest.
6. Vor- und Geburtsname der Mutter: / Prénom et nom de famille de la mère: / Nome e cognome di nascita della madre: Fanny Meisel,gest.
7. Geburtsdatum: / Date de naissance: / Data di nascita: 17.4.84.
8. Geburtsort: / Lieu de naissance: / Luogo di nascita: Polhora (Slovakai)
9. Früherer Wohnort: / Ancien domicile: / Domicilio precedente: Mantua
10. Beruf: / Profession: / Professione: Hausfrau
11. Zivilstand: / Etat-civil: / Stato civile: Wittwe von Ludwig Schlesinger
12. Konfession: / Confession: / Religione: Jüdin
13. Begleitende Familienangehörige: / Membres de la famille accompagnant l'intéressé: / Congiunti che accompagnano l'interessato: Sohn Guido, Schwiegertachter und 2 Enkelinnen
14. Ausweispapiere: / Papiers d'identité: / Documenti di legittimazione: Identitätskarte N 5,273,507 Mantova,20.4.42. Aufenthaltsbewilligung von Mantua, 15.3.1940
15. Militärische Einteilung: / Incorporation militaire: / Incorporazione militare:
16. Grund und Umstände der Flucht sowie eingeschlagener Weg: / Motifs et circonstances de la fuite ainsi que route suivie: / Motivi e circostanze della fuga come pure percorso seguito: Seit dem 25.9.43 hatte ich mich mit meiner Familie in der Gegend von Vercelli und Biella versteckt, da ich befürchtete aus Rassengründen verfolgt zu werden. Am 15.1.44 verliessen wir Biella und begaben uns über Intra und Scarena nach Piaggko Valmara, wo wir übe nacht - eten. Tags darauf setzten wir den Weg fort und marschierten die ganze Nacht bis uns die Führer sagten, wir seien in der Schweiz angelangt. Am 17.1.44 begab sich mein ~~Mann~~ Sohn allein, da wir zu erschöpft waren, auf die Suche der Grenzwache. Da er nicht zurückkehrte und ich nicht wagte, den vereisten und steilen Abhang hinter zu steigen, wartete ich während 2 Tagen. Meine Tochter fand endlich eine Patouille, und wir konnten Schweizr Gebiet errei - chen. Wir wurden nach Cortaccio gebracht und am 20.1. nach Brissago, am 2.1 nach Bellinzona.

F 115 / 82868

Document issued by the Police of Bellinzona:

Reason and circumstances of the escape as well as the route taken:

Since September 25th, 1943 I hid with my family in the area of Vercelli and Biella because I feared of being persecuted for racial reasons. On January 15th, 1944 we left Biella and went via Intra and Scarena to Piaggio Valmara, where we spent the night. The next day we continued on our way and walked all night until the guides told us that we had arrived in Switzerland. On January 17th, 1944 my son went on alone because we were too exhausted to search for the border guard. Since he didn't come back and I didn't dare to climb the icy and steep slope, I waited for 2 days. My daughters finally found a patrol and we were able to reach the Swiss territory. We were brought to Cortaccio on January 20th and to Brissago on January 2nd and on to Bellinzona

17. Ort und Zeit des Grenzübertrittes:
Lieu et date du passage de la frontière:
Località, data e ora dello sconfinamento: Cortaccio, 19.1.1944, 24 Uhr.

18. Gesundheitszustand:
Etat de santé: gut
Condizioni di salute:

19. Verwandte und Bekannte in der Schweiz:
Parents et connaissances en Suisse: keine
Parenti e conoscenze nella Svizzera:

20. Allfällige Garanten in der Schweiz:
Répondants éventuels en Suisse:
Eventuali garanti nella Svizzera:

21. Genaue Zusammenstellung der Vermögensmittel im In- und Ausland:
Liste exacte des ressources à l'étranger et en Suisse:
Specificazione esatta dei beni patrimoniali in Svizzera e all'estero: Ich habe weder im Ausland noch in der Schweiz irgendwelche Vermögensmittel.

22. Vermerk ob Mitteilung über Verhalten der Flüchtlinge bekanntgegeben:
L'« avis au réfugié » a-t-il été porté à la connaissance du réfugié? Ja.
La « Communicazione ai rifugiati » è stata portata a conoscenza dell'interessato?

Einvernommen durch:
Interrogé par:
Interrogato da:
[illegible]

Der Flüchtling:
Le réfugié:
Il rifugiato:
Laura Schlesinger
geb. Hammermüller

Guardie di Confine
IV. Circondario.

DICHIARAZIONE D'AMMISSIONE PROVVISORIA

Stato nominativo completo, nazionalità, categoria di profughi:

SCHLESINGER LAURA nata Hammermüller, 17.4.84. di razza ebraica, apolide (ex cecoslovacca) domiciliata a Mantova Ita., casalinga e nuora:

CALO' ENRICHETTA in Schlesinger, 13.9.14 di razza ebraica, italiana, casalinga, dom. a Mantova It.

coi figli: ANNA nata il 31.9.35 e LEA nata il 11.11.42

Disponibilità in denaro: nessuna

totale persone quattro

ammesse dal Posto Guardie Federali CORTACCIO

Data: 20.1.44

timbro del posto Posto Guardie Federali CORTACCIO

firma: [illegible]

copia alla Direzione generale delle dogane, Berna, p.v.d.s.

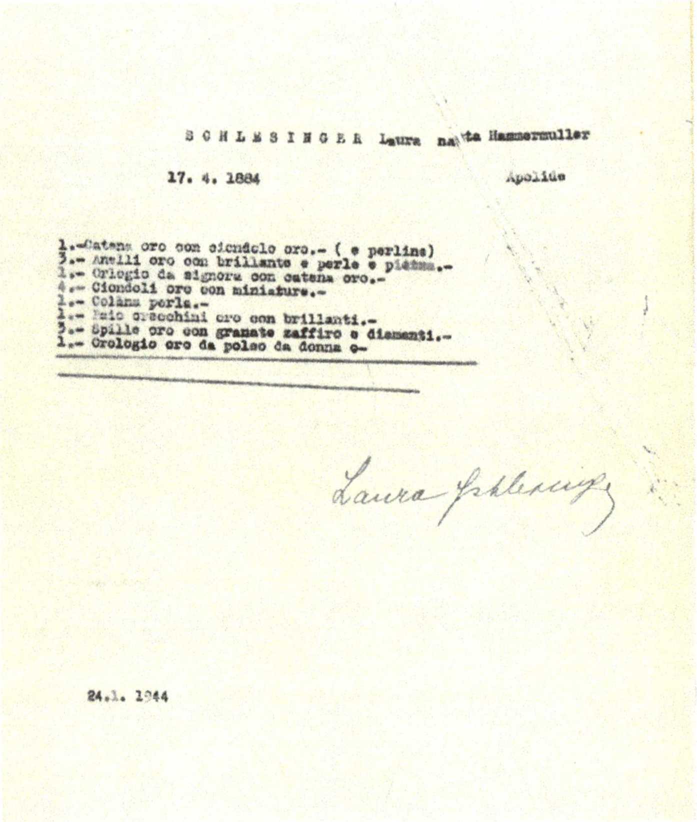

S C H L E S I N G E R Laura nata Hammermuller

17. 4. 1884 Apolide

1.-Catena oro con ciondolo oro.- (e perline)
3.- Anelli oro con brillante e perle e pietre.-
1.- Orlogio da signora con catena oro.-
4.- Ciondoli oro con miniature.-
1.- Colàna perle.-
1.- Paio orecchini oro con brillanti.-
3.- Spille oro con granate zaffiro e diamenti.-
1.- Orologio oro da polso da donna o-

Laura Schlesinger

24.1. 1944

1 gold chain with a gold pendant (and little pearls)
3 gold rings with diamonds and pearls and stones
4 gold pendants with miniatures
1 pearl necklace
1 lady watch with gold bracelet
1 pair gold earrings with diamonds
3 gold brooches with sapphires and diamonds,1 gold lady watch

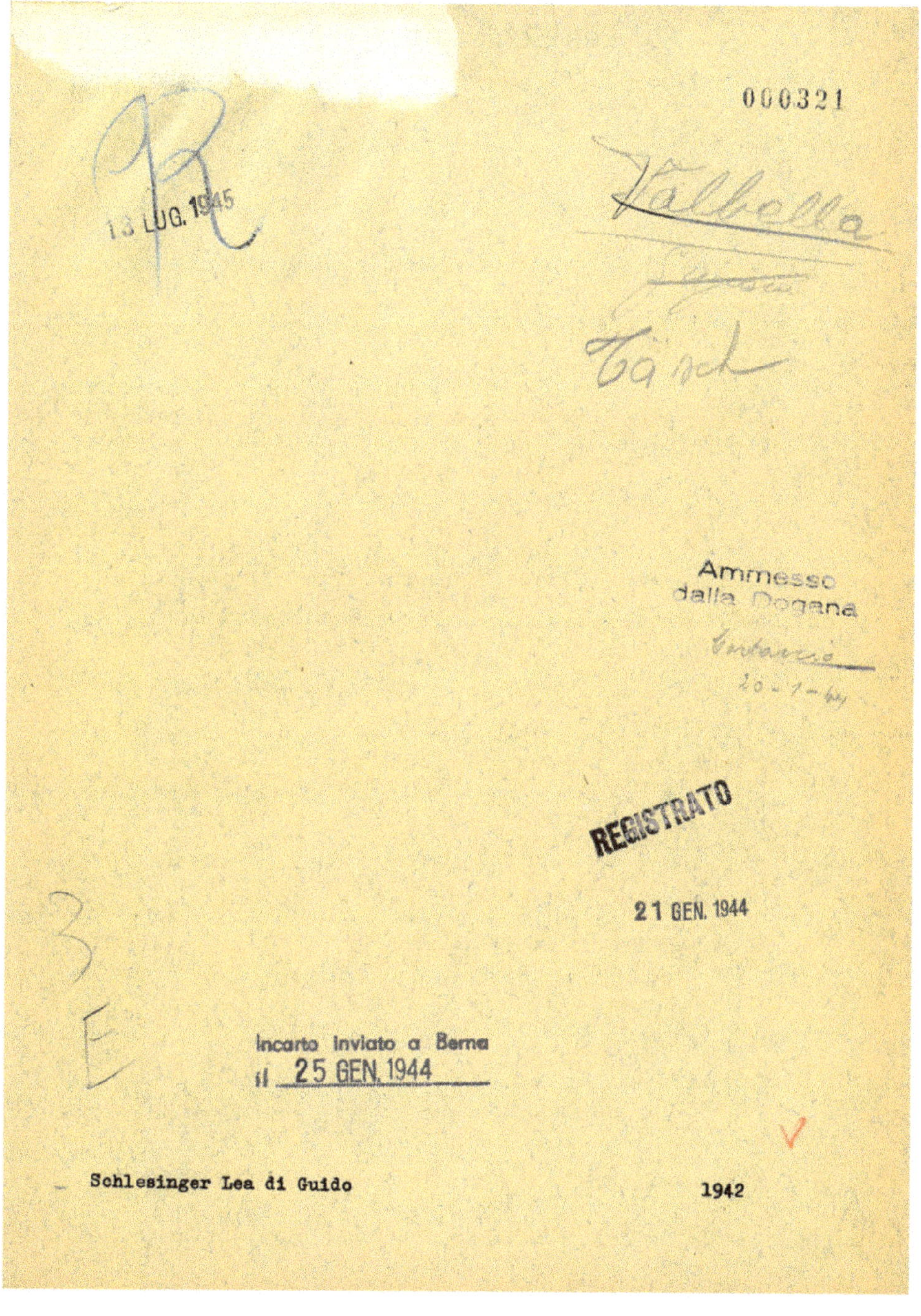

000321

13 LUG. 1945

Valbella

Ammesso
dalla Dogana

20-1-44

REGISTRATO

21 GEN. 1944

Incarto inviato a Berna
il 25 GEN. 1944

Schlesinger Lea di Guido

1942

Lea Schlesinger

Uff. di Pol.
Cdo. Ter. 9 b.

P. C., il 12. 5. 1944

Cdo. Terr. 9 b.
Serv. Int.-

Vorrete disporre affinché le rifugiate :

Schlesinger	Laura	1884	(Campo Majestic Lugano
Schlesinger	Léa	1942	" " "

possano partire il giorno 15. 5. 44 dimodoché possano raggiungere il campo di Valbella (GR) in giornata prima dalle ore 18.00.-

Vi preghiamo di ritornate il buono di trasporto No. 102611 per Tüsch, dove la Schlesinger doveva recarsi in un primo ordine,-direttamente alle Zentralleitung der Arbeitslager, Zurigo.-

Annesso : No. 2 buoni di trasporto.-

Eidgenössisches Justiz- und Polizeidepartement
Polizeiabteilung

Département fédéral de justice et police
Division de police

Dipartimento federale di giustizia e polizia
Divisione della polizia

N 29046 Be

Berna, 11 4 luglio 1945

Sig. Guido SCHLESINGER
con Lea
Home Schweizerhof
Bostenberg. (BE)

Le autorità di occupazione alleate in Italia permettono il vostro ritorno in patria.

V'invitiamo a volervi presentare il

giorno 12 luglio 1945

a Chiasso

alle ore 16.30 al più tardi. In ogni caso siete tenuto a presentarvi all'Ufficio della Polizia Militare alla stazione di convocazione subito dopo l'arrivo del vostro treno. Non vi sarà nessuna possibilità di rinvio della data di partenza. Non vi sarà modo di essere spostati da una lista sull'altra, perchè le liste sono state verificate ed approvate dagli alleati secondo un ordine determinato e perciò, nostro malgrado, non potremo apportare modificazione alcuna agli ordini di partenza. Ugualmente è inutile vi presentiate prima della data fissata, perchè non vi sarà la possibilità di partire e l'Ufficiale di Polizia dovrà arrestarvi e punirvi.

Vi facciamo noto che, se il vostro ritorno in Isvizzera si rendesse necessario, potrete presentare una domanda di entrata regolare ai nostri Consolati in Italia; la vostra domanda sarà trattata dalla Polizia Federale degli Stranieri.

I vostri documenti vi sono già stati spediti. Per disposizione delle autorità di occupazione alleate vi facciamo noto che i rifugiati celibi od isolati potranno portare seco un bagaglio del peso che sono capaci loro stessi di trasportare. Le famiglie dei rifugiati, invece, potranno portare con loro bagagli del peso massimo di 45 kg per persona. Per tutte le altre disposizioni da parte svizzera, concernenti le merci o i quantitativi esportabili, vi invitiamo ad attenervi alle istruzioni impartite al riguardo alle autorità di polizia ed alle direzioni dei campi e delle case per rifugiati, con nostra circolare del 25 maggio 1945. (Vi rendiamo tuttavia attenti al fatto che, mentre da parte svizzera si permette l'esportazione di 5 orologi per persona, da parte italiana, si autorizza ad ogni rifugiato l'importazione di un solo orologio.)

La Svizzera ha avuto il privilegio di potervi accogliere nel momento in cui vi siete trovato in difficoltà. Non è stato possibile, nostro malgrado, offrire ad ognuno, quanto avremmo voluto offrire; abbiamo tuttavia fatto del nostro meglio per darvi tutto quanto ci era possibile in relazione ai nostri mezzi limitati. Abbiamo grata questa occasione per formularvi i migliori auguri per il vostro rimpatrio e ci permettiamo di esprimere i migliori voti per l'avvenire del vostro Paese.

Il capo della divisione della polizia
p. o.

Copia a:

Polizia cantonale degli stranieri,
Direzione centrale dei campi di lavoro, Zurigo;
Ufficio comunale di razionamento,
Campo od home di Schweizerhof, Bostenberg, BE
Statistica;

F. 110 - 23040 fe

Majestic

EIDGENÖSSISCHES
JUSTIZ- UND POLIZEIDEPARTEMENT
POLIZEIABTEILUNG
Zentralleitung der Arbeitslager

DEPARTEMENT FEDERAL DE JUSTICE ET POLICE
DIVISION DE POLICE
Direction centrale des camps de travail

DIPARTEMENTO FEDERALE DI GIUSTIZIA E POLIZIA
DIVISIONE DELLA POLIZIA
Direzione centrale dei campi di lavoro

PA 20046
PA 20046

Zurich, le 11 mai 1944

Express

Of. Pol. Ar. Ter. 9b

Poste de campagne 5394

Ihr Zeichen / V. réf. / V. ref.:

Unser Zeichen / N. réf. / N. ref.: Pi/do
Bitte in der Antwort anzugeben.
A rappeler dans la réponse s. v. p.
Da richiamare nella risposta p. f.

Concerne : ZL 18555 Schlesinger Laura, 17. 4.1884
ZL 18556 Schlesinger Léa, 11.12.1942

Nous vous informons que nous modifions notre convocation du 5 mai 1944. Ces réfugiées devront se rendre le 15 mai 1944 non pas au home de Täsch, mais à celui de Valbella.
Nous vous remettons ci-joint de nouveaux bons de transport et vous prions de nous retourner le bon no.102611.

DIRECTION CENTRALE DES CAMPS DE TRAVAIL
Le chef p.o. :

Galay

2 bons de transport nos. 102296-97.

Copie à :

Division de Police, Berne
Cdt. du camp d'accueil "Hôtel Majestic"Lugano,poste de Campagne
Direction du home de Täsch
Direction du home de Valbella .

32

Zentralleitung der Arbeitslager, Zürich 2
Direction centrale des camps de travail, Zurich 2,
Direzione centrale dei campi di lavoro, Zurigo 2,
Beethovenstrasse 11, Telefon 7 38 50

Silvia Vitale

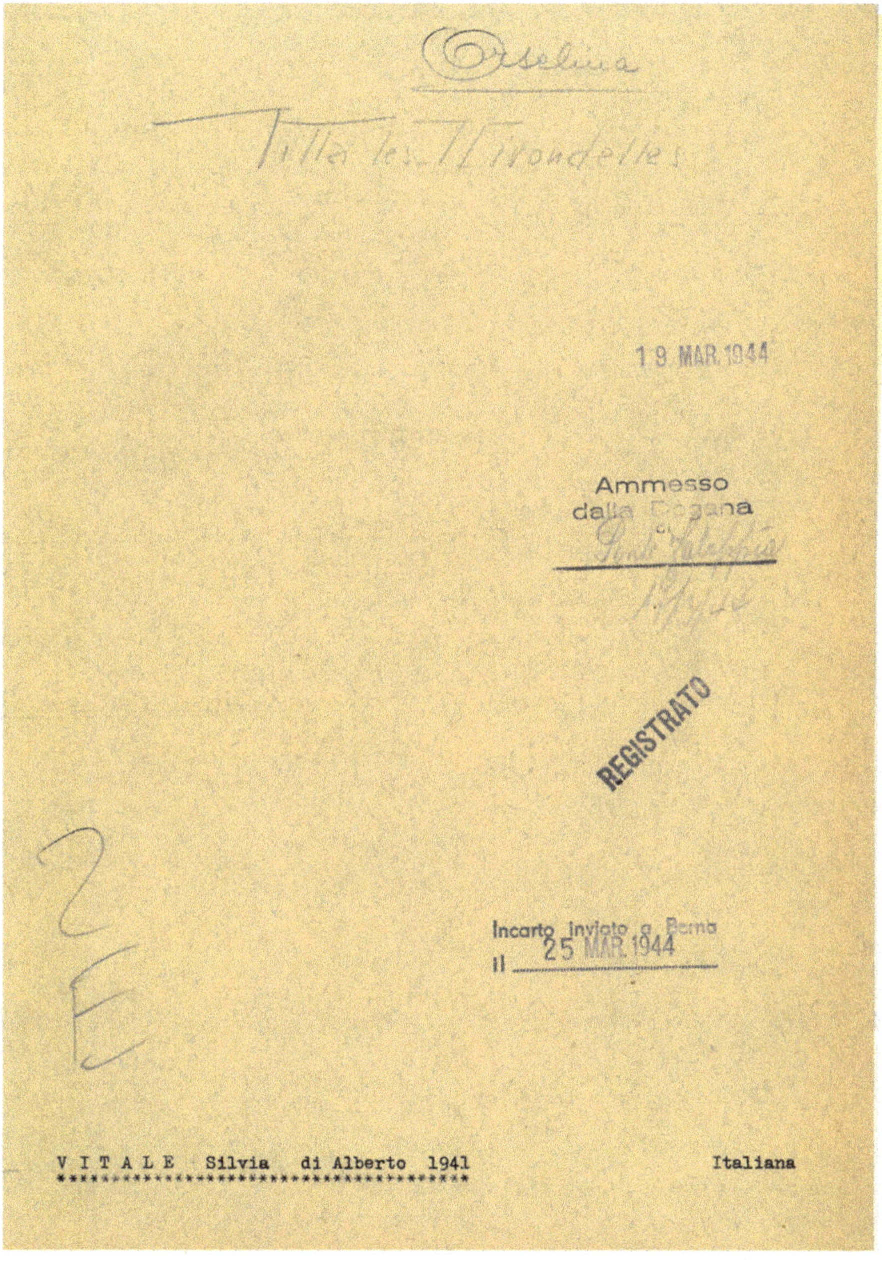
Orselina

Villa les Hirondelles

19 MAR 1944

Ammesso
dalla Dogana
di

REGISTRATO

Incarto inviato a Berna
il 25 MAR 1944

V I T A L E Silvia di Alberto 1941 Italiana

Cdo.Terr. 9b
Uff. Pol.

Name
Familienname VITALE
Cognome

Christian Name
Nome Silvia
Vorname

Father
Padre di Alberto
Vater

Mother
Madre Calo' Elsa
Mutter

Born at
nato a Biella (Vercelli)
geboren zu

The date
il 27. 5. 1941
den

domicile
dimorante a Biella (Italia)
Wohnhaft in

Street
via Torino No. 55
Strasse

Profession
Professione ********
Beruf

Maried or Not
ammogliato o celibe *******
verheiratet oder nicht

Incorporation-Military service
Incorporazione militare *****
Militäreinteilung

Internet in
Internato in Svizzera

in camp
nel campo di Bellinzona Casa Italia

Data. 19. 3. 1944

Firma: p. Vitale Silvia Calo' Elsa

DIPARTIMENTO CANTONALE DI POLIZIA

UFFICIO CANTONALE STRANIERI

Bellinzona, 5 maggio 1944

Alla Gendarmeria cantonale

No. 167.

Orselina

Vi trasmettiamo annesso il decreto d'internamento emanato dalla Divisione di Polizia del Dipartimento Federale di Giustizia e Polizia nei confronti dell'attinente italiana

V I T A L E Silvia, nata il 27 maggio 1942

Lo stesso è autorizzato a dimorare in Orselina

presso Villa Les Hirondelles

sino nuovo avviso, ed alle seguenti condizioni:

1. Astensione da qualsiasi attività politica di atto e contegno contrario alla neutralità della Svizzera.
2. Divieto di esercitare qualsiasi attività lucrativa o anche di accettare un impiego non retribuito.
3. Divieto di esercitare una pubblica attività (Conferenze, scritti per giornali, pubblicazioni, collaborazioni alla radio, al teatro, ai cinema).
4. Divieto di abbandonare la località di residenza fissata e di cambiare residenza nella località di soggiorno.
5. Deposito presso la Banca Popolare Svizzera a Berna di tutti i mezzi liquidi e degli oggetti di valore posseduti in Svizzera o che possono loro pervenire dall'estero.
6.

Il rifugiato rimane sottoposto al controllo della Divisione Federale di Polizia del Dipartimento Federale di Giustizia e Polizia.

Non è necessario che vengano regolate le condizioni della sua dimora.

TESSERA DI RAZIONAMENTO - Per la sussistenza ogni interessato riceverà per ogni 15 giorni, dall'Ufficio cant. Forestieri, una dichiarazione di sussistenza (Modulo UGV AF 1) che dovrà essere consegnata all'Ufficio dell'Economia di Guerra del Comune di dimora per ottenere le corrispondenti tessere di razionamento, qualora non fosse ancora in possesso del Libretto per rifugiati.

UFFICIO CANTONALE DEGLI STRANIERI

COMUNICAZIONE:

all'interessato per il tramite della Polizia cant. di Orselina

alla Polizia cant. di Orselina

alla Municipalità di Orselina

all'Ufficio comunale dell'Economia di Guerra di Orselina

Al Comando Terr. 9b. - Uff. di polizia - Posta da Campo.

Allegato menzionato.

44 853 2000

Ludovico Schlesinger

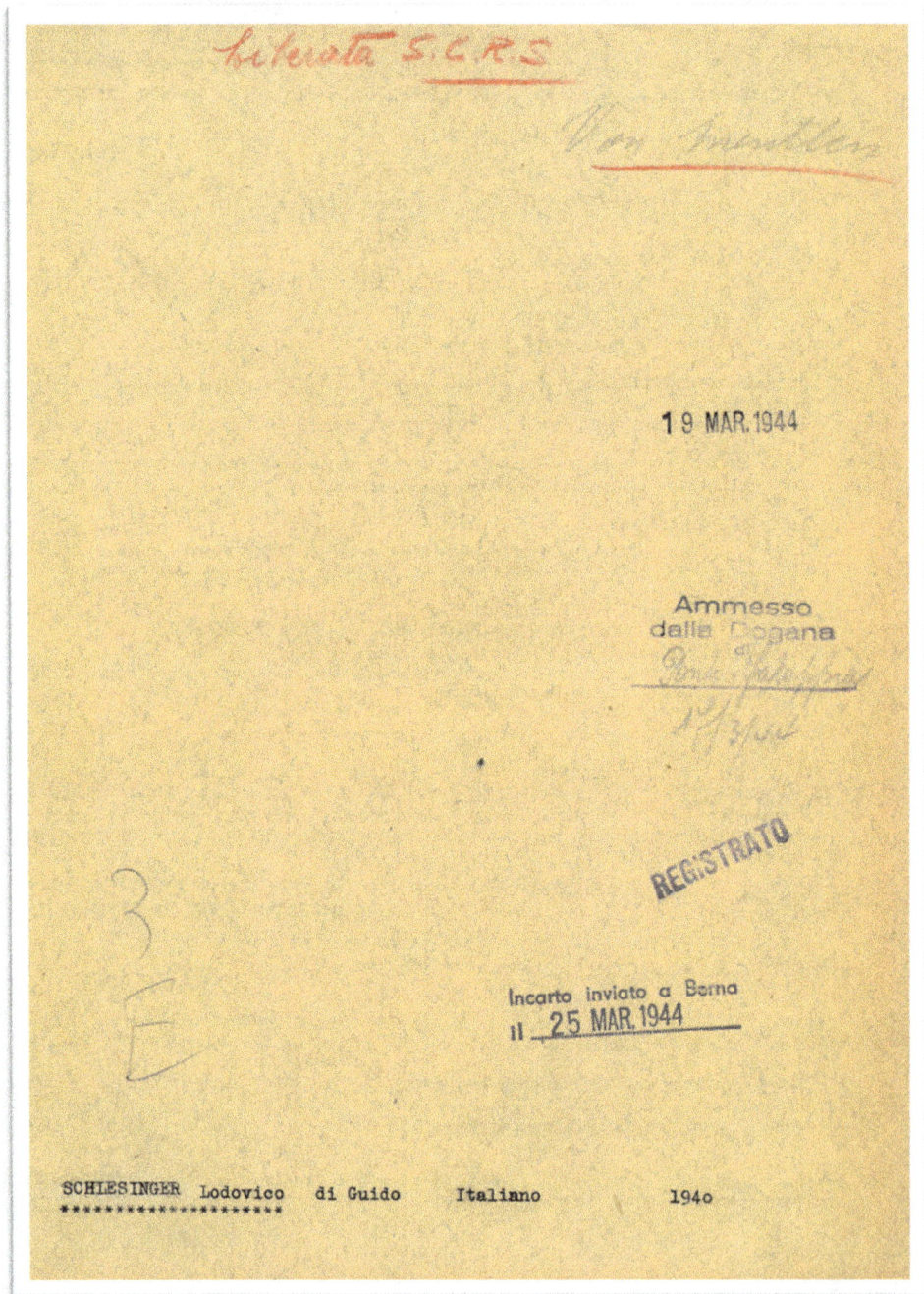

Liberata S.C.R.S

19 MAR. 1944

Ammesso
dalla Dogana
di

REGISTRATO

Incarto inviato a Berna
il 25 MAR. 1944

SCHLESINGER Lodovico di Guido Italiano 1940

Cdo.Ter.9b.
Uff.di Pol.

P.C. 11.11.44.

ORDINE DI LIBERAZIONE

S c h l e s i n g e r Lodovico, di Guido e Enrichetta Calò, nato a Mantova il 21.3.1940, già dimorante a Mantova, italiano, att. a Bellinzona, Von Mentlen,

é l i b e r a t o

e passa sotto il controllo della Croce Rossa Svizzera, Soccorso ai fanciulli, Berna.

E' liberato a Bellinzona presso Ricovero Von Mentlen " Soleggio "

Cdo Ter 9 b
Uff. di Polizia
Cap. Ferrario

Copia:
Divisione di Polizia, Berna. 20046 Cs.
Cdo.Ter.9b. Servizio Inter.
Ricovero Von Mentlen, Bellinzona.
C.R.S. Soc.ai Fanc. Sez.Ticino.
Interessato.
Incarto.-

Cdo.Terr. 9b
Uff. Pol.

Name
Familienname SCHLESINGER
Cognome

Lodovico

Christian Name
Nome
Vorname

Father
Padre di Guido
Vater

Mother
Madre Enrichetta Calo'
Mutter

Born at
nato a Mantova (Italia)
geboren zu

The date
il 21 marzo 1940
den

domicile
dimorante a Mantova (Italia)
Wohnhaft in

Street
via Gilberto Govi No. 9
Strasse

Profession
Professione ******
Beruf

Maried or Not
ammogliato o celibe ******
verheiratet oder nicht

Incorporation-Military service *******
Incorporazione militare
Militäreinteilung

Interned in Svizzera
Internato in

in camp Bellinzona Casa D'Italia
nel campo di

Data. 19. 3. 1944

Firma: p. Schlesinger [illegible]
[illegible]

Guardie di Confine
IV. Circondario.

DICHIARAZIONE D'AMMISSIONE PROVVISORIA

Stato nominativo completo, nazionalità, categoria di profughi:
Federico Bernheimer di Guido e di Enrichetta
ebreo nato il 21.3.1940 a Mantova.

I genitori si trovano al [illegible] a Lugano dal
gennaio scorso

Disponibilità in denaro: –

totale persone 1

ammesse dal Off. Botta

timbro del posto Posto Guardie F. PONTE FALOPPIA

Data: 17.12.44

firma: Off. Botta

copia alla Direzione generale delle dogane, Berna, p.v.d.s.

Anna Schlesinger

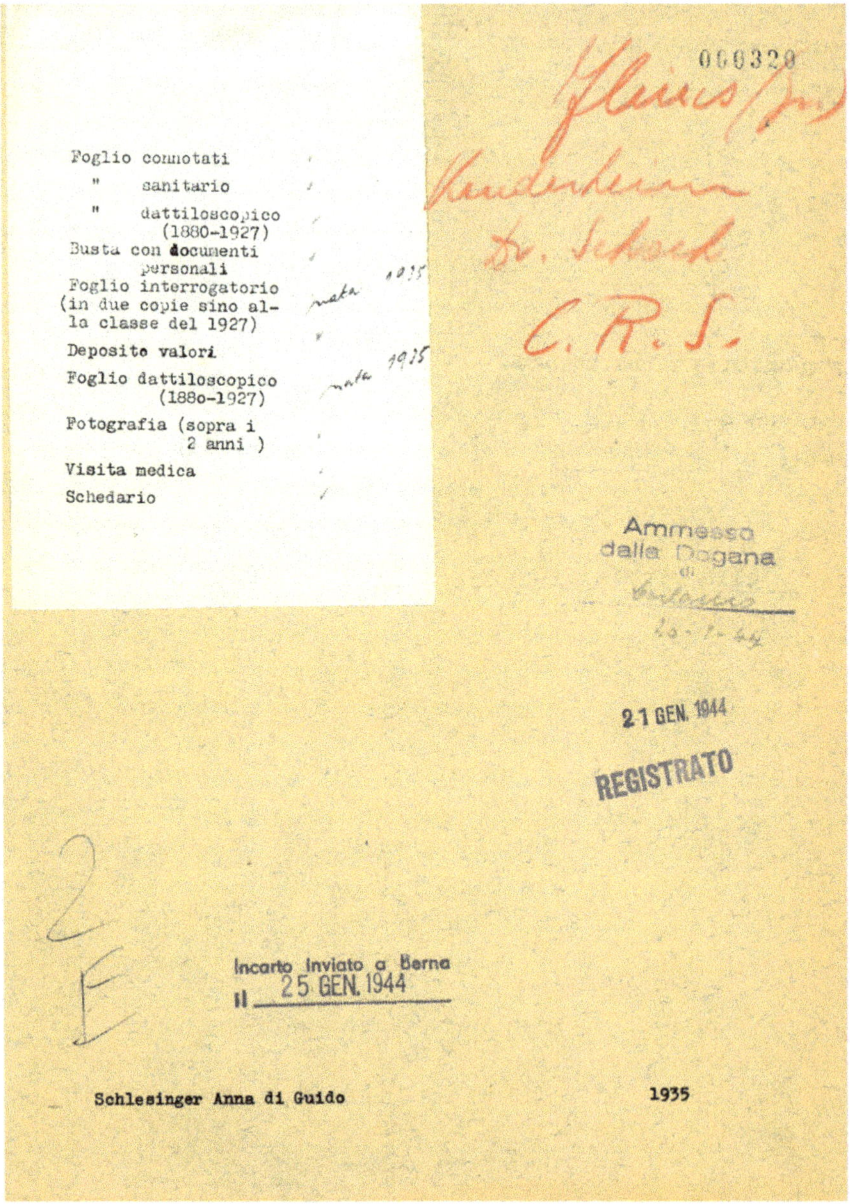

000329

Foglio connotati
" sanitario
" dattiloscopico (1880-1927)
Busta con documenti personali
Foglio interrogatorio (in due copie sino alla classe del 1927)
Deposito valori
Foglio dattiloscopico (188o-1927)
Fotografia (sopra i 2 anni)
Visita medica
Schedario

C.R.S.

Ammesso dalla Dogana di

21 GEN. 1944

REGISTRATO

Incarto Inviato a Berna il 25 GEN. 1944

Schlesinger Anna di Guido

1935

SWITZERLAND DURING THE SHOAH

My father Aldo Caló was born to Gustavo Caló and Alba Milla Caló on December 28, 1912 in Corfu, Greece.

Aldo Caló, to the right of the cannon, with a book under his arm

Aldo Caló, first row lying on the ground, first on the left

He graduated from university and worked in Milan for an insurance company until 1943.

In 1943, the Germans occupied Italy and my father and the rest of his family tried to find refuge in Switzerland.

The Swiss Government did not welcome the arrivals of Jews that were fleeing for their lives from all over Europe but felt pressured to at least admit some.

"During the Holocaust 23,000 Jews found temporary shelter in Switzerland, but 35,000 were turned away. The country remained neutral during the war, yet the Swiss treated Jewish refugees differently. They persuaded the Germans to stamp the letter "J" on German and Austrian Jewish passports to make it easier for the immigration authorities to deny them entry."3

Crossing the border into Switzerland was extraordinarily difficult. Any movement needed to be clandestine. One needed to find locals that were familiar with the mountains, smugglers that crossed the border illegally and sometimes did business with the border guards. These alpinists knew where to stop; they knew how the border was controlled, when and where to cross, when the border guards changed shifts. Basically, one had to trust quite unreliable people.

---

[3] Robert Hersowitz, The Jerusalem Post, July 29, 2020

My father found someone to take him across the Alps and reach the Swiss border. Unfortunately the border officers collected a fee which he did not have so he was refused entry. He tried again, this time paying the Swiss border guards who let him cross the border.
He was taken to a labor camp in Aarau, a town between Basel and Zurich, where he was made to chop wood in the forest to pay for his stay.

I found this postcard in his books after Mamma z"l passed away. It refers to Olsberg, a town in Northern Switzerland and I do not know who these people are or why he kept the postcard.

A photo taken during a post war reunion of refugees from Olsberg. (in the photo below)

Olsberg, Switzerland

COMUNE DI MANTOVA

MANTOVA LIBERA

Squarciata la tenebra della duplice oppressione
la città dei Martiri è restituita alla Patria

Il Consiglio Comunale
con deliberazione unanime
del 14 marzo 1977
ha espresso

RICONOSCIMENTO CIVICO

a

CALO' ALDO

per la persecuzione subita
durante la dittatura fascista

IL SINDACO

Mantova, 25 aprile 1977.

XXXII° DELLA LIBERAZIONE

A certificate issued to Aldo Caló by the Italian government in 1977 in recognition of persecutions during the Fascist regime.

NEW BEGINNINGS

Via Petrella 8, Milano

At the end of the war he came back to Milan and on March 28, 1948 he married my mother.

I was born in Milan, on January 10, 1949. We lived on via Petrella 8, off Corso Buenos Aires. It's a small street off a main and busy commercial avenue.

We lived in Milan four or five years, I am not exactly sure. Although I was a little girl some scenes are vivid in my mind. I remember the layout of the flat. I remember riding my tricycle down the "long" hallway. I remember the day my brother David was born in 1953. The Brith must have taken place at the house because I remember a lot of people gathered in the bedroom at the end of the hallway, on the left.

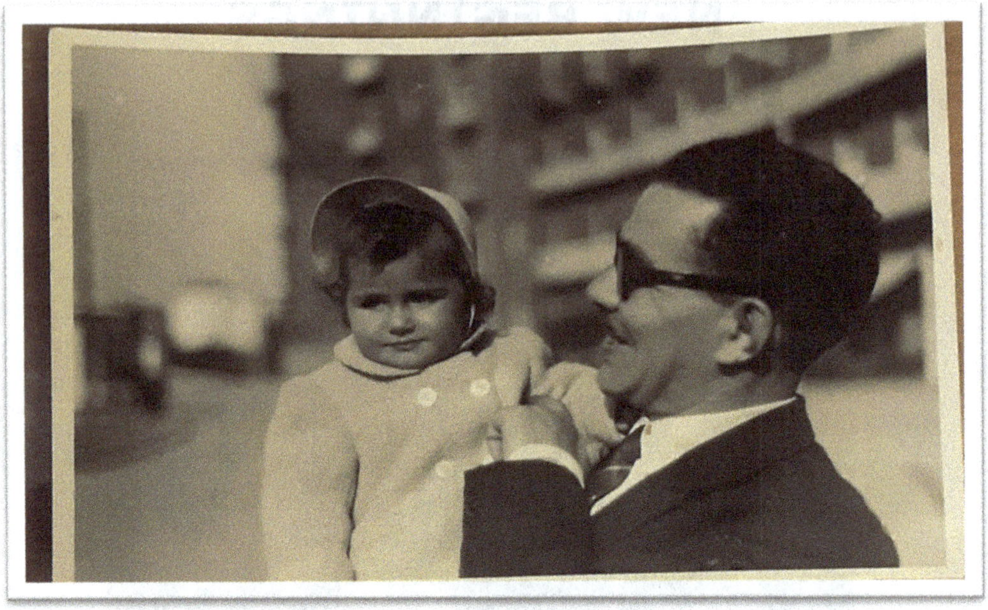

1949 Milan. My father and I

Sunday mornings my father would take me for hot chocolate at Motta, a coffee shop.

I also remember that I had a red and white checkered apron for kindergarten.

One Purim celebration I dressed up as a Dutch girl and David as Harlequin. I vividly remember the white starched Dutch cap with the sides flipped up and the wooden clogs. I must have been three or four.

In the summer time we used to go to Bormio, a mountain village with a population of about 4,100 close to the border with Switzerland on the western side of the Dolomites, 90 miles from Milan.

.

Bormio 1953

Bormio, Nonna Olga, Mamma, David and I, 1953

THE SHOAH OF ANCONA JEWS

Bice Ascoli, my mother, was born on January 28, 1922 in Ancona, on the Adriatic Sea, a quiet town of 100,000 inhabitants with a small Jewish population but an interesting Jewish history.

In 1569 Ancona was one of only three towns in the Papal state, along with Rome and Avignon, where Pope Pius the fifth decreed that Jews were allowed to live.

My maternal grandmother, Olga Russi, was also born in Ancona in 1893. She was one of the 11 children of Davide Russi and Sara Moscato, a family of pharmaceutical industrialists who had come to Ancona from Ragusa, (today Dubrovnik) across the Adriatic, in the 1700s. In 1845 Jacob Russi, Davide's father, founded the company Russi & C. in via Saffi, the first modern pharmaceutical distribution, also known for pioneering studies on infectious diseases. In the 1940s it had 600 employees and a share capital of 8 million Italian Lire, over shading Italian pharmaceutical brands such as Linetti, Robert's and Farmitalia.

Front row left to right: Vito, Sara Moscato Russi, Davide Russi, Annina
2nd row: Raffaele, Rodolfo, Stella, Olga, Franco, Giacomo
3rd row: Valentina, Enrica, Franca.[4]

[4] Link for the Russi family tree: https://drive.google.com/file/d/16LmVUooQlm2V931lyt472v2UNeSGJNI_/view?usp=sharing

The golden wedding anniversary of Davide and Sara Russi. Olga is sitting at the table on the right, the last on the left, holding baby Bice on her lap.

My maternal grandfather, Giuseppe Ascoli was born in Ferrara in 1900, to Moisé Ascoli and Bice Modigliani. He had one sister, Renata that died when she was just 2 years old.

He owned a wholesale business for men's fabrics on the third floor of a 3 story house in via Indipendenza 18.

I remember him, Nonno Beppino. He was a stern looking man, with a big aquiline nose who taught me and my brother David table etiquette and how to walk properly. We had to hold a book under our arms and walk without swinging our arms around. And as far as table etiquette of course we were reprimanded each time our elbows would rest on the table. There was a somewhat compulsive aspect to his personality as I remember him saying that in order to promote good digestion food needs to be chewed seven times before being swallowed.

He was self-taught; he read Shakespeare in English. I have the edition of the full works of Shakespeare that belonged to him. He was an avid art connoisseur. He collected art, some of which I still have in my house. Although he was an atheist, a view my mother also held, he was responsible for the preservation of the religious furnishings of the Levantine and Italian synagogues of Ancona in the early days of the German occupation, in collaboration with the secretary of the community Alberto Pacifici, who was later murdered in Auschwitz.

English china

Chinese art.

Presidente della
dell' Ordine di
su proposta del Ministro per la Difesa
con Decreto in data
ha conferito l'onorificenza di
Cavaliere
dell' Ordine di Vittorio Veneto
Roma
Il Presidente
del Consiglio dell' Ordine

This medal was assigned to Giuseppe Ascoli, my grandfather.

The military Order of Vittorio Veneto was founded as a national order by the fifth President of the Italian Republic, Giuseppe Saragat, in 1968, "to express the gratitude of the nation" to those decorated with the Medal and Cross of War for Military Valor (Medaglia e Croce di Guerra al Valor Militare). The medal was assigned to those who had fought for at least six months in World War I and earlier conflicts.

Did Nonno Beppino fight in WWI?!

Bice Ascoli on the higher chair, Giuliana on the smaller chair

Nonno Beppino and Nonna Olga had two daughters, Bice and Giuliana and lived a very comfortable life.

Bice Ascoli Caló is the first girl on the left, Ella looks like her

Giuseppe and Olga Russi Ascoli

They were totally integrated within the Italian society and identified themselves as Italian Jews, Italians first and proud to be so.

It is 1938. Bice is a red head slender teenager, not a worry in the world, living a normal peaceful life, surrounded by an extended family of aunts, uncles and cousins, looking forward to a whole new world that awaited for her, friendships, first love, graduation, young adulthood.....

But things would change and gradually their world would come crushing down. It will never be the same for Bice.

Mussolini issued the infamous racial laws against Jews. In the spring my mom would have graduated from high school, she wanted to go to university. But things started to deteriorate. First she was told that she could only sit in the back of the class. Then she could not find her name on the list of the finals' results; Ascoli should have been at the top of the list but her results were published at the very end, in a totally separate category! And then she was forbidden from attending school altogether!

The Jewish community of Ancona set up a "school" in which students of different ages were taught by Jewish teachers expelled from their teaching positions. She was not allowed to take the matriculation exams in Ancona and had to travel to Pesaro, 60 miles North of Ancona, to take them. Because of the racial laws she was also forbidden to attend university.

Bice Ascoli High School Diploma

And then the unexpected betrayal of her friends, people she had known from kindergarten. Her non-Jewish friends all of a sudden would not speak to them, would not hang out with them and would cross to the other side of the street...

So the Jewish kids hung out among themselves. One of my mom's uncles had a villa in the outskirts of town. They would get together there on a weekend night and dance. But they could not be seen or heard by the neighbors......, so they kept the shutters closed, kept the music down and danced.

But the worst was yet to come.

In 1941 the authorities confiscated Nonno Beppino's business; he was forced to work in a factory that manufactured the accordions "Soprani" by "Castelfidardo". Later he was incarcerated in the Ancona jail. Food was scarce. In July he was released from prison, the family got false identity cards under the name Asoli and in August they fled. Run. Hide. My mother, seventeen years old, found herself forced to leave her home and go into hiding.

They found refuge, most of the Russi family did, with the help of Don Pio Duranti, the parish priest of Santa Cosma and Damiano, in peasants' houses in Loreto, south of Ancona. They could not go outdoor least they be seen by the local fascists. In October they left Loreto and always with the help of Don Pio Duranti found refuge in Recanati.

"Raconta sempre mì madre che Don Pio Duranti, paruco de San Cosma e eroe dela Resistenza, cui fascisti nu jé la guantava più de tanto, ma sicome era 'n pezo d'omo che nun ciaveva paura de nisciuno e ciaveva el pugno proibito che 'n giorno aveva steso gió longo a 'n fascista che j'aveva dato da dì, alora el lasciavane in pace. De sciguro, se tratava de na mosca bianca, perché invece el clero cul fascio era papa e cicia... e figuràmoce: i fascisti era queli che aveva fato stà zziti ai rosci nemighi dela religió!"

"My mother always said that Don Pio Duranti, the priest of San Cosma and the hero of the Resistance, whom the fascists didn't really like a lot, but being a man that was afraid of nobody and had a fist which he had already used against a fascist, they left him alone. Undoubtedly it was quite rare, because instead of the fascist armband he wore the church emblem, as he was stubborn. He silenced the fascists as the red enemies of religion!" [5] (My translation from Anconetano, the local dialect of Ancona).

I think Don Pio Duranti should have been recognized by Yad Va-Shem as a Righteous Gentile. I did contact them to this end but unfortunately they needed more concrete evidence which I did not have.

With a new name, they got away by introducing themselves as displaced Catholics whose house had been bombed. On Sundays they went to mass. All except Nonno Beppino who was taken in by nuns in the Loreto convent, because his nose.... would have given him away. There he helped in the library.

They paid for their stay in peasants' houses by selling their grandmother's jewelry and by sewing aprons. Fortunately the allies arrived in Ancona relatively early, because by then they had nothing left to sell.

Meanwhile in Ancona, on September 22, 1943, the Germans deported Giacomo Russi who managed the Russi's pharmaceutical company and his son Sergio to the Meppen Versen camp, to never come back. Somebody denounced him, perhaps the pharmaceutical "competition" jealous of the success of the Russi's company, despite the fact that everyone knew of his "fascist and anti-Zionist" militancy,

In November an allied bomb destroyed the Russi's establishment, at that time deserted. Only the arch at the entrance to the establishment still remains, the Russi's Arch ("Arco dei Russi"), incorporated today in the entrance to the headquarters of the Police Headquarters (Guardia di Finanza) in Lungomare Vanvitelli.

In 1944 the Ascoli returned to Ancona to a small house in the outskirts of the city because their house had been bombarded by the Allies.

---

5 https://www.anconanostra.com/vernaculo/storia_ancona/17_venteniofascista.h

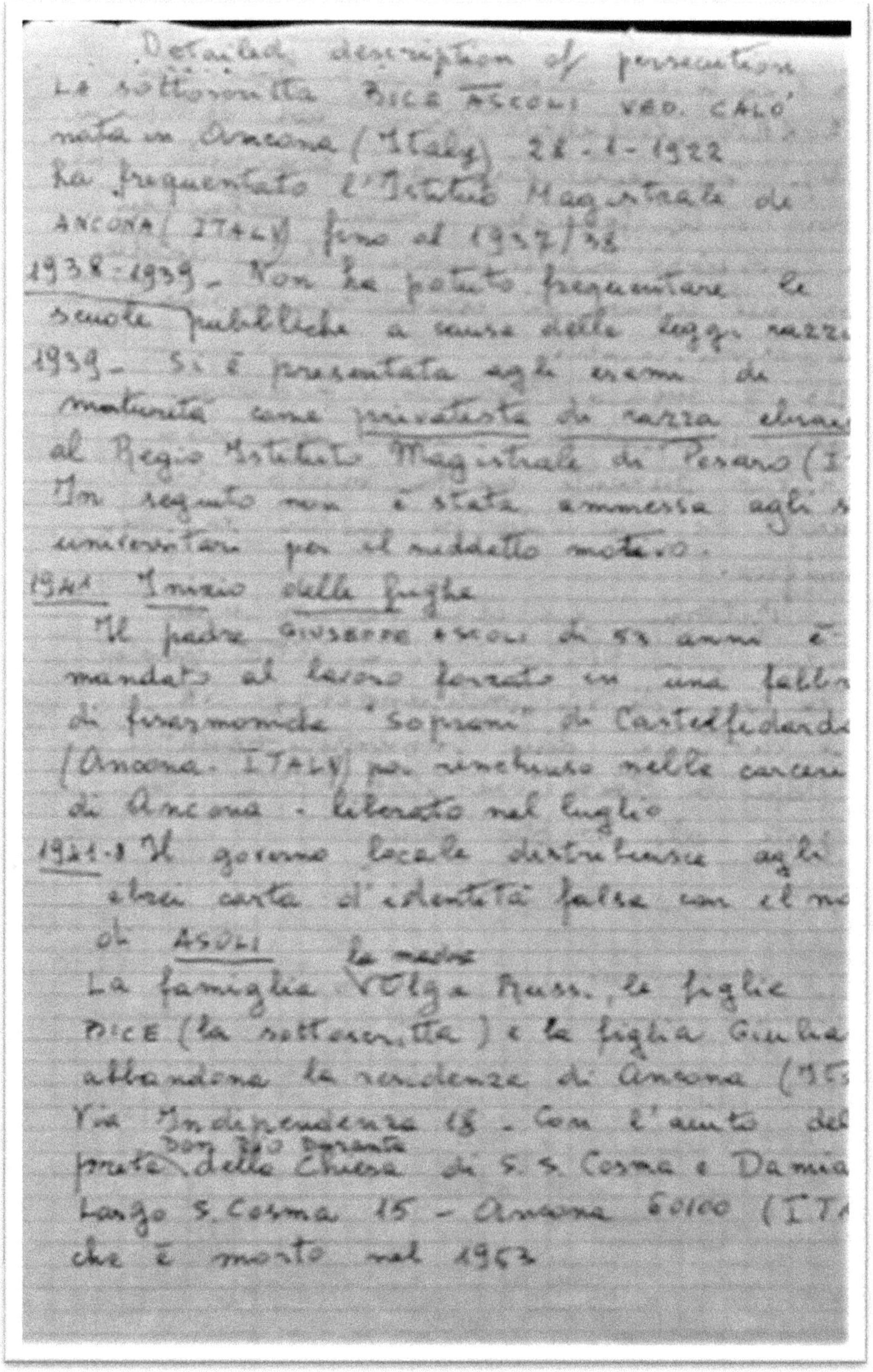

Detailed description of persecution
La sottoscritta BICE ASCOLI VED. CALÒ
nata in Ancona (Italy) 28-1-1922
ha frequentato l'Istituto Magistrale di
ANCONA (ITALY) fino al 1937/38
1938-1939 – Non ha potuto frequentare le
scuole pubbliche a causa delle leggi razzi
1939 – Si è presentata agli esami di
maturità come privatista di razza ebrai
al Regio Istituto Magistrale di Pesaro (I
In seguito non è stata ammessa agli s
universitari per il suddetto motivo.
1941 Inizio della fughe
Il padre GIUSEPPE ASCOLI di 53 anni è
mandato al lavoro forzato in una fabb
di fisarmoniche "Soprani" di Castelfidardo
(Ancona. ITALY) poi rinchiuso nelle carceri
di Ancona. liberato nel luglio
1941-? Il governo locale distribuisce agli
ebrei carta d'identità falsa con il no
di ASOLI
La famiglia la madre Volga Russi, le figlie
BICE (la sottoscritta) e la figlia Giulia
abbandona la residenza di Ancona (ITA
Via Indipendenza 18 – Con l'aiuto del
prete Don Pio Doranti della Chiesa di S.S. Cosma e Damia
Largo S. Cosma 15 – Ancona 60100 (ITA
che è morto nel 1953

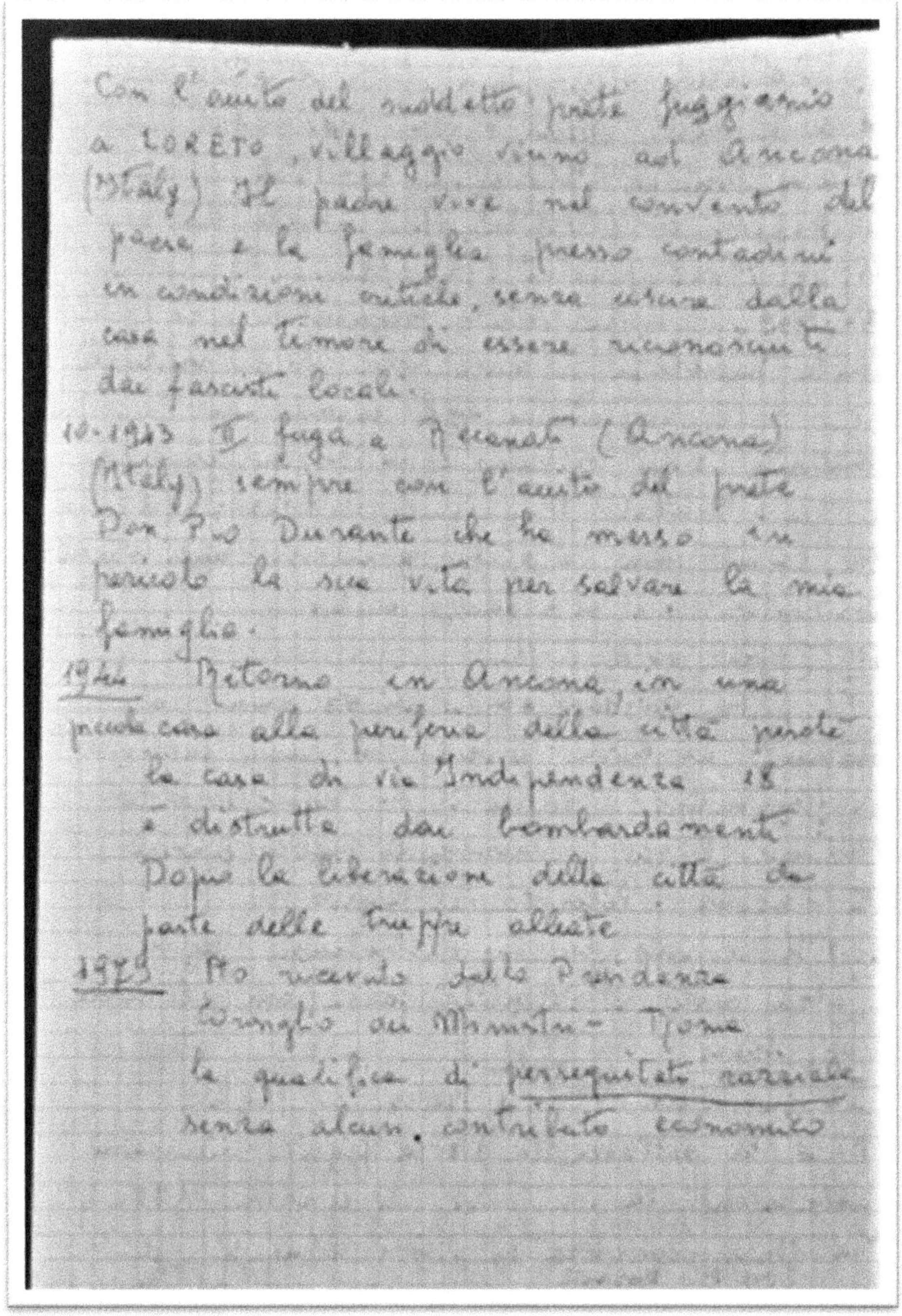

Con l'aiuto del suddetto prete fuggiamo
a LORETO, villaggio vicino ad Ancona
(Italy) Il padre vive nel convento del
paese e la famiglia presso contadini
in condizioni critiche, senza uscire dalla
casa nel timore di essere riconosciuti
dai fascisti locali.
10-1943 II fuga a Recanati (Ancona)
(Italy) sempre con l'aiuto del prete
Don Pio Durante che ha messo in
pericolo la sua vita per salvare la mia
famiglia.
1944 Ritorno in Ancona, in una
piccola casa alla periferia della città perché
la casa di via Indipendenza 18
è distrutta dai bombardamenti
Dopo la liberazione della città da
parte delle truppe alleate
1975 Ho ricevuto dalla Presidenza
Consiglio dei Ministri - Roma
la qualifica di perseguitato razziale
senza alcun contributo economico

My mother's description of the years 1939-1943

My parents's graves in the Segula cemetery, Petach Tikva, Israel,
Nonno's grave is plot 11 Row 143 (יא.קמג)
Savta's grave is plot 11 Row 144 #2 (יא.קמד.2)

http://famigliarussi.com/

Calo/Livni/Weisz family tree – geni.com

The Russi Ascoli family tree

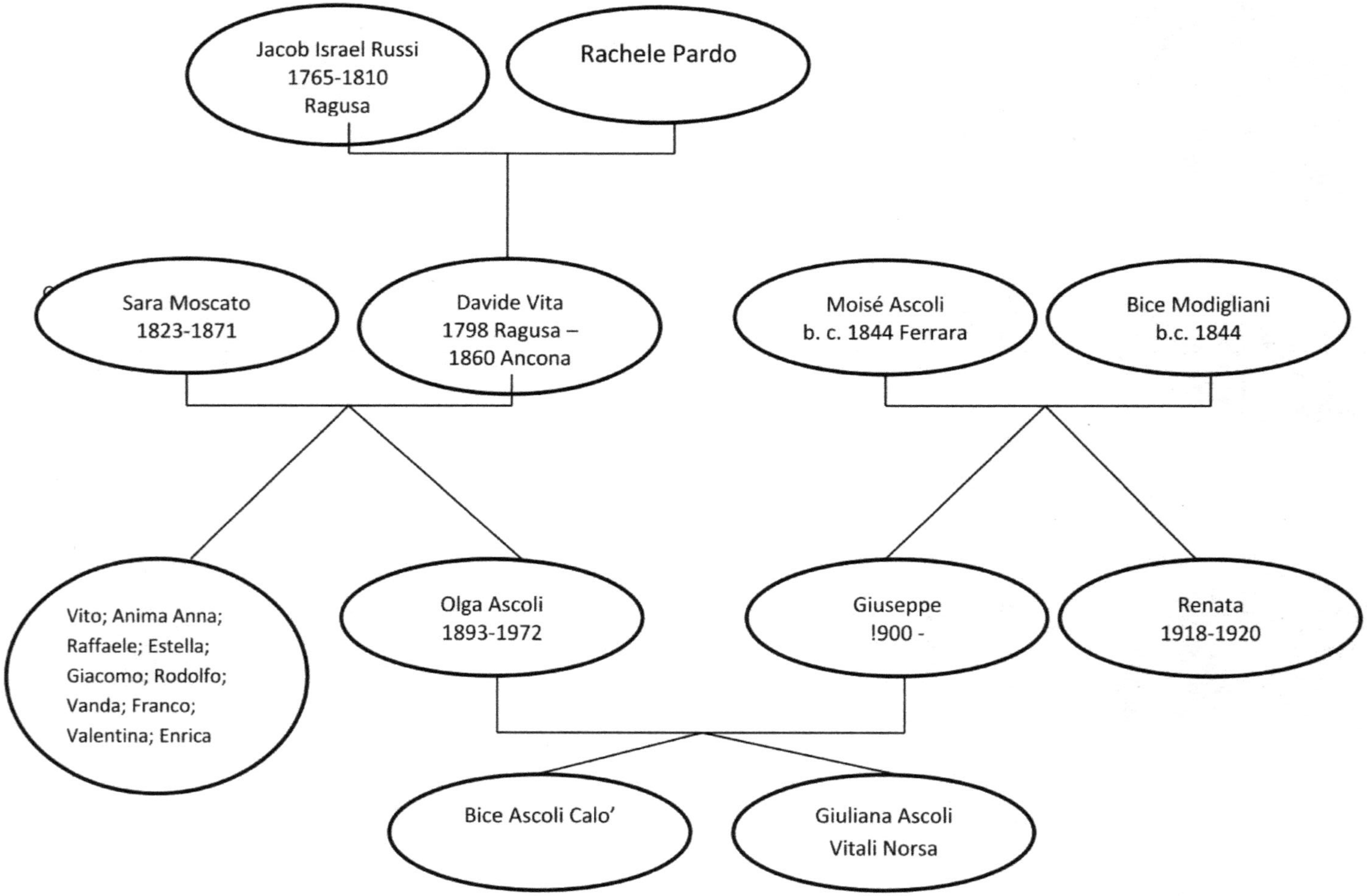
Jacob Israel Russi
1765-1810
Ragusa
Rachele Pardo
Sara Moscato
1823-1871
Davide Vita
1798 Ragusa –
1860 Ancona
Moisé Ascoli
b. c. 1844 Ferrara
Bice Modigliani
b.c. 1844
Vito; Anima Anna;
Raffaele; Estella;
Giacomo; Rodolfo;
Vanda; Franco;
Valentina; Enrica
Olga Ascoli
1893-1972
Giuseppe
!900 -
Renata
1918-1920
Bice Ascoli Calo’
Giuliana Ascoli
Vitali Norsa

AM ISRAEL CHAI

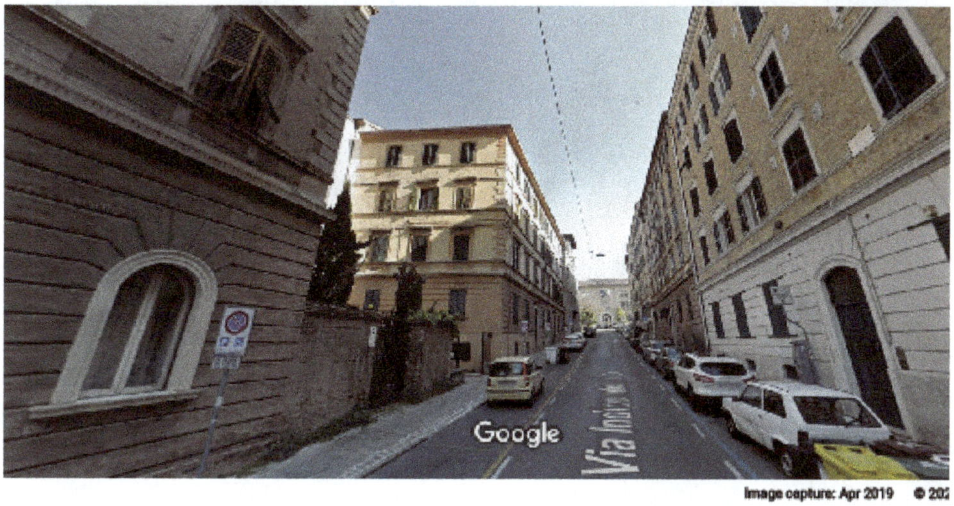

Via Indipendenza 18, Ancona

When I was four or five we moved to Ancona. We lived with my grandparents. At the top of this very "steep" street there was an army barrack and at the bottom on the left there was an ice cream shop. A short walk from there was Piazza Cavour. In the winter my mom used to take us there to get roasted chestnuts in a cone of newspaper.

When we visited Ancona many years later I navigated the streets and got to the house and Piazza Cavour without the help of any navigator and Via Indipendenza was rather short and ...not steep at all as I remembered it.

I have fond childhood memories of Ancona. A young family with two kids probably more or less our age lived downstairs and we played with them in the attic or outside in the backyard.

The kids from downstairs in Ancona

For the high holidays we went to Zio Vito in Viale della Vittoria. I remember a very long table that ran across more than one room, or maybe it just seemed very long and....lots of noisy kids.

I did not attend first grade and was home schooled instead for the simple reason that I am left handed. The first grade teacher came to our house to teach me how to write with my right hand. Yes, indeed. It sounds very strange and would be totally unacceptable today but that was the norm then and nobody gave it a second thought. Actually, in retrospect it turned out to be worth it as I am now ambidextrous.

I remember the flat. You walked into a large hallway. To the right on the wall there was a long black wooden coat hanger, beneath it "la cassapanca", a long black chest. At the corner there was the black stool which is now in my house and the umbrella holder that is at Dafna's.

Also to the right of the entrance, there was the cold dark room. No windows and shelves ran all around it, loaded with jars and jars of tomato sauce.

The kitchen was further on to the right, after the coat hanger. There was a big table in the center of the room and a huge black stove on which Nonna

Olga warmed a black metal iron. My brother David and I used to have hot chocolate milk in red plastic bowls.

The dining room was right across the entrance. The door to the dining room was always closed and all I remember is the "credenza" (buffet) on the right on which there was a clock and the console on the left which is now in my living room.

Nonna Olga's console.

In the summertime we went to the beach of Palombina on the outskirts of Ancona it seems to me daily, or probably a lot. As a child I was a very bad eater and rather small and the doctor said that the sea air will improve my appetite.

I don't remember how we got there because my mother didn't have a car so it must have been by bus or by train; I think we went by train. It is a beautiful long and wide sandy beach on the Adriatic. I went back years later. The sea is always calm and you can actually walk hundreds of yards and the water only reaches your ankles or knees. At Palombina we learned how to swim. My mother who was a good swimmer took us on a sailing boat, tied a rope to our waist and simply dropped us into the water.

For some reason many of these memories are related to food. Back from the beach we would have spaghetti all'olio and for a snack in the afternoon we would have a slice of bread with olive oil, salt and pepper. To this day when we go to Italian restaurants and they serve bread with a dish of olive oil to dip I always add a dash of black pepper...

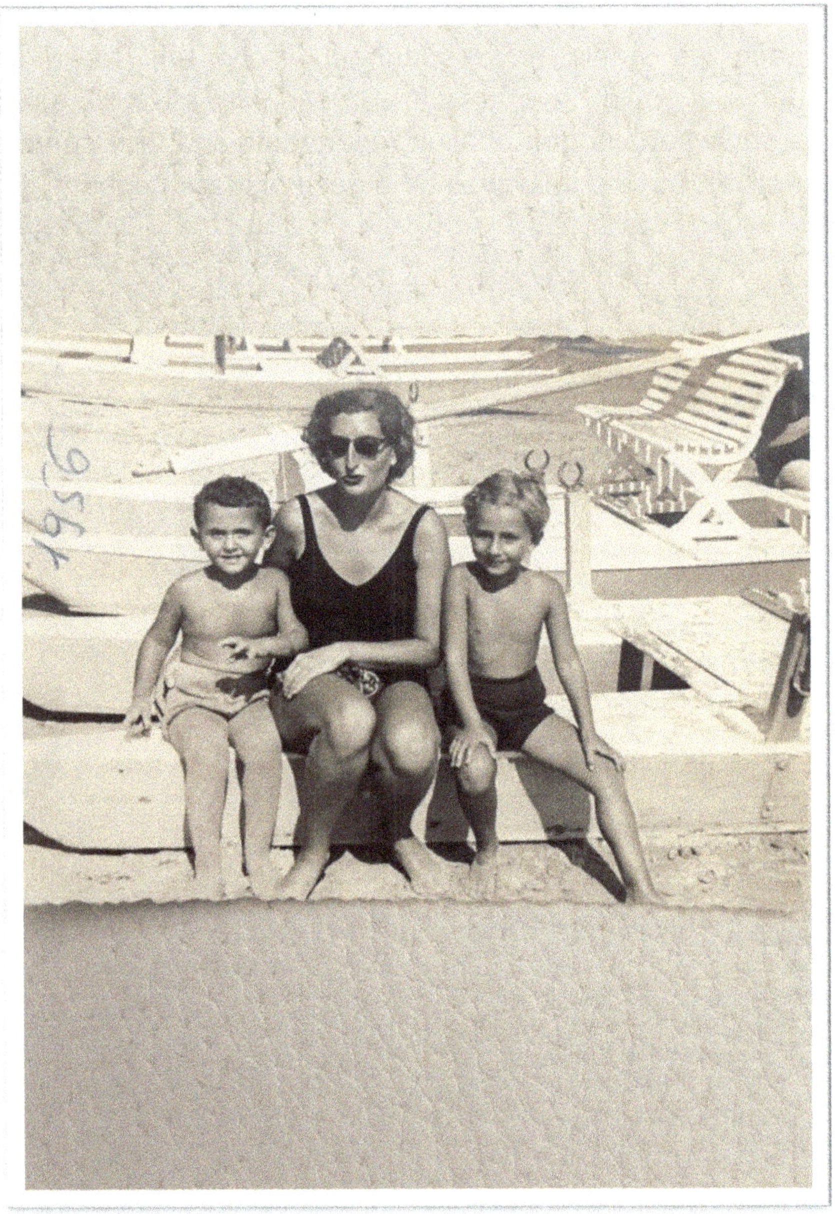

Bice Caló, David and I at Palombina,

Ancona 1956

That doctor must have also prescribed a daily glass of orange juice so my Mom must have found the biggest glass in Ancona for that. At meal times they would sit me by the window and play with the alarm clock to distract me and make me eat. Years later, I found the clock, which was still filled with grains of rice. And if I still didn't eat they would put my little rattan table and chair outside the door, in the staircase landing until I finished my meals. They used to say that at five in the afternoon I was still chewing on the last bite of my lunch.

THE SHOAH OF SATU MARE JEWS

Satu Mare

Ilona (Ilu) was born in 1912 in Oradea, Romania to Yoseph and Josephine Reitzer. She had nine siblings, Ela, Aidi, Leibi, Wolvie, Fradu, Zisu, Pinhas and Leizer and grew up in a very strictly observant household.

The Reitzers were quite poor. Ilu's father was not a very successful merchant and life was hard.

Yoseph and Josephine Reitzer

Erno (Bubi) was born in 1909 in Satu Mare, Romania to Haim and Helen Weisz. He had five siblings, Leibi, Irene, Adele, Rozsi and Aranka.

Bubi's grandparents lived on 6 Lacrimioare Street which was once called 6 Perenyi Street. When we visited Satu Mare we found the house. It was quite emotional when the new owners let us in although we had no idea what the house had looked like as the house was totally remodeled.

Bubi and Ilu married and had two kids who died as toddlers before WWII. Bubi ran a lumber warehouse in Timisoara, in Salva and later in Cluj. They led a comfortable life with numerous friends surrounded by a big family.

Bubi (Ernő) and Ilu (Ilona) Weisz

But in 1944 everything changed. Bubi was drafted to the Munkaszolgálat, a labor unit of the Hungarian army which was basically set up to persecute Jews. Ilu was determined to keep him at home and bribed somebody to get him released. The commander of the unit, Revicky Imre, a Hungarian nobleman who happened not to be an anti-Semite, advised her against it. He promised her that as long as he is the commander, no harm will come to any Jew in his unit. He also told her that worse times for Jews are yet to come and the safest would be to stay with him. But Ilu insisted. How could she have known? It wasn't long before she unfortunately lived to regret her decision.

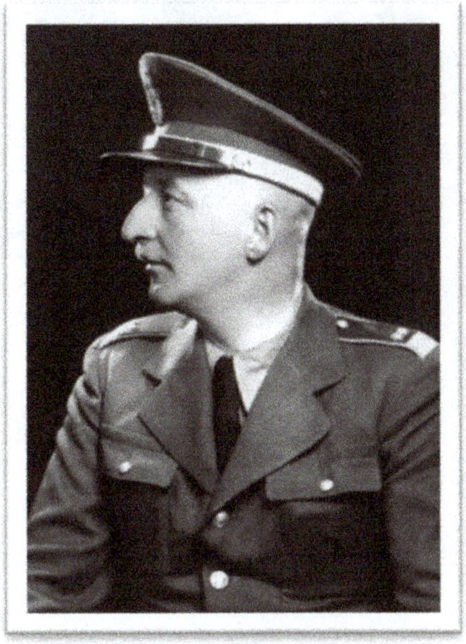

Revicky Imre - A Righteous Gentile.

The term "Righteous Gentile" refers to non-Jews who risked their lives to save Jews during the Holocaust. They are honored at the Yad Vashem Museum in Jerusalem and Revicky Imre is amongst them. [6]

6

https://righteous.yadvashem.org/?searchType=righteous_only&language=en&itemId=4017151&ind=NaN

Amon Leopold Göth, the commandant of the Kraków-Płaszów concentration camp.

In May 1944 the German army invaded Hungary. Ilu and Bubi missed a second chance to avoid deportation and save their lives when two German soldiers that quartered in their house offered to

take them in their tank from Cluj where they lived then across the border to Romania where it was safer. (Cluj was part of Hungary from 1940-1945). Unfortunately they preferred to stay.

It wasn't long before the SS followed the German army and the Jews of Satu Mare, Oradea and Cluj were swiftly deported to concentration camps.

Bubi's parents and sisters were deported from Satu Mare, Bubi, Ilu and Irene were deported from Cluj to Auschwitz. Ilu and Irene were further transferred from Auschwitz to Plasow and towards the end of the war they were transported further on to Bergen Belsen where Irene died. Ilu's parents, her brother Pinhas and her sisters Aidi and Zisu were deported to Auschwitz.

Years later, on Saturday afternoons, with the first bus out of Ashdod, Ilu and Bubi would come to visit us in Hod Hasharon. Dafna and Michal were toddlers when over coffee and cake Ilu would tell of her ordeals. That is how we learned about the cruel camp commander of Plasow, Amon Leopold Göth, long before Steven Spielberg made the movie Schindler's list.

Meanwhile Ilu's sister Ela had moved to Roanne, France and Leibi had crossed the border to Switzerland. Volvie had been in Strasburg, France since 1940. He was amongst millions of other refugees that ran away towards Paris. As an observant Jew, he stopped along the way to pray and covered himself with the tallit, the prayer shawl. It wasn't long before the French servicemen arrested him accusing him of signaling to the Luftwaffe, the German Air Force. He was tried and sentenced to death as a German spy. But the French colonel that had to sign the execution order asked to see the evidence of his crime, namely the suspicious cloth. You see, the colonel's grandfather was Jewish and the colonel remembered him praying with the Tallit. He cancelled the order and Volvie was set free.

The last week before the camps were liberated Bubi's sister Rozsi was taken on a march. This fragile petite young woman managed to escape and hide in a hay stack. Although the suspecting German guards picked the hay with their bayonets they did not find her and she was not harmed.

Within one year Ilu lost her parents and two of her siblings, Eidi and Pinhas.

Ilu was liberated by the British in May 1945. She was almost given for dead and she was taken to a hospital in Sigtuna, Sweden where she stayed for about a year. She suffered from typhoid fever and thrombosis.

Bubi returned to Satu Mare with his brother Leibi and his sisters Aranka and Rozsi.

Those were chaotic times. Survivors had no information about their loved ones, who perished and who survived. Neither Bubi nor Ilu had any idea whether their spouse had survived.

Bubi and Ilu's story of reunification is extraordinary. They both started to look for each other any way they could, to no avail. Eventually Ilu wrote Bubi's sister Adele who lived in Tel Aviv. The only information Ilu had about her was the name of the street she lived on ....Weisz Street. Six months later, when Adele finally got the letter, she notified Bubi in Satu Mare ...and the rest is history.

Yossi (Ivan) and his twin brother Haim (Bandi, Andre) were born on February 22, 1947 in Satu Mare, Romania. They lived on 28 Iuliu Maniu Street which was earlier called, in Communist Romania, 32 Pushkin Street.

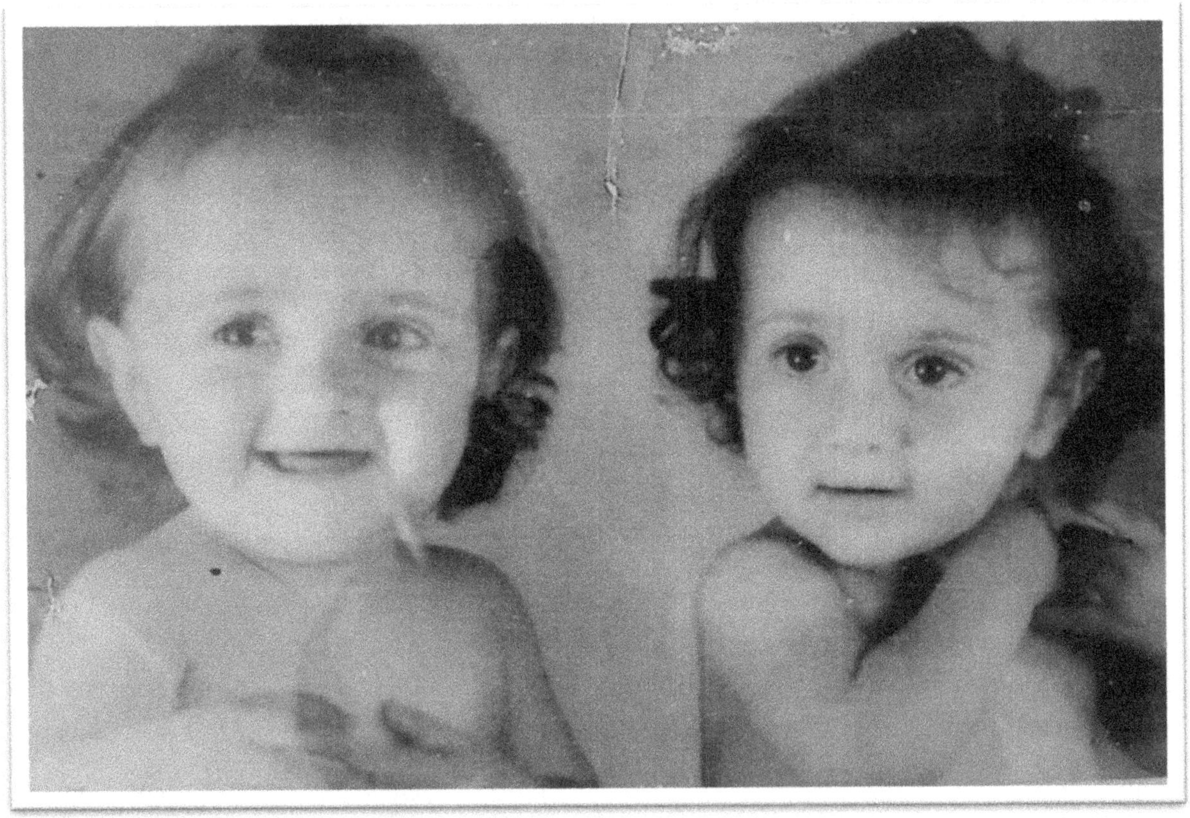

Yossi (Ivan) and Haim (Bandi) Livni (Weisz)
Which one is Yossi?
Doesn't Tamar Livni look like them?

Yossi and Haim – Who is who?

By 1947 most Romanian Jews and the Weisz amongst them wanted to leave Romania. Unfortunately, in 1948 the Romanian Communist regime closed the borders and did not let Jews leave the country. In 1951 they let a few leave but then they closed the borders once again.

Nine years later, in 1958, the Romanian authorities decreed that Jews have one day, one day only, to apply for permission to emigrate, on the holiest of days, on Yom Kippur! The Rabbi of Satu Mare allowed the Jews to go and apply on this the holiest of days. The Weisz applied but only six years later they got permission to leave. In August 1964 the Weisz left Romania, spent six months in Naples and Rome and in December arrived to Israel to once again rebuild their lives.

Bubi passed away Sukkot 1984 and Ilu passed away Erev Rosh Hashana' (the night of) 1985. They are both buried in the cemetery of Ashdod, Israel, plot 19, site 5.

The Weisz Reitzer family tree

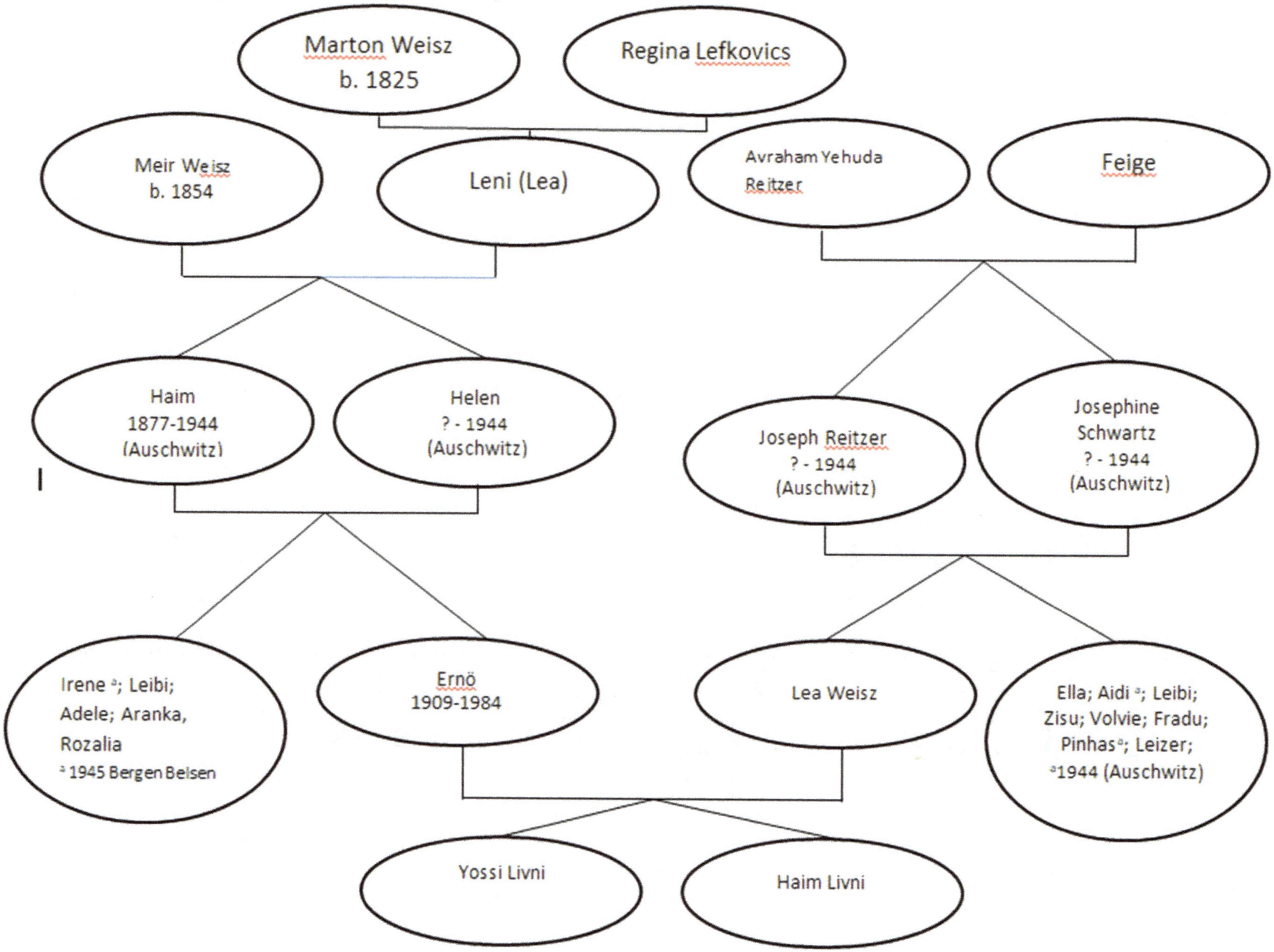

Marton Weisz
b. 1825
Regina Lefkovics
Meir Weisz
b. 1854
Leni (Lea)
Avraham Yehuda
Reitzer
Feige
Haim
1877-1944
(Auschwitz)
Helen
? - 1944
(Auschwitz)
Joseph Reitzer
? - 1944
(Auschwitz)
Josephine
Schwartz
? - 1944
(Auschwitz)
Irene [a]; Leibi;
Adele; Aranka,
Rozalia
[a] 1945 Bergen Belsen
Ernö
1909-1984
Lea Weisz
Ella; Aidi [a]; Leibi;
Zisu; Volvie; Fradu;
Pinhas[a]; Leizer;
[a]1944 (Auschwitz)
Yossi Livni
Haim Livni

Documentation of the Orthodox Jewish Cemetery from Sathmar

Introduction Ortodox Cemetery Status-Quo Cemetery Szatmari Memento

Catalogue of every Tombstone in the Orthodox Jewish Cemetery from Szatmarnemeti (Satu Mare) Romania. The main intention was to give a helping hand to those who are looking for the graves of their ancestors, then to help each documentary work regarding to Jewish burial sites, genealogy, etc. For that purpose, each readable gravestone (more then 2,300) - standing, fallen or broken, beginning with the oldest ones – have been photographed. The main purpose of the present work is to link the data from the Orthodox Cemetery Registry pages with those photos (photographer Alexander C. Huzau), of the gravestones.

The Orthodox Cemetery Registry

Show 10 entries
Search: Weisz

Name	Mother	Father	Death Date	p/s/h	Tomb	Obs.
Weisz Marton, Lefkovits Regina a neje, Minaj, szatocs, Perenyi u.50			1899.03.25		NA	74 years old, State Archive
Weisz Marton Mordechaj			1899.03.26	06 01 06	NA	reg.1358, 74 years old, kerekedo, Mihalyi
Weisz Marton Majer		Samuel	1946.08.28	13 07 15	Tomb	28 years old
Weisz Marton Jozsef Mordechaj Benzion	Weinstok Eszter	Zoltan Zalman Lejb	1933.04.08	12 08 23	Tomb	14 years old
Weisz Marton			1880.11.22		NA	61 years old
Weisz Marton		Izsak	1872.09.12		NA	0 years old
Weisz Maria, Eotvos u.7	Neufeld Hermina	Ignatz, szabo mester	1899.11.01		NA	27 napos, another baby, Salamon, Born on dead in 1898.06, reg.1358, State Archive,
Weisz Mari Bernathne			1873.10.12		Tomb	36 years old
Weisz Malka Itzhackne		Samuel	1923.02.06	11 14 06	Tomb	
Weisz Malka Eli Martonne		Kalman Moshe	1935.10.22	16 01 22	Tomb	felsoresz keszito
Name	Mother	Father	Death Date	p/s/h	Tomb	Obs.

Showing 121 to 130 of 591 entries (filtered from 6,751 total entries)
FirstPrevious1112131415NextLast

Legend

- Death Date - yyyy.mm.dd
- p/s/h - parcel/row/place of the tomb
- Color *rose* - culturally renowned person
- Color *purple* – renowned religious leader

Click on the *map* to view the Map of Orthodox Cemetery in Satu Mare

Please refer to the *Szatmari Memento* for full information about the deportation from Szatmar Ghetto.

Groom Bride	Groom's Father / Mother Bride's Father / Mother	Groom Age Bride Age	MarriageDate Marriage Town Registration Town Jaras Megye	Comments	Source Record Image#
			Abaúj-Torna		
VEISZ, Jakab **MARKOVITS**, Betti	Jozsef / WEISZ (Mattel) Majer / MAJER (Regina)	21 17	09-Dec-1863 Szatmar Szatmar Local Gov't. Szatmár	groom student from [father teacher in]/born in Turterebes, bride from Szatmar, born in Zsadany, parents farming in Gorbed	Romanian Nat'l Archives - Satu Mare, Reg.1349 190-4
WEISZ, Jakob **KATZ**, Leni	Aron / -- (--) David / Majer / -- (--)	23 18	23-Jul-1870 Szatmar Szatmar Local Gov't. Szatmár	Groom student from/born in Kisvarda, father teacher. Bride from/born in Szatmar. Witnesses Abr. FREUND, Jakob DAVIDOVITS	Romanian Nat'l Archives - Satu Mare, Reg.1349 196-8
FRIEDMAN, Majer **WEISZ**, Leni	Moritz / -- (--) David / -- (--)	26 18	24-Mar-1874 Szatmar Szatmar Local Gov't. Szatmár	Groom merchant from/born in Nagysomkut. Bride from Szatmar. Witnesses David WEISZ, Mozes HERSKOVITS	Romanian Nat'l Archives - Satu Mare, Reg.1349 202-4
BRAUN, Majer **WEISZ**, Sali	Farkas / -- (--) Jozsef / -- (--)	28 26	24-Jan-1876 Szatmar Szatmar Local Gov't. Szatmár	Groom tailor in Szatmar, from/b Csenger; bride living in Szatmar, from/b Beregszasz. Witnesses Moritz FRIEDMAN, Jakob FISCH	Romanian Nat'l Archives - Satu Mare, Reg.1349 206-2
WEISZ, Majer **WEISZ**, Leni	Moritz / -- (--) Marton / -- (--)	22 18	05-May-1876 Szatmar Szatmar Local Gov't. Szatmár	Groom student [Talmud?] from/b Nagykaroly, father tailor; bride from/b Szatmar, father distiller. Witnesses Majer PERLSZ, David WEISZ	Romanian Nat'l Archives - Satu Mare, Reg.1349 207-10
WEISZ, Majer **HIRSCH**, Zseni	Farkas / -- (--) Adolf / -- (--)	28 20	18-Apr-1883 Szatmar Szatmar Local Gov't. Szatmár	Groom merchant from/b Feketeardo; bride from Szatmar, born in Szamosujvar; Witnesses are Adolf WEISZ, Simon BEER	Romanian Nat'l Archives - Satu Mare, Reg.1349 219-9

Szatmár, 1909. február 17. SZATMÁR-NÉMETI 3-ik oldal

January 1909 Local newspaper in Hungarian, notice of birth of Weisz Erno

ISRAEL

We left Italy for Israel in the fall of 1958, I don't know the month but it must have been summer or fall, early fall. We came, David, my Mom and I by boat from Naples to Haifa. Zia Giuliana, my Mom's sister, came to see us off. The only memorable event from the trip is that my Mom hurt her finger on the boat, she must have closed a door or a window on it and she was probably hurting because it got impressed in my mind.

My father preceded us in 1957. He was waiting for us when we got to Haifa and I remember the plum red grapes on the table when we got to the house in Kiriat Matalon.

The road into Kiriat Matalon splits into four. The first on the right leads to the Youth (Noar Ha-oved) clubhouse, the second leads to a short strip of stores, amongst them the grocery store and the produce store and further on the Iraqi synagogue. We would go there with my parents on high holydays. It was of course an orthodox synagogue, men downstairs and women upstairs and the kids stayed outside playing in the courtyard. I remember that on Kippur my mother would carry chocolates in her purse that we would eat on the way home. I mostly remember my father taking me and David under his tallit, placing his hands over our heads and bless us.

The third road led to my friends, Shula Zeituni and Avigail Fleischer. I spent a lot of time at Shula's house. Her parents were Syrians.

The first road on the left led to our house and the school. It was the industrial area of Kiriat Matalon and there were a couple of factories on the left hand side of the road. Issargo, a plant owned by Alberto Vitale's family (my father's brother in law, Elsa's husband) was the last one, right across from an orchard. Beyond Issargo there was a large open field where we lit campfires on Lag Ba'Omer. Issargo was a large square building surrounded by a wire fence and an electrical gate that opened sideways in the front on the left. The entrance led straight ahead into the factory. On the left hand side there was a staircase that led to the office. On the right hand side of the building, around the corner, there were stairs that led to our apartment. On the left hand side of the building there was another set of stairs but I don't remember where they led to. All around the building the ground was covered by gravel. We spent a lot of time playing outside on the grounds of the factory. They made fabric and I remember playing with big thread cones left outside on the grounds.

Thinking about those days makes me sad.

David and I shared the one bedroom. There were shelves above our beds stacked with die cast model cars that David collected and enjoyed throwing at me. Mom and dad slept in the living room. There was a small kitchen; I remember it being dark as it had no window. There was one bathroom and no dining room.

The living room had a double glass door that opened onto a long outdoors corridor. There were two doors to get into the apartment, the main door and a door at the end of the corridor that led into the bedroom. There was also a door from the bedroom into the office. I guess there were more doors than windows.

Downstairs, adjacent to the house by the staircase there was a small garden where my father planted a fig tree, a blackberry tree and strawberries. David and I used to climb the blackberry tree. There was a faucet under the staircase that constantly leaked so that frogs were frequent visitors. David would catch a few and put them in a jar with holes in the lid for me to bring to school to dissect during biology classes. I actually liked doing that, we would anesthetize the frogs and then pin them to a table.

Abba would build a Sukkah for Sukkot where we sometimes ate. I remember him shaking the palm branch and holding the citron.

The plant itself was walking distance to the elementary school and my friends' houses. Shula's house was just across the orchard in front of our house; a little further away would be Esther Peretz's house, Nira Hevdeli's and others.

From school I remember two things, the choir and agriculture lessons. You think the concept of inclusiveness started in the 21st century? Well, you're wrong. The music teacher didn't exclude anyone, regardless of their music inclination. As I was short he placed me on the first row, but noticing right away that I was hopelessly out of tune he told me to just move my lips.

I also remember we would attend these youth meetings held by youth leaders of the young wing of the Labor movement (Ha-noar Ha-Oved). The labor party was basically in control of many aspects of Israeli life those days and there was quite some political indoctrination going on but as kids we did not care for that, we had fun and went on lots of trips.

Notwithstanding my overall good memories from those days I remember three disturbing occurrences. I had a small collection of tiny Murano glass animals. One day, after my friends left, one of the animals was missing. Why would they take it? The other episodes equally disturbing happened at school. I guess it was shortly after I arrived. I must have looked different, dressed different cause I remember standing in the center of a circle looked upon by many other kids. It must have felt terrible being watched like a spectacle!

The third episode also took place in school. Before we left Ancona my mother had made for us some nice winter coats. Brown checkered, double breasted with a hood. Nothing of the kind one would ever see in Israel in 1958! And sure enough, it didn't take long before a kid sitting behind me in class slit the lining of the hood with a razor blade! How terrible!

Bice Caló, David and I in Piazza Cavour, Ancona. I am wearing the coat that was damaged in Israel, 1957

We lived in Kiryat Matalon from 1958 until 1965.

Those were difficult years in Israel, what they call the "tsena" (shortage) years. I remember the food stamp booklet, all greasy. One could only purchase limited quantities of basic food supplies, flour, sugar, eggs and milk per month, according to the size of your family. We didn't have a fridge but an ice box and a man would bring ice blocks on a cart pulled by a donkey. We didn't have a washing machine, let alone dryer or dishwasher. We had no phone either but we were allowed to use the phone in the office.

Years later when Ella interviewed me for a school project she was surprised to learn that I didn't have a favorite T.V show when I was growing up because ...we didn't have a T.V.

My father, who in Italy worked for an insurance company, worked in Israel in the laundry of Ramat Aviv Hotel. He would leave very early in the morning, and I remember the big rubber boots he used at work. It was only about 10 years later that he was promoted to be in charge of the purchasing of kitchen supplies at the hotel. My Mom worked part time jobs and night shifts on the production floor of Osem and Hagor. She did that for a couple of years until she started to teach Italian to adults. First she taught evening classes at Berlitz and then she taught at the Instituto Italiano di Cultura (The Italian Culture Institute) in Tel Aviv. She taught until she was 78 years old. When we sat Shiva for her, her ex-students told us how much they loved her. No wonder she kept on working.

She was a tough practical woman, always living up to her obligations, never displayed an outpour of emotions or feelings so one could not easily tell what she thought or felt. But there are two events that stand out in my memory. I cannot remember my mother ever being sick except for one day when she stayed in bed in the middle of the day. She suffered from back pains but never complained. The other event was when her mother passed away. I remember that day vividly. She was in the midst of washing the floors when a telegram arrived. I see her. She opened it, read it, not a word. She then picked up the mop and went on washing the floors.

My parents could not afford to buy me clothes but I was still the best dressed girl in town because twice a year my cousin Paola would ship me all her clothes.

Notwithstanding these hardships I had a happy childhood. I never felt that I was missing anything and never thought we were poor. My parents who never bought anything for themselves bought me my first pair of high heel shoes at Mikulinski, a fancy shoe store in Tel Aviv. They were white, sling stile with a two inches curved heel and the front was sort of perforated.

Looking back I admire my mother and give her lots and lots of credit. She never confined me or forbade me to do whatever I wanted. I don't think there was a trip or a get together that I did not attend. When I went out at night to meet my friends in Petach Tikva she would take me to the bus stop. It didn't occur to me then that she had to go back home in the dark by herself. Only once, I was already in University, only once did my father raise his voice and explicitly forbade me from seeing this boy. He was most probably right.

In 1963 I went on to Ahad Haam high school in Petach Tikva. Those were happy years. In 1965, when I was a sophomore we moved to Givat Schmuel, to a small flat my parents bought, with subsidies allocated from the government to new immigrants.

I remember my high school years with nostalgia. I was fifteen when I fell in love for the first time. Together with other kids in our class we would spend Friday nights dancing slow, rock and roll and slow fox to the tunes of Elvis, the Beatles, Paul Anka and Cliff Richard. Saturday mornings we would go for walks in Yad Le'Banim Park or to Antipatros fortress. In those days Petach Tikwa was not densely populated and there were plenty of orange and grapefruit orchards. We would go for walks in the orchards and enjoy the juicy fruit or the prickly pear cactus.

During my senior year I befriended my neighbor Mira that introduced me to people my age in Givat Schmuel. They were also new immigrants from Romania, some actually from Yossi's hometown Satu Mare. Friday nights we would go to the local club house and have dance parties. The girls would come to my house before the party to do their hair.

I think our parents were happy then and proud. They had sacrificed a lot, endured hard times but it would be different for us children.

I graduated High School in June 1967, when the Six Day war broke out. I watched Maya graduate from high school. Everybody was so busy with graduation plans, parties, celebrations, prom, the dress.... Well that is the way it is supposed to be. When I was in my senior year at high school all men were called for active service so all our male teachers were away. We had our finals with little or no supervision. As of May 1967 all buses had been reassigned for military use so I had to walk to school, usually a twenty minutes car drive. There was no prom, no celebrations, and no dress. Eventually we did have some kind of graduation celebration at city hall in Petach Tikvah where we got our diplomas.

At night there was black out and as it was summer time Ibi and I preferred to spend the evening outside walking down the main street. In the dark one could see and hear the lighting bombs or perhaps shells in the distance, merely ten miles away.

Nobody went into shelters, everybody was outside and I don't particularly recall that time as scary.

With my friend Ibi I also went on numerous trips around the country and to many dancing clubs in search of ....boys of course.

I was exempted from military service. After the Six Days War all the girls that were supposed to be drafted in 1967 were released. They did suggest that I could still volunteer but I wanted to go to University so in the fall of that year I started my undergraduate studies at Bar Ilan University. I loved biology and that's what I really wanted to study but I wasn't accepted as my grades in physics were low. The physics teacher, well I didn't like him and he didn't like me. But I was good with languages so I enrolled in American and English literature, political sciences as the minor and a teaching certificate.

Those were also good years. Bar Ilan university was walking distance to Ghivat Schmuel and I made new friends.

I met Batia Kotlicki, Gabby Fiks and Yocheved. I still keep in touch with Batia and Gaby.

We had a weekly routine. Every Saturday night we would have coffee in Tel Aviv, in a coffee shop called "Tsapihit Bi-Dvash" (A Plate of Honey) on Frishman Street, watching people go by and then we would go to the movies or the other way round, I don't remember.

I graduated in 1972. I couldn't wait to start working and feel independent. I had ...big plans. For years all I wanted was contacts lenses and a car, a Mini Cooper, or as Anna used to say when she was a baby, a Mini Tooper. I had a teaching certificate but I didn't want to teach. I was convinced that I could not face a whole classroom of rowdy kids so I became a secretary instead. I didn't last long, about one year, because I just hated it and the last straw was when the Executive Director of a big firm asked me to …peel some oranges for him. Really?! By this time I was already dating Yossi who encouraged me to go into teaching.

So in 1973 I started teaching English as a second language, first Middle School then High School. I taught for 31 years until I retired in 2010. For the last 6 years I was elected to be the President of the Federation of Teachers of Jewish Day Schools in Montreal. Those were the best years of my career and the work I loved the most. I loved dealing with the school administrators, negotiating for renewal of teachers' contracts and filing grievances on teachers' behalf.

I was 61 when I retired. I wanted to be able to see the kids that by then were all in Boston without being tied to a schedule and move on to do other things before… I needed a wheel chair.

In the summer of 1972 a mutual friend, Miriam Hershkovits Shelef introduced me to Abba. I had had a couple of boyfriends but Abba was different from the start. He was different from the very first phone call. He wasn't boring. We would spend hours and hours talking and it wasn't boring.

At that time he was in the army and didn't have a penny to his name. I don't remember the occasion, maybe my birthday; probably my birthday and we went to a restaurant, Shaul's. There were two choices of dining rooms, upstairs and downstairs. I don't know why but I picked the wrong venue. It turned out to be outrageously expensive because he kept the receipt for many years.

He proposed in September and we got married in the Ramat Aviv hotel on March 27, 1973. For our honeymoon we spent a week in Tiberias. We were the only young couple in the hotel, all the other guests I believe were quite older, or so we thought at that time and I think they enjoyed watching the young couple.

We bought our first apartment in Hod Hasharon, a peaceful town which was then sparsely populated. In the back of our house on Ben Gurion Street number 51 there were open fields and chicken coops. When we moved in all we had was a cooler that served as a fridge and hardly any furniture. But hey, we were very proud and in love. The first time I made dinner for our friends was a total fiasco. I don't really remember what I made but I do remember what I didn't make, potatoes of course. Well, anybody that knows Yossi would have known better so I still had a few things to learn.

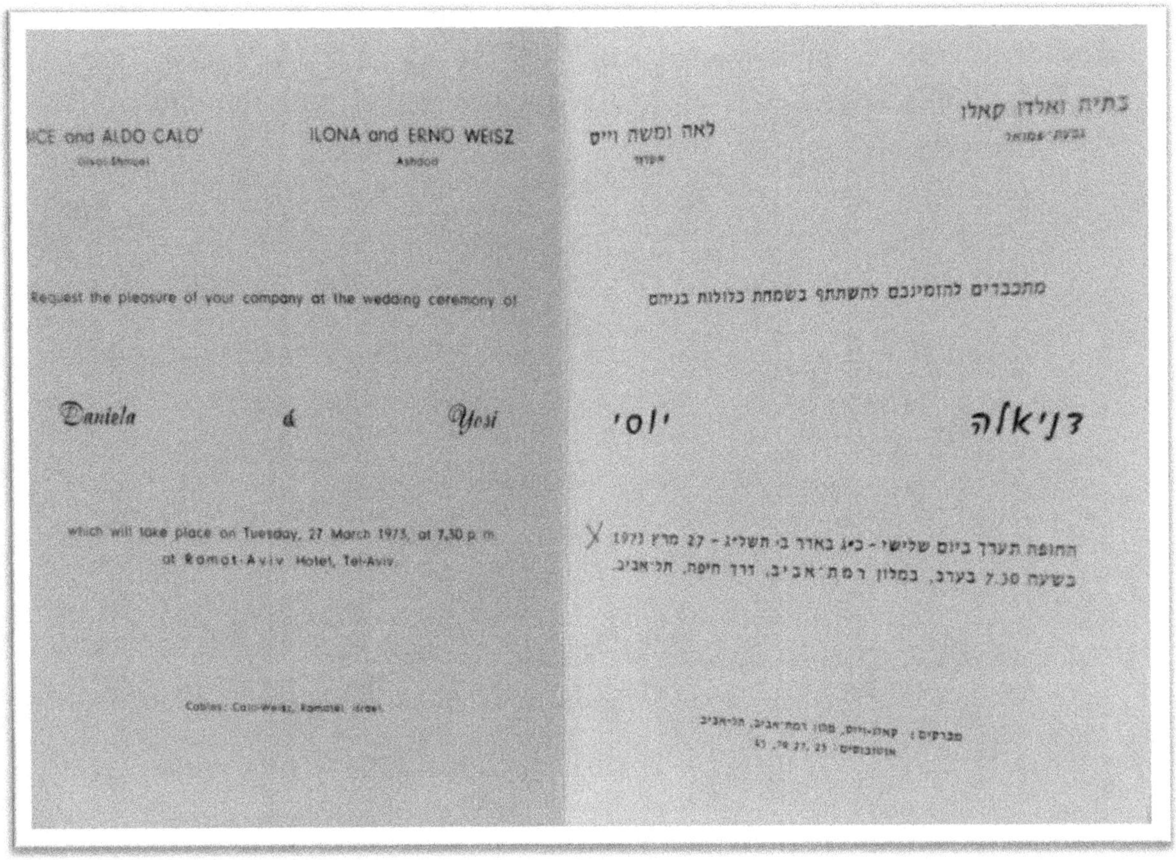

...ICE and ALDO CALO'
Givat-Shmuel

ILONA and ERNO WEISZ
Ashdod

Request the pleasure of your company at the wedding ceremony of

Daniela & *Yosi*

which will take place on Tuesday, 27 March 1973, at 7,30 p.m.
at Ramot-Aviv Hotel, Tel-Aviv.

Cables: Calo-Weisz, Ramotel, Israel.

בתיה ואלדו קאלו
גבעת־שמואל

לאה ומשה וייס
אשדוד

מתכבדים להזמינכם להשתתף בשמחת כלולות בניהם

דניאלה יוסי

החופה תערך ביום שלישי - כ״ג באדר ב׳ תשל״ג - 27 מרץ 1973
בשעה 7.30 בערב, במלון רמת־אביב, דרך חיפה, תל־אביב.

מברקים: קאלו־וייס, מלון רמת־אביב, תל־אביב
אוטובוסים: 25, 27, 79, 45

Our wedding invitation, March 27, 1973

Daniela and Yossi Livni

The wedding cake

We didn't stay long in our new apartment because the Yom Kippur War broke out. We did not have a phone and Yossi was told to stay close to a phone. In those days it took a couple of years to get a phone line, so we moved back to my parents' apartment for a couple of months.

On July 15, 1975 Dafna was born. The Kupat Holim nurse showed up for a home visit and left us with instructions, some useful, others less. "Why don't you turn on the AC?" she asked. It was July, the peak of a humid hot summer. So we did that. Then she said that I have to learn how to breast feed her. Ok. That didn't work. Dafna was hungry and kept crying, I cried because she cried and this went on for a good two weeks. Eventually I decided enough is enough and I'll do it my way. Sterilizing bottles became Yossi's job. Dafna was happier and so was I. Pretty soon she started sleeping through the nights.

Dafna

Dafna

Mamma with Maya

Michal

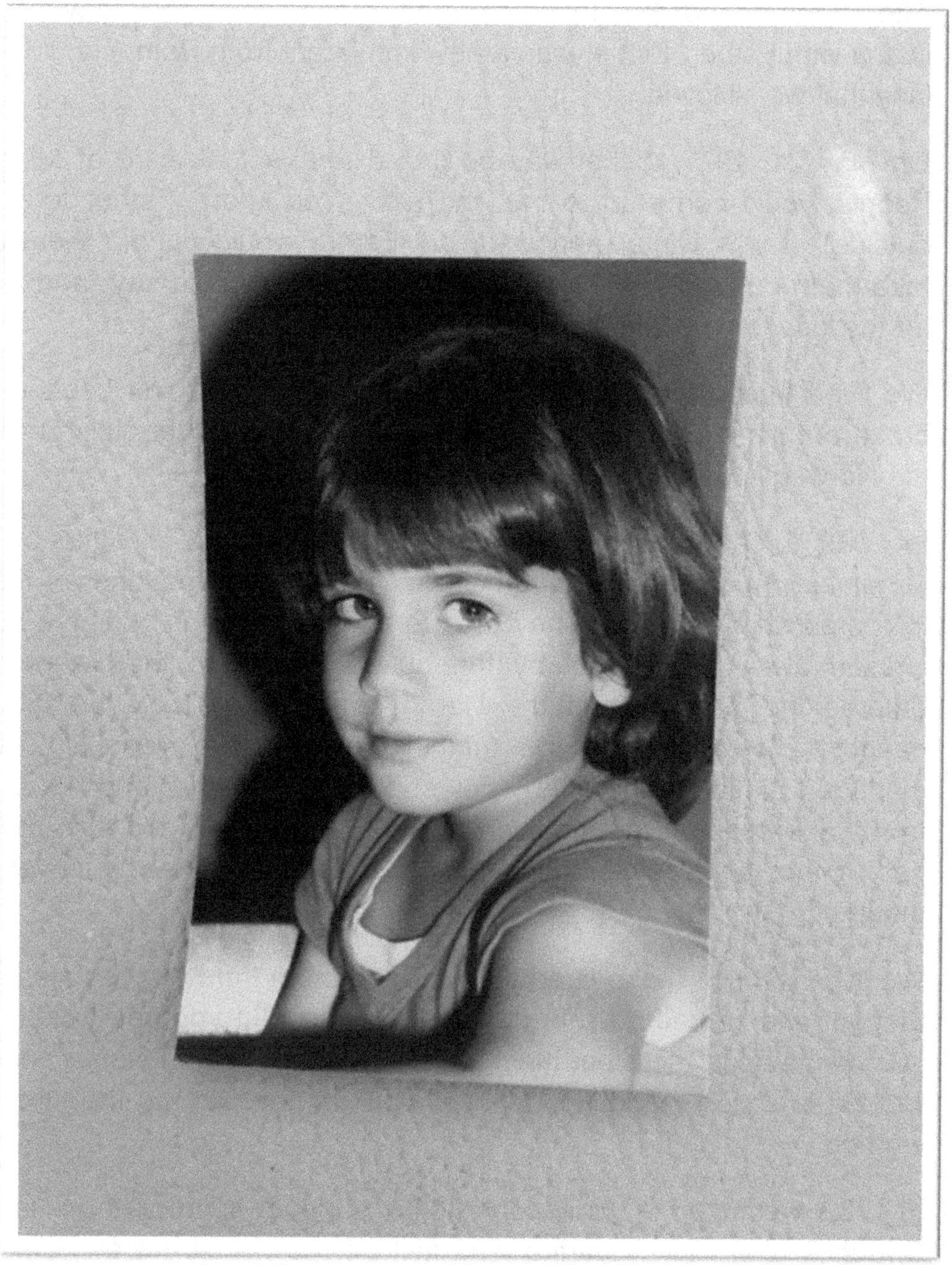

Michal

After the three months of paid maternity leave I went back to work and left Dafna with Esther. Esther was a new immigrant from Romania, a very nice lady that we all loved.

On May 21, 1977 Michal was born and Esther took care of Michal too. People would come up to me and say: "You know, Esther took Michal outside!" It was winter and cold, but Esther would bundle them up and take them out. "Its way colder in Romania!" she would say "and it's good for the kids to be out in the fresh air."

We lived through several wars. Operation Litani, the first Lebanese war, broke out in 1978. Yossi was drafted and served as the liaison officer to the Norwegian UN Peace Corps in Lebanon.

In 1979 three Arabs that were parts of the PLO (Palestine Liberation Organization) led by Mahmud Abbas (yes, todays President of the PLO) infiltrated from Lebanon. They tried to enter a house in Naharya but were chased away by gunshot by the house owner; so they went on and entered the apartment of the Haran family. They took the father and daughter hostage while the mother and her two year old daughter managed to hide in the attic. They shot both the father and his daughter. In the apartment in the meanwhile Yael, the two year old also died while her mother was desperately trying to keep her quiet by covering her mouth.

We lived through these events, dismissed them from our psyche or so we thought and carried on with our daily routine. But you see I didn't forget, you can subdue them but they leave a mark and when Dafna and Michal walked to school about 15 minutes' walk all the way up the street I was worried.

In 1982 we moved to our second home, a bigger apartment on Ha-Gheula Street. Michal's kindergarten was just across the street and Dafna who was already in first grade had a key and picked her up at noon. They played with the neighborhood kids until I was back from school.

We moved in the summer and in the fall Operation Peace for Galilee started. Yossi was drafted again. This time I recall one day, or two. As an officer he escorted the IDF supplies convoys in Lebanon, which meant he was in the front jeep that led the convoys. The route to the base followed a mountain road and more than once they would come onto a turn in the road where, being in unfriendly territory, one could not predict what would await them beyond the curve.

And then, still in Lebanon, he escorted these two guys in civilian clothes, Yossi sitting in the back of an unmarked car, with a gun on his lap. They came up to a non-descript building, double parked and told him to wait in the car. While they were gone some kids approached the car and peeked inside. Yossi thought nothing of it until a second car parked in front of him, a third car parked behind him and yet another one parked just.... besides him. Well, by now he was convinced that this is it, they have him surrounded and... and he should get ready for the worst. He grabbed his gun when a very loud bell rang. Lots of kids came running out of the building towards the parking cars.....to be picked up by their parents.

While Yossi was away, one Saturday I went with Dafna, David and Haviva to the beach. We were just walking along the beach when I suddenly realized Dafna wasn't there. I confess I panicked. The beach was packed and she was nowhere in sight. We looked for her and after a while we decided to go the police. We made our way back to the spot where we had left our bags and low and behold Dafna is sitting there! Later she said that when she realized she had lost us, she understood that we will have to come back for the car keys!!!

Michal used to get time out in the bathroom. We thought it was a good way to teach her a lesson but it was only many years later that she "confessed" that it was no punishment at all as the bathroom had a back door to the balcony where she spent her punishment!

Our life evolved into a routine. Friday nights we went for dinner to my parents and Saturday mornings we drove to Ashdod to be with Yossi's parents. Quite often, on weekends or when we went away on vacation, we left the girls with my parents and Mamma would take them by bus to the beach in Tel Aviv, go for pizza in Ramat Gan or go to the local library. Whenever we went to my mother she used to drop everything she was doing and play with them. She would let them do whatever they wanted in her tiny apartment, build a fort in the living room under the coffee table and over the armchair and make a total mess. "I will have plenty of time to clean up when you go home", she would say. They loved her for that and have sweet memories of her.

In the summertime, when Dafna and Michal came to Israel they would stay with her. So it came as no surprise to me that when I called early in the morning the day she passed they booked a flight to Israel to be at her funeral. Wherever she is I hope she knows that.

MONTREAL

In 1986 we moved to Montreal, Canada. At first I thought it would be an easy, smooth move but I very soon found out that it was quite complex. We knew we were doing it for the right motives; we wanted Dafna and Michal to have a better chance to a good life. I look now at Dafna and Michal and their families and I am content. We did well, they did well and we are proud of their achievements, both personal and professional. But everybody paid a price, maybe some more than others. First and foremost, the move was difficult on Dafna and Michal. Dafna was eleven and Michal was nine. The adjustment was difficult as not only they did not speak the language but there was a significant cultural shock. In Israel kids did not need their parents to set up a play date, in Israel the school day ended at lunch time and everybody played outdoors until dinner time. What a different world these two little girls suddenly had to adjust to! And as if this was not enough within the first two years they switched schools twice! They say kids adjust easily to changes but it's not true. The move was definitely difficult on them.

My parents also paid a hefty price. Only when I became a Savta I understood what our move to Canada meant to our parents. We deprived them of a great source of happiness and fulfillment. The relationship between grandparents and their grandchildren is unique. You want to do with them only what they love, you don't have that sense of responsibility, you get pure joy from spoiling them rotten and letting them have ice cream for breakfast! They are happy, you're happy! And we deprived our parents of that happiness!

HEIRLOOMS and MORE

Well yes. I know you don't care for all the knicks and knacks I keep but I want to tell you something. Don't throw anything out, yet. Put everything in boxes and keep them in the basement for a while. Some have no monitary value, others do but this is not the reason why I want you to keep them, albeit in the basement. They are me. Nonna Olga's console is more than just a piece of furniture, Nonno Gustavo's cutlery with the initials GC is not just forks and knives, and so is my mother's tea set and many more. They are a constant reminder of a life that once was and I want you to keep alive. Two of these items though I hope will stay upstairs. The first if this silver hannukiah which was my father's and the second is the engagement ring of my mother. The ring holds no significant monitary value but this is how I remember my mother. This is how I would like you to remember her too.

And if you forget her voice or what she looked like the link below includes a very short video of her recorded by my second cousin Michal Dviri Rosenblatt, the daughter of Manuela Vitali Norsa Dviri.

The link for my mother's video clip:

https://drive.google.com/file/d/1IMNcb5UstdB8vv8a7ShURWeP18zJKX-j/view?usp=drivesdk

My father’s hannukiah

My mother's ring

TRADITIONS and HOLIDAYS

Vincisgrassi or cappelletti? No family get together can be even remotely considered respectable without ... food. Food and Holidays or Holidays and food bring us together and make our family unique.

Some of the dishes in this book I learnt from my mother and others from Ilu and I know who in our family likes what. Maya likes meat and pasta, Ella likes rakot krumpli, Ben likes chocolate cakes and cookies and everything else and Anna likes...pasta.

ROSH HA-SHANA'

The most important thing we make for Rosh Ha-Shaná is the hand, "la manina" which we display from Rosh Ha-Shana' Eve until the end of Sukkot. The hand made of water and flour symbolizes the blessing of the Priest for the New Year, the rice and the pomegranate (with all its seeds) symbolize plentitude.

The menu for Rosh Ha-Shana' dinner includes apples with honey, a round Challah and chicken soup with cappelletti

The "manina" (small hand) for

Rosh Ha-Shaná

HANNUKAH

The menu for Hannukah dinner includes sufganiot (Doughnuts) and levivot (Latkes, potato pancakes).

PURIM

The menu for Purim dinner includes Hamman Tashen.

PASSOVER

For Pessach we carry on the tradition of finding the hidden Hammetz (bread, forbidden during the eight days of Passover). The kids, each holding a flashlight, follow Saba around the house trying to find pieces of bread left suspiciously in conspicuous places. And the Affikomen, we do it Bubi's style. In our house the kids hide it and not the leader of the Passover Seder, like in other families. And now it's Saba that has to find the Affikomen in order to resume the reading of the Haggadah and finally get to the meal itself. Since he "cannot" find it without the kids' help they offer to help him out, for a price. Surprisingly, he has gifts ready for each of them and all ends well.

The menu for Passover dinner includes harroset, hard boiled eggs, potatoes served with an individual small bowl of salted water, just before the meal, horseradish (white and red), matzas and chicken soup with matza balls.

The Seder plate:

Chicken bone (roasted drumstick), harosset, egg, maror (boiled potato), horseradish (white and red)

RECIPES

PASTA AND SOUP DISHES

VINCISGRASSI (my mother taught me)

According to the Italian tradition, the name of the dish derives from the name of the Austrian general Alfred von Windisch-Graetz who won over the Napoleonic troops that besieged Ancona in 1799. A lady from Ancona prepared this dish in his honor and named it after him.[7] Notwithstanding this wonderful story, the dish was probably already present in the culinary tradition of the Marche, and in particular of Macerata since a recipe of a particular lasagna called "princisgrass" already exists in a 1779 cooking book "Il cuoco maceratese" (The cook from Macerata).

---

[7] Wikipedia

Ingredients: (serves 6)

Fresh pasta (see recipe below) or 1 box of commercial lasagna.
Ragout (see recipe below).
Besciamelle sauce (see recipe below)
Turn on the oven to 350°F.
In a big pot bring water and salt to boil. Cook the pasta al dente.

In a baking dish, spread some ragout to cover the bottom of the dish then place layers of pasta, ragout and besciamelle sauce. The last should be ragout. You can actually mix the ragout and the besciamelle and spread between the pasta layers.

Bake uncovered in 350°F for 45 minutes.

CHICKEN SOUP (serves 4, Hanna taught me)
Ingredients:

2 medium carrots, peeled
1 big onion, peeled
1/2 celery root, peeled
3 celery stalks
1 medium parsnip, peeled
1 kohlrabi (optional, since hard to find)
1 lb. chicken bones or 4 chicken drumsticks
4 quarts water.
Salt, pepper, paprika

Place all ingredients in big stock pot, cover with water, bring to a boil, and cook for 2 hours on low heat.

Cool, discard all vegetables except carrot, remove chicken bones and strain soup to remove tiny bones.

Can be served with vermicelli, cappelletti or stracciatella (recipe below).

HUNGARIAN MUSHROOM SOUP

Ingredients:

4 tablespoons unsalted butter
2 cups chopped onions
1 lb. fresh mushrooms, sliced
2 cups water
1 tbs. paprika
1 cup milk
3 tbs. all-purpose flour
½ cup sour cream
2 tsp. lemon juice
1 tsp. salt
Ground black pepper to taste

Melt butter in a large pot over medium heat. Add onions; cook and stir until softened, about 5 minutes. Add mushrooms and sauté for 5 more minutes. Stir in water and paprika; reduce heat to low, cover, and simmer for 15 minutes.

Whisk milk and flour together in a separate bowl; stir into soup until blended. Cover and simmer for 15 more minutes, stirring occasionally.

Add sour cream, lemon juice, salt, and ground black pepper; stir over low heat until warmed through, about 3 to 5 minutes. Serve immediately.

HUNGARIAN BEAN SOUP (Bableves)

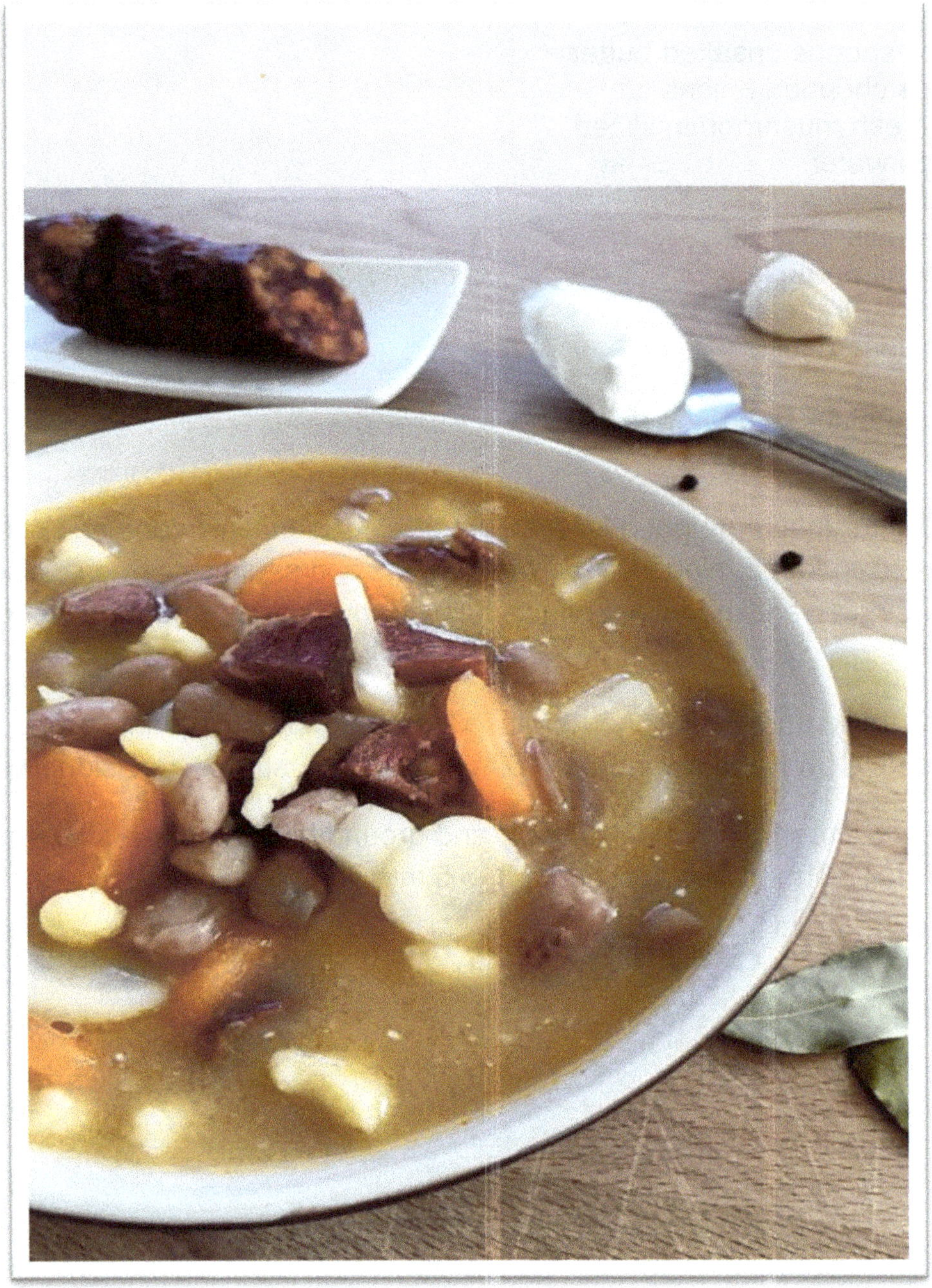

Ingredients:
¾ cup dried pinto beans (or any kind of beans, soaked overnight)
½ cup pancetta, or bacon cubed into ½ inch cubes
2 bay leaves
10 black peppercorns
5 cloves of garlic
2 medium carrots – peeled and cut into ¼ inch slices
1 medium parsnip – peeled and cut into ¼ inch slices
Vegetable oil
2 tbs. flour
1 tsp. sweet paprika powder
Salt to taste
Sour cream

Soak the beans overnight.

In a large pot sauté' the cubed bacon with the peppercorns, 4 cloves of garlic and bay leaves for 5 minutes until bacon becomes crunchy. Add 4 ½ cups of water. Pour off the soaking water of the beans and add the beans to the pot. Cover and cook for 2 hours until the beans are almost tender.

When the beans are almost tender, add the carrot and the celery root cubes. Cover and bring back to a boil, reduce the heat and keep cooking until the vegetables are tender. Add salt if necessary. I discard the parsnips.

Roux (to thicken your soup):

Heat oil in a pan; add 2 tablespoons of flour, stirring constantly. After 2-3 minutes when it starts to brown, take it off the heat, add 1 clove of minced garlic and stir. Allow to cool and add 1 teaspoon of red paprika powder. Now add some soup to the roux to thin it. Pour this mixture back to your soup pot and bring the soup back to a boil.

Serve with sour cream.

CAPPELLETTI (serves 8, my mother taught me)

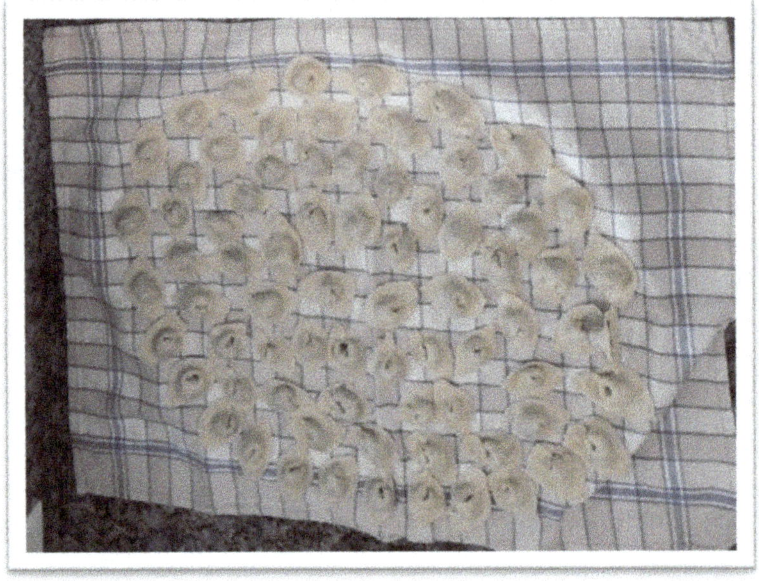

Ingredients:

Fresh pasta (see recipe below)
1/2 lb. ground beef or pork
2 strips of bacon
1 small onion
Salt, pepper
Chop the onion and sauté. Add the meat, salt and pepper. Grill / fry the bacon and chop it.
Combine the cooked meat with the chopped bacon.
Make sheets of pasta approximately 1/16' thick. Work a small quantity (fist size) at a time and keep the rest of the dough covered with a tea towel so it doesn't dry.
Cut the pasta sheets into 1½' x 1½' squares.

Put ½ tsp. of meat on each square, fold in half to create a triangle. Hold 2 extremities of the triangle; fold them to the back around your finger and stick together to get the shape of the cappelletti. Squeeze all edges to close tight. You have to work fast or the pasta will dry out and it will be difficult to close the cappelletti.

To cook, drop into boiling salted water. Cook until soft, remove and immediately add either melted butter/olive oil/sauce so they don't stick to each other.

PASSATELLI – For Passover's soup

Ingredients: **(serves 4, my mother taught me)**

6 tbs. matza meal (can be replaced with bread crumbs for the rest of the year)
3 tbs. grated parmesan
2 eggs
½ lemon zest
Salt, pinch of nutmeg

Combine all ingredients and pass through a rice masher into boiling soup.

STRACCIATELLA (Egg droppings for soup, serves 4)

Ingredients:

2 tsp flour
2 eggs
1 tsp lemon zest
½ tsp nutmeg
3 tbsp. parmesan

Combine all ingredients, drop into boiling soup while stirring with fork.

SFOGLIETTI (Pasta for Passover, serves 4)

Ingredients:

2 egg
1¼ cups + 1 tbs. flour

Combine ingredients and flatten with rolling pin or pasta machine to a thin leaf. Randomly cut into hand size pieces. Turn on oven to 400°F and bake on a baking sheet lined with parchment paper for a couple of minutes until you see bubbles on leaves. Flip them and bake for 2 minutes more. Randomly break them into boiling soup.

CHALLAH BREAD

Ingredients:

2 lbs. flour
3 tbs.oil
1 egg
½ stick soft butter, room temperature
2 tbs. dry yeast
5 tbs. sugar
1 tsp. salt
2-2 ½ cups water

For brushing:

1 egg
½ cup poppy seeds or sesame seeds (optional)
Melt yeast in ½ cup lukewarm water (109°F) with 1 tbs. of sugar. Let stand for 10 minutes to activate.

In a mixer bowl combine flour, oil, egg, butter and yeast. Mix slowly while adding water. Add salt for last. Stop mixing when dough detaches from bowl.

Place dough in lightly oiled bowl, cover with saran wrap and let stand in warm place (turned off oven) until doubles in size or in fridge overnight.

Shape into desired form (braid or round). Put on baking sheet lined with parchment paper, cover with a tea towel and let stand for 20 minutes.

Brush with beaten egg and bake for 25-30 minutes in 350°F, until golden.

RAGOUT (MEAT SAUCE) (serves 4)

Ingredients:

1 lb. ground beef
1 medium carrot
1 celery stalk
1 medium onion
1 tbs. dried tomatoes
1 big can crushed tomatoes
Salt, pepper, red hot pepper flakes
2 tbs. fresh basil

Chop onion in food processor and sauté in big pot.

Add meat and brown for 5 minutes.

Chop carrot, celery and dried tomatoes in food processor and add to pot. Add all other ingredients. Simmer on very low heat for 2 hours.

TÖLTÖT KAPOSZTA (stuffed cabbage, serves 4)

Ingredients:
1 lb. ground beef
1 curly cabbage
1 medium onion
1 cup rice
1 jar sauerkraut (optional)
Salt, pepper, paprika
Hot red pepper flakes to taste.
Freeze the cabbage a couple of days before you plan the make the dish and defrost it the night before.
Cook the rice until almost done.
With a sharp knife cut around the stalk of the cabbage and gently separate the leaves from each other. Chop up the smaller leaves that are too small to be stuffed.
In a large bowl combine all ingredients, except the sauerkraut.
Place 2 tbsp. of the meat at the wide base of one leaf. Fold the right side of the leaf to the left and the left to the right. Then start rolling the leaf from the base towards the edge of the leaf, quite tightly.

In a big pot, put the sauerkraut first (and/or the chopped smaller leaves) and then the cabbage rolls on top. Sprinkle salt, pepper and paprika and cover with water. Cook for 90 minutes on low heat. Serve with sour cream.

CHCKEN PAPRIKAS (serves 4)

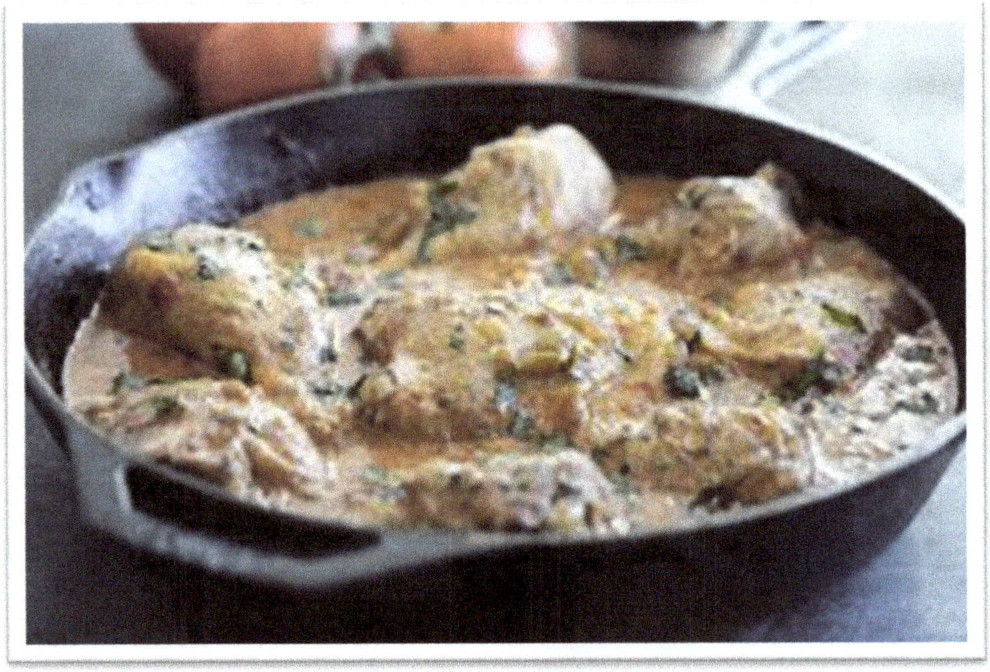

:

Ingredients

4 chicken drumsticks or thighs.
4 small onions
1 red pepper
2 tbs. flour
3 tbs. sour cream
Salt, pepper and 1 tbs. paprika

Chop the onion and sauté. Add chicken pieces and brown for 5 minutes each side. Add chopped pepper, salt, pepper and paprika. Half cover with water. Cook for 1 hour on low heat. Towards the end, stir the flour and sour cream in 1/2 cup of cooking liquid and add to the pot. Serve with nokerli (recipe below) and sour cream.

CHOULENT (serves 4)

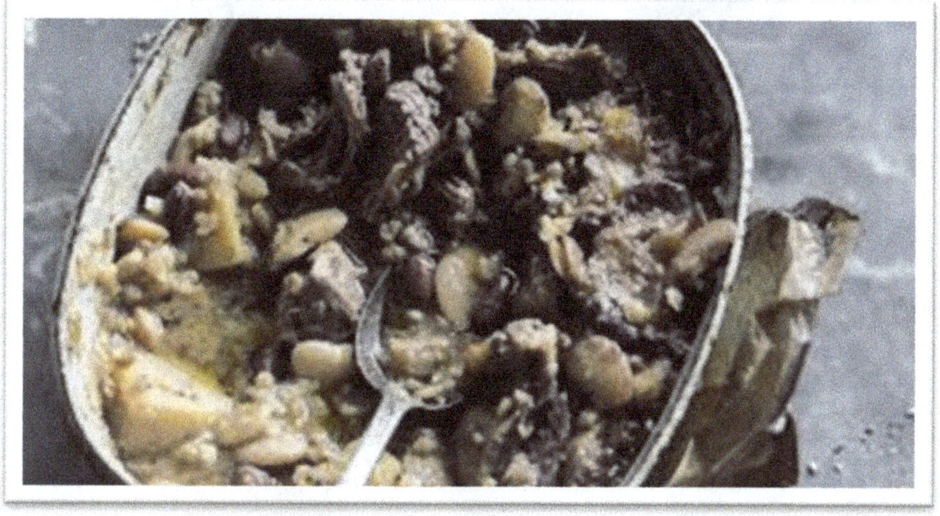

Ingredients:

1 lb. beef cubes
2 beef bones (optional)
½ cup diced pancetta
2 cups red beans
½ cup barley
2 tbs. baking soda
1 medium onion
Salt, pepper, paprika, 1/4 tsp. hot paprika flakes.

Two nights before soak the beans with baking soda in a bowl covered with water.

Cooking starts the night before. Turn on oven to 350°F. Combine all ingredients in a Dutch oven or other deep baking dish. Cover with water, cover and bake until bubbling then reduce to 200°F and bake overnight or at least for 12 hours. Bake uncovered for the last 5 hours.

GOULASCH

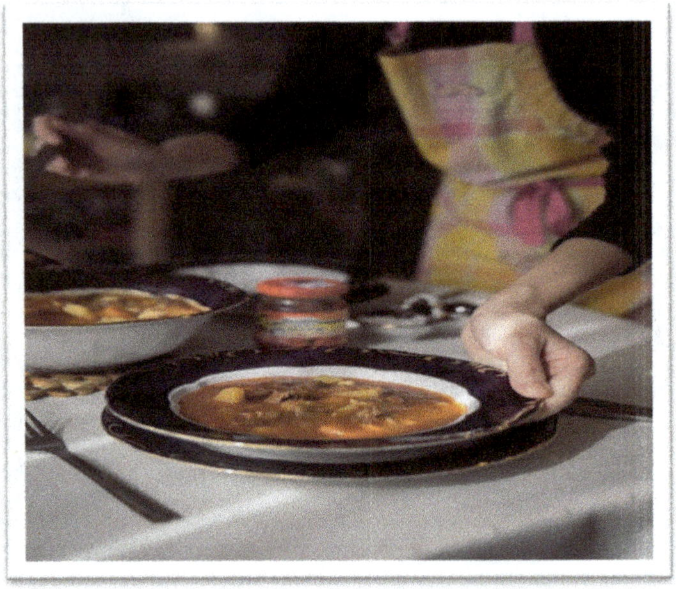

Ingredients:
⅓ cup vegetable oil
3 onions, sliced
2 tbs. sweet paprika
3 tsp. salt, divided
½ tsp. ground black pepper
3 lb. beef stew meat, cut into 1 1/2 inch cubes
1 ½ cups water
1 clove garlic, minced

Heat oil in a large pot or Dutch oven over medium heat. Cook and stir onions in oil until soft, 2 to 4 minutes. Remove onions and set them aside. Coat beef cubes with paprika, 2 teaspoons salt, and pepper, and cook in the onion pot until brown on all sides.
Return onions to the pot with beef; pour in water, tomatoes, garlic, and remaining 1 teaspoon salt. Bring to a boil, and then reduce heat to low. Cover and simmer, stirring occasionally, until meat is tender, 3 hours.

Can be cooked in slow cooker on low heat for 6 hours.

RAKOT KRUMPLI (serves 4)

Ingredients:

4 big potatoes
4 eggs
1 lb. sour cream
½ stick butter, diced
Salt and pepper.

Cook potatoes and eggs until potatoes are soft. Peel and slice potatoes and eggs. Sprinkle with salt and pepper.

In a deep baking dish put some butter first. Then alternate layers of potatoes, eggs and butter. Cover with sour cream. Bake uncovered at 350°F for 40 minutes.

PICKLES

Ingredients:
12 mini cucumbers
12 garlic cloves
2 tbsp. black pepper grains
Salt
Glass container
1 bunch of dill.

Place cucumbers in glass jar, cover with salted water (1 tbs. of salt /cup) and cover with dill. Put a slice of bread on top of everything (to prevent mold) and close jar.

Leave on countertop for 5 days and then refrigerate.

GNOCCHI (serves 6, with Angie Calós help)

Ingredients:

2 lbs. Russet potatoes
1 1/2 cups flour
The ratio potatoes/flour in weight is 3:1 (1/3 flour, 2/3 potatoes, the more flour you use the harder the gnocchi will be)
Salt

Cook unpeeled potatoes until soft for about 40-50 minutes. Don't pierce potatoes while they cook. Peel potatoes while still hot, without cooling them under water (not easy).

Mash hot potatoes with rice masher. Add flour and salt. To get soft gnocchi knead as little as possible, until all ingredients are incorporated. Cover with tea towel.

Work a small amount at a time (fist size). On a flour dusted surface, make 1 finger thick logs and cut into 1' pieces.

Using a flour dusted fork, (or special gnocchi tool to make indentations) slide gnocchi onto the fork to make indentations.

Bring salted water to a boil in a big pot. Drop some gnocchi in the water until they float and remove promptly. As you remove gnocchi spray with olive oil so they don't stick. Don't cook all gnocchi at once because it will cool the boiling water.

FRESH PASTA

Ingredients: (For 4)

1¾ cups flour
2 eggs
Salt

Combine flour, eggs and salt and knead until smooth for about 5 minutes. Cover with tea towel. With pasta machine work a small amount at a time to make desired leaves.

BESCIAMELLE SAUCE (serves 4)

Ingredients:

3 ½ tbs. butter
4 ½ tbs. flour
2 cups milk
1 cup grated parmesan
Salt, pepper and a dash of nutmeg.

Melt butter in medium pot. Add flour and milk. Continuously stir for 5 minutes or until sauce thickens. If not thick enough add flour, 1 tbsp. at a time. Remove from heat and add salt, pepper, nutmeg and parmesan.

KRUMPLISH NUDLI (Hungarian gnocchi, serves 6)

Ingredients:

2 lbs. Russet potatoes
1 1/2 cups flour
1 egg
Salt
4 tbsp. olive oil
1 cup bread crumbs

Make nudli (like gnocchi recipe above). In a medium size pot heat oil and bread crumbs. Toss in nudli until well covered.

NOKERLI (serves 4)

Ingredients:

2 eggs
2 cups flour
¾ cup water
½ tsp salt

Combine all ingredients to get a sticky mix.

Bring salted water to boil in big pot.

Using the side of a teaspoon, spoon small amount of dough into boiling water.

Dipping the spoon in the hot water will remove the dough from the spoon (it is easier if you have a spaetzel maker, as you want very small noodles).

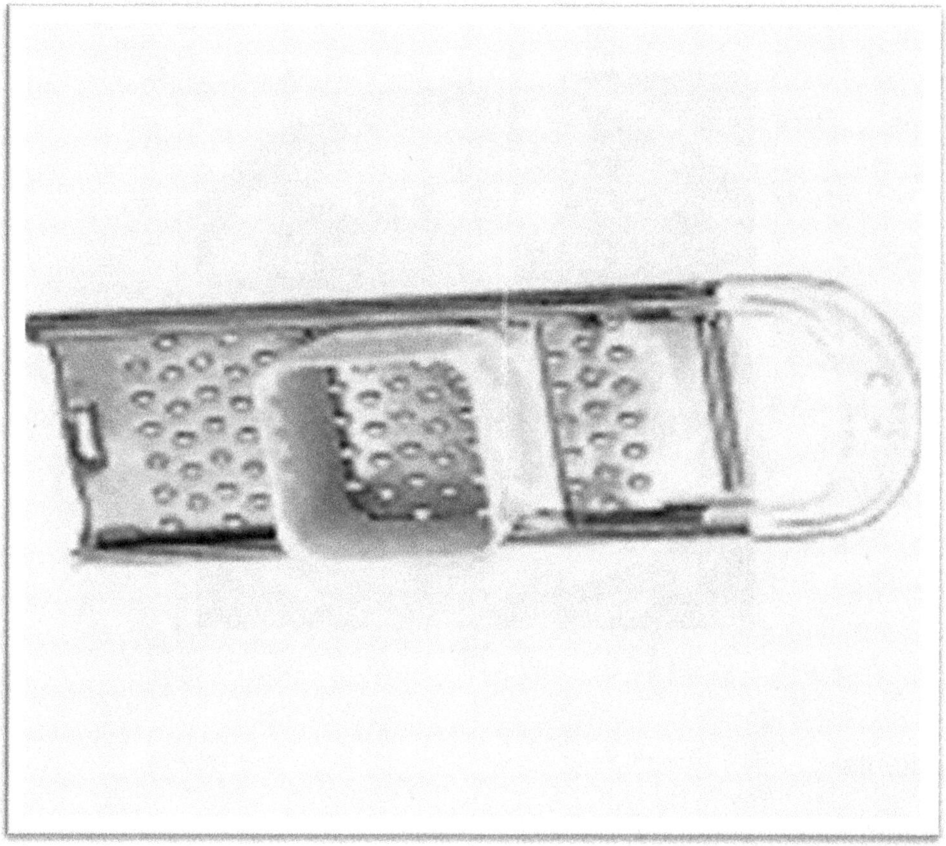

The noodles are done when they float to the top.

Remove from water with large slotted spoon, and place in colander.

Rinse with cold water. Can be served with sauce of chicken paprika.

LATKES (Potatoes pancakes, makes 8)

Ingredients:

4 medium russet potatoes, peeled
1 egg, beaten
¼ cup flour
1 medium onion, chopped
1 tsp. salt
Pepper
Oil for frying
Apple sauce or sour cream for serving

Grate potatoes. Squeeze and drain accumulated liquid. Combine with rest of ingredients.
Heat oil in a large skillet.
Drop batter in dollops of 3 tbs., flattening with spatula.

Fry for 3-4 minutes each side.

Drain on paper towels.

GNOCCHI ALLA ROMANA (serves 6)

Ingredients:

2 cups milk
5 cups semolina flour
1 butter stick
2 tbs. grated parmesan
3 egg yolks
Salt, pepper, a pinch of nutmeg.

Combine milk and semolina flour in a pot over low heat and stir continuously for about 10 minutes until it solidifies. Remove from heat and add ½ stick of butter, 2 tbs. of parmesan, salt, pepper and nutmeg. Let cool and then add egg yolks. Lightly wet countertop and spread gnocchi dough to ¼ thick.

Melt the rest of the butter.

Wet the edge of a glass under cold water and cut circles. Oil a baking dish, place the circles and in between each layer brush with melted butter and parmesan. Finish with parmesan. Bake at 350°F for 45 minutes.

HOUMMUS

Ingredients:

1 cup chick peas
1 tbs. tahini (optional)
½ cup water
1 tsp. lemon juice
2 cloves garlic
1 tbs. olive oil
½ tsp salt
¼ tsp. pepper
¼ tsp. cumin

Mix all ingredients in food processor.

TUROS RETES (Cottage Cheese Strudel)

Ingredients: (makes 2 rolls)

1 package puff pastry (16 oz)
2 cups cottage cheese
2 eggs
3 1/2 tbs granulated sugar
1 tbs semolina flour
1 1/2 tbs sour cream
1/2 tsp salt
1 tsp vanilla extract
1 lemon's zest
raisins (optional)

Confectioner sugar for serving

Preheat oven to 375°F.

In a large mixing bowl, mix the cottage cheese with sugar, lemon zest, salt, and vanilla extract.

Separate egg yolks from the egg whites. Add the yolks to the cheese mixture. Beat up egg whites until they hit firm peaks. Fold egg whites into cheese mixture.

Stretch the puff pastry a little bit and sprinkle with semolina. Pour on your filling leaving about 2 inches at one side so you can tuck them in later. If you're using 2 sheets, pour half of the filling onto each. Roll the pastry into a log shape, tucking in the sides and pressing down on the edges so they fuse together.

Place strudel log onto parchment paper and bake for 25-35 minutes, or until the top gets brown.

Let it cool at room temperature at least 30 minutes before cutting. Serve topped with powdered sugar.

HUNGARIAN BISCUITS (pogácsa)

Ingredients:

2 cups flour
½ tsp. Salt
1 ¾ sticks butter
2 tbs. sour cream
1 egg for brushing
Mix flour, salt and butter until you get a mixture of like peas. Add yolks and sour cream. Wrap the dough with saran wrap and refrigerate overnight.

Remove dough from fridge and let rest for 1/2 hour. Flatten to 1/8 inch. Fold into 3 parts, then in half and refrigerate for ½ hour. Remove from fridge and flatten into rectangle, Place on baking dish with parchment paper. With a fork make marks lengthwise and width wise. With a shot glass cut circles. Wet the shot glass so dough doesn't stick to it. Flatten left over dough and make more circles.

Pre heat oven to 350°F.
Brush with egg with a few drops of oil. You can spread Kosher salt or sesame seeds.

Bake for 20-25 minutes until golden

HUNGARIAN PANCAKE (Palacsinta)

Pancakes:

2 cups all-purpose flour
2 eggs
1 cup milk
1 pinch salt

Can be filled with savory or sweet fillings:

Sweet cheese filling:
1 cup cottage cheese or farmer's cheese.
4 tbs sugar, to taste
1 package vanilla sugar
½ cup raisins

Chocolate Topping:
¼ cup water
½ cup white sugar
½ cup chopped bittersweet chocolate
2 tablespoons butter

Blend the flour, eggs, milk, and salt in blender.

Heat a lightly greased frying pan over medium heat. Pour 1/4 cup of the batter into the pan and cook the pancake for about one minute. Flip it over and cook for another minute, or until golden brown. Remove the pancake from the pan. Repeat with the remaining batter, stacking the pancakes while keeping them separate with waxed paper.

For the chocolate topping, combine the water, 1/2 cup sugar, and chocolate in a saucepan and cook over low heat just until the chocolate melts. Remove the pan from the heat and add the butter, stirring until melted and combined.

HUNGARIAN FLOATING ISLAND (Madártej)

Ingredients:

6 eggs
4 cups milk
6 tbsp sugar
1 tbsp vanilla extract
1 tbsp corn starch
1 pinch salt
lemon zest when serving

Heat milk in a big pot until hot but not boiling.

Separate the egg yolks from the whites.

Beat the egg whites with a little pinch of salt until stiff peaks form. When the milk is hot, using a spoon, put 4 dollops of egg-white foam in the milk (they will look like dumplings). Cook one side for about 2 minutes, then flip to the other side, cover the pot and cook for another 2 minutes. When the egg-white foam dollops have boiled, take them out of the milk and place them in a strainer or colander.

Make sure that the milk is not boiling. If it is too hot, you would overcook the egg white the dollops will shrink and be flat and thin once you take them out.

Keep cooking the dollops.

Beat the egg yolks with sugar and vanilla extract until thick and the color is light yellow. Add the cornstarch. Pour some of the hot milk into the egg yolks, stir continuously. Now pour this mixture back to the rest of the milk, put back on the heat, and do not stop stirring. Do not let it boil; this prevents the eggs from scrambling. Keep stirring until you get a creamy consistency. Turn the heat off and keep stirring for another minute.

Let it cool down, pour the content into nice serving bowls.

Place the dollop on the cream. Sprinkle with lemon zest.

HUNGARIAN GERBAUD CAKE (Zserbó szelet)

Ingredients:

For the dough

2 cups flour
8 tbs butter
1 tbs dry yeast
1 egg
2 yolks
1 tbsp sugar
1/2 cup milk
1/2 lemon zest
1 pinch salt
½ cup ground walnuts
3 1/2 tbs powdered sugar
1 ¾ cups apricot jam

In a saucepan heat milk until lukewarm (109°F) and dissolve 1 tablespoon of sugar and the yeast.

In a large bowl mix the flour and cubed butter by hand. The mixture will be quite crumbly.

Add the egg, 2 egg yolks, the dissolved sugar and yeast mixture, pinch of salt and the lemon zest. Knead thoroughly.

Divide the dough into 4 balls, cover and let rest for 30 minutes.

Heat the oven to 355°F. Butter and flour a 16×10 inch baking pan.

On a floured surface roll out one part of the dough to the size of the baking tin, then lay it in.

Mix the ground walnuts with the powdered sugar. Spread one third of the apricot jam on the first layer of dough. Sprinkle with 1/3 of the walnut-sugar mixture.

Roll out the second piece of dough and gently put it on top of the first layer. Put the jam on it and sprinkle with walnut-sugar mixture.

Roll out the third piece of dough and gently put it on top of the second layer. Spread the jam on it and sprinkle with walnut-sugar mixture.

Roll out the fourth layer and place on top.

Bake the cake for 30 minutes, until the top is light-brown. You can test it with a tootpick, if it comes out clean, then the cake is baked. Let it cool completely.

For the chocolate glaze:

In small pan melt 8 tablespoons butter, add 4 tablespoons of cocoa powder, 4 tablespoons of sugar and 4 tablespoons of water and stir until the sugar melts and the mixture thickens. Cover your cake with the chocolate sauce. The butter will make the chocolate have a glassy look. Cut into squares.

KINDLI (Nuts or poppy seeds cake)

Ingredients:

Dough:

1 tbs. yeast
1/3 cup lukewarm milk (109^{0}F)
½ cup sugar
4 cups flour
Salt
2 ½ sticks butter
2 yolks

½ cup sour cream
1 yolk, for glazing

Poppy seeds filling:

¼ cup sugar
1 tsp. vanilla
½ tbsp. Flour
Zest of ½ a lemon
1 tbsp. lemon juice
¼ butter stick less 1 tbs
¼ tsp cinnamon
½ cup milk
1/2 cup poppy seeds
1 grated granny smith apple

Nuts filling:

1/2 cup sugar
½ cup milk
2/3 cup ground nuts (in food processor)
1 bag vanilla sugar
Zest 1 lemon
2 tbs crushed cookies

To make poppy seeds filling:

Cook sugar and water for a couple of minutes. Add honey, butter, lemon juice and zest. Add and stir poppy seeds and cinnamon. Add some crushed cookies if to liquid to spread.

To make nuts filling:

Cook milk and nuts for a couple of minutes. Remove from heat and add while stirring nuts, vanilla sugar, zest and cookies.

To make dough:

Dissolve yeast in milk with 1 tsp sugar. Let stand for 10 minutes to activate, until fluffy. Combine flour, butter and rest of sugar until you get crumbles. Add yeast, yolks and sour cream. Add salt for last. Mix until you get a smooth consistency.

Divide dough into 4. Flatten each into a thin rectangle. Spread 2 rectangles with shredded apple and half the poppy seeds mixture and the other two with the nuts mixture. Roll and close ends tightly so filling doesn't come out. Glaze with egg yolk. Pierce with fork in 4-5 places to let air out. Refrigerate overnight.

Bake on baking sheet lined with parchment paper in 375^{0}F oven for 40 minutes until golden. Slice when cooled down. Sliced cake can be frozen.

ALMAS PITE (Hungarian apple cake)

Ingredients:

2 1/2 butter sticks
1 ¾ cup + 2 tbs. flour
2 yolks
2 tbs. ice water
Salt
1/3 cup sugar
1/3 cup sour cream

Yolk + 1 tsp. water for glazing

Filling:

5 lbs. granny smith apples
1 jar pitted sour cherries (or frozen or raisins)
½ stick butter
½ cup walnuts
1/3 cup sugar
2 tbs. flour
4 tbs. bread crumbs
1 tsp. vanilla
½ lemon juice

In a mixing bowl combine flour and diced butter. Add sugar, salt and yolks. Add sour cream. Wrap the dough in saran wrap and refrigerate for 1 hour.

Peel and grate apples. Add cherries, lemon juice, butter, sugar and nuts and cook on low heat.

Divide the dough in 2 parts. Roll between 2 floured parchment sheets of paper to the size of an oven baking sheet, one slightly bigger.

Line an oven baking sheet with parchment paper and place bigger half on bottom. Sprinkle with bread crumbs, spread apple filling and cover with second half. Glaze with egg wash and pierce with fork to let air out while baking.

Bake in 350°F oven for 55 minutes.

TIRAMISU

Ingredients:

1 lb. mascarpone cheese
3 tbs. sugar
2 tbs. liquor (optional)
1 cup whipping cream
1 ½ cup cold brewed espresso or strong filter coffee
24 lady fingers (savoiardi)
6 ounces semi-sweet chocolate finely chopped in food processor

In a large bowl combine mascarpone, sugar, liquor. Beat until smooth. In a second bowl whip cream. Gently fold whipping cream into cheese.

In an 8' square cake pan layer quickly coffee moistened lady fingers, ½ cream mixture and ½ chopped chocolate, repeat same 3 layers. Finish with chopped chocolate.

ROGELACH

Ingredients:

3 ½ cups flour
2 tbs. yeast
2/3 cup lukewarm milk
2 eggs
1/3 cup sugar
1 tsp. vanilla.
¾ soft (room temperature) butter stick + 1 tbs
1 tsp. salt

½ container of Hashar Haolé chocolate spread or:

1 cup sugar
¾ cups cocoa powder
1 scarce tsp. cinnamon
1 ½ stick melted butter

For glazing:

1 egg with ½ tsp oil

For syrup:

½ cup water
1 cup sugar

Dough:

Dissolve yeast in 1/2 cup lukewarm milk and 1 tbs. sugar. Let stand 10 minutes until fluffy. In a mixer bowl combine flour and yeast. Add milk, eggs, sugar, vanilla and butter. Mix for 5 minutes and add salt for last. Cover and refrigerate overnight.

Next day roll dough to ½' thick rectangle. Spread 2 soft butter sticks on 2/3 of the dough. Fold the 1/3 without butter onto the middle third, and then fold the other 1/3 onto these. Now fold horizontally 1/3 towards the center then the other 1/3 onto them. Wrap in saran wrap and refrigerate for 1 hour. Repeat, without butter, and refrigerate for another hour. Divide dough into 6 parts and roll each into 1/8' thick circle. Cut circle into 12 small triangles. Spread chocolate and roll from outer longer edge towards tip. Brush with egg wash.

Warm the oven to 350°F. Bake for 15-20 minutes until golden.

In the meantime prepare the syrup. In a small pot dissolve water and sugar over medium heat while stirring. Brush the rogelach with syrup immediately when taken out of oven.

SUFGANIOT (Doughnuts, makes 20)

Ingredients:

3 cups flour
1 tbs. yeast
¼ a cup lukewarm (108^{0}F) water
4 tbsp. sugar
2 eggs
1 lemon zest
1 tsp. salt
2 tbs. liquor (optional)
4 cups of canola oil
Confectioner sugar.
Strawberry jam or chocolate spread

Dissolve yeast and 1 tbs. sugar in water. Let rise for about 10 minutes. In a mixer bowl combine the flour, yeast, rest of sugar, eggs, liquor and lemon zest. Mix slowly for 1 minute. Add salt and mix until detaches from bowl. Cover with saran wrap, let stand in warm place for 1 hour until doubles in size.

Make 20-30 balls egg size, cover with lightly oiled saran wrap and let stand until doubles in size.

Fry in hot oil about 2 minutes per side, until golden. Put on paper towels. With pastry syringe fill with jam or chocolate, sprinkle with confectioner sugar.

HAMMAN TASCHEN (Chiacchere, Italian version)

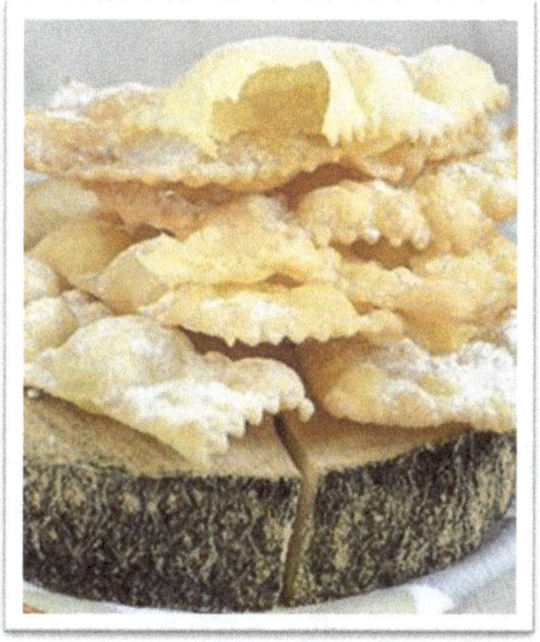

Ingredients:

3 eggs
3 tbs. sugar
1½ cup flour
½ cup oil
Salt

½ tsp cinnamon
Zest of 1 lemon
Confectioner sugar.

Combine all ingredients. With a rolling pin (or pasta machine) flatten into 1/8' leaf. Cut into 1' x ¾' strips. Fry in hot oil. Sprinkle with confectioner sugar while still hot.

OZNEI HAMAN (Israeli version)

Ingredients:

For the dough:
3 cups flour
1½ sticks butter, room temperature
1 cup confectioner sugar
1 egg
1 yolk
1 tsp. vanilla
1 tsp. baking powder
1/8 tsp. salt

For the filling:

25 gr. butter
1 tsp. honey
¾ cup sugar
½ cup finely crushed nuts (walnuts or pecans)
1 ½ cup ground poppy seeds
½ lemon grated peel
1 egg white

Make the filling:

In a small pot, warm milk with honey, butter and sugar until the sugar is melted, until boiling. Then lower heat, add nuts and cook for 1 minute. Remove from heat; add poppy seeds and lemon and mix. Add yolk and mix well. Cover with saran wrap and leave in fridge for 1 hour.

Make the dough:

Mix all ingredients in electric mixer at medium speed for 2-3 minutes.
Cover with saran wrap and leave in fridge for 1 hour.
Pre heat oven to 350oF.
Flatten the dough on a floured surface to a 1/8 in. Cut dough to 3 in. circles. Put 1 tsp of filling in the center of every circle, fold to a triangle leaving a small opening on the top and close tight.
Place on a baking dish covered with parchment paper with 1 in. spaces.

Bake for 15 minutes until golden.

Let cool and then sprinkle confectioner sugar.

BABKA

2 English cake baking dishes (12 in. long)

Ingredients for the dough:

1 tbs. dry yeast
¼ cup
Warm water (109oF)
1½ stick butter, cut into cubes
1 cup milk
2 cups flour
1 tbs. vanilla
2 eggs
8 tbs. sugar
¼ tsp salt
½ cup chocolate chips or crushed nuts

Ingredients for the filling:

½ container Ha-Shahar Ha-Ole' chocolate spread or
1 ¼ stick butter, cut into cubes
1 cup confectioner sugar
5 tbs. cocoa powder, sifted

For brushing:

1 egg with 3 drops of oil

For glazing:

1 cup confectioner sugar
4 tbs. water
1 tsp. vanilla
1 tsp. lemon juice

Dissolve the yeast in lukewarm water.

In small pot, melt butter with milk on low heat.
In electric mixer, slowly mix flour, dissolved yeast, vanilla, eggs and sugar.
Add salt at the end.
Add melted butter. Cover with saran wrap and leave soft dough in fridge overnight or 5 hours at least.
Prepare the filling:
In an electric mixer, mix butter and confectioner sugar until you get a smooth cream. Add the cocoa powder and continue to blend.
Divide dough into 2. On a floured surface flatten ½ of dough into ¼ in width. Spread half the filling all over.
Roll dough.
With a sharp knife cut each roll length wise into halves;
Place both cut sides to same direction and twist.

Place into baking dishes and brush with egg.

Let rise in warm place for 30 minutes.

Bake in pre-heated oven (350oF) for 30 minutes until a toothpick inserted is dry.

Mix glaze ingredients in small bowl and brush babka while still hot

CHEESE CAKE (Israeli style)

Ingredients:
2 cups cheese (farmers' cheese or Philadelphia)
1 cup sour cream
4 tbs. corn flour
1 package instant vanilla pudding
5 eggs, separated
¾ cup sugar

For the glaze:

½ cup whipping cream
4 tbs. confectioner sugar

Syrup:

1 cup berries (also frozen)
½ cup sugar
1 tbs. corn flour
1 tbs. water.
1 tsp. lemon juice

Pre-heat oven to 350oF.

Blend cheese, sour cream, corn flour and vanilla pudding powder. Add yolks.

Beat whites and slowly add sugar.

Gently fold whites into cheese mixture.

Oil a 26 in. baking dish. Pour mixture into baking dish.

Bake for 50 minutes, turn off oven, and keep cake in oven for one additional hour.

Whip cream with confectioner sugar and spread over cool cake.

Dissolve corn flour in water. Cook in small pot sugar, berries, lemon juice and corn flour until sugar is dissolved and syrup gets thicker.

HAROSSET (Ancona)

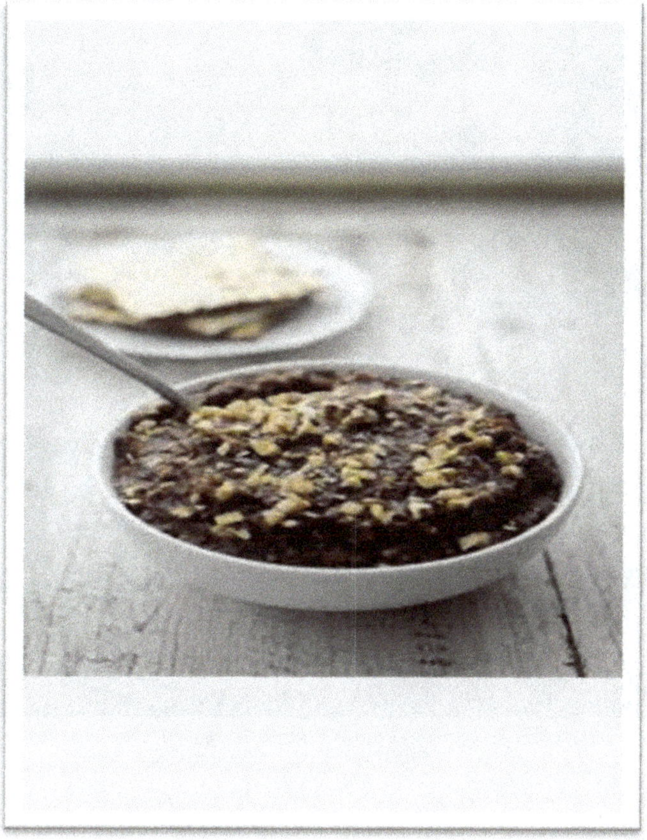

Ingredients:
2 granny smith apples
1 cup pitted dates
1/2 cup nuts (walnuts, pecans or hazelnuts)
½ cup orange juice.
Peel and core the apples and grate in food processor.
Grind the nuts in food processor.
Mash the dates with ½ the orange juice in food processor.

Combine everything. Add orange juice if needed to get a smooth consistency.

APPLE STRUDEL

Ingredients

1 package puff dough
5-6 apples
1/2 cup crushed walnuts
1/3 cup raisins
1/2 cup sugar
1 tsp cinnamon
1 tsp vanilla sugar
1 egg

Preheat the oven to 350 degrees.
Peel and dice the apples. In a small pot, cook apples with sugar on low heat until soft, about 15 mins.
On a floured surface, roll dough to 1/8 in thick to a rectangle.
Mix all ingredients and spread over dough.
Fold short sides 1/2 in. Roll dough lengthwise.
Place on a baking loaf pan with parchment paper.
Brush on egg wash. Bake for 35 minutes until golden and an inserted toothpick is dry.

"Life does not end with death. What you pass on to others remains. Immortality is not the body, which will one day die. That does not matter; of importance is the message you leave to others. That is immortality."
Rita Levi-Montalcini

RECIPES INDEX

www.ingramcontent.com/pod-product-compliance
Lightning Source LLC
Chambersburg PA
CBHW082010150426
42814CB00005BA/276
* 9 7 8 1 9 5 4 1 7 6 7 6 8 *